Crossing Continents

Crossing Continents

Between India and the Aegean from Prehistory to Alexander the Great

Robert Arnott

OXBOW | books
Oxford & Philadelphia

Published in the United Kingdom in 2022 by
OXBOW BOOKS
The Old Music Hall, 106–108 Cowley Road, Oxford, OX4 1JE

and in the United States by
OXBOW BOOKS
1950 Lawrence Road, Havertown, PA 19083

Paperback Edition: ISBN 978-1-78925-554-6
Digital Edition: ISBN 978-1-78925-555-3

A CIP record for this book is available from the British Library

Library of Congress Control Number: 2022933274

Printed in the United Kingdom by Short Run Press, Exeter

Typeset in India by Lapiz Digital Services, Chennai.

For a complete list of Oxbow titles, please contact:

UNITED KINGDOM
Oxbow Books
Telephone (01865) 241249
Email: oxbow@oxbowbooks.com
www.oxbowbooks.com

UNITED STATES OF AMERICA
Oxbow Books
Telephone (610) 853-9131, Fax (610) 853-9146
Email: queries@casemateacademic.com
www.casemateacademic.com/oxbow

Oxbow Books is part of the Casemate Group

Front cover: Unfired Mature Harappan Phase steatite seal from Mohenjo-daro (DK 10355) depicting a flat-bottomed boat with rower and oar of the type used to sail from the ports on the Indian Ocean that served the Gulf [Mohenjo-daro Museum inv. no. MM 4890] (© Harappa.com 1995-2021); background image: Map Of Asia 1896 (© iStock/traveler1116)

In memory of Sir John Marshall CIE FBA
Minoan and Harappan

Contents

List of Tables and Figures

Acknowledgements

I owe a great debt of gratitude to those who have given freely of their knowledge and time or other innumerable kindnesses, especially Mrs Helen Hughes-Brock, who advised me about beads, read an early version of the manuscript and offered many invaluable suggestions for improvement, and Professor Dr Claus Reinholdt of the University of Salzburg, the excavator of the Aegina Hoard. Others include Professor Eric H. Cline, Dr Nicole Pareja Cummings, Professor Costis Davaras, Professor Klaus Karttunen, the late Professor Wilfred Lambert FBA, Dr Jacke Phillips, the late Professor Gregory L. Possehl, Dr Yannis Tzedakis and Professor John G. Younger, although any mistakes or solecisms are mine alone. My earlier conclusions were presented to the Asian Archaeology Group of the McDonald Institute for Archaeological Research of the University of Cambridge, on 27 February 2017 and I should like to thank the participants for a stimulating discussion.

A study like this can only be successfully undertaken with access to several excellent libraries and other resources. In India, I would like to thank the American Institute for Indian Studies at Gurgaon, Haryana (near New Delhi) and the Central Archaeological Library of the Archaeological Survey of India for the opportunity to make use of their unrivalled library holdings. I should also like to acknowledge the British School at Athens, of which I was a student for many years and the Departments of Ancient History and Classical Studies and of Classical and Early Aegean Archaeology of the University of Salzburg. Finally, in Oxford my thanks go to Green Templeton College (where I am a Fellow and which provides a solid base for my work), the Bodleian Library, the former Bodleian Indian Institute Library, the Sackler Library and the Oriental Institute Library for all the facilities kindly put at my disposal.

As I was preparing the final manuscript, I had the opportunity to consult Richard Stoneman's *The Greek Experience of India: from Alexander to the Indo-Greeks* (2019) and I should like to express my admiration for such a masterly work. I must also warmly thank my editor at Oxbow Books, Mrs Jessica Hawxwell, who made this book a reality.

Much of the writing of this book was undertaken during several very agreeable stays in India and Greece; at the hill station of Shimla in the foothills of the Himalayas and on the Greek islands of Aegina and Naxos and I should like to thank all those who made it possible.

Introduction

The first contacts between Greece, the Aegean and India[1] were thought to have occurred sometime at the beginning of the sixth century BC. This was when Greek merchants, explorers and adventurers travelled along the trade routes that linked Ionia in Western Anatolia with what was later to be the Persian Achaemenid Empire and then with India. They then established themselves south of the Hindu Kush Mountains in that part of the rich Northern Indian plain, now called The Punjab, from where flowed the River Indus and its four major tributaries.

These early travellers and traders brought back not only exotic goods, but also fantastic tales often linked to the mythical journey to India of Dionysus and Heracles,[2] evidence of great wealth and strange peoples and by doing so expanded the boundaries of Greek geographical knowledge.[3] There is now growing evidence, however, of much earlier and indirect contacts, stretching far back into prehistory. These were between India and its Indus or Harappan Civilisation,[4] the Near East and finally westwards through Syro-Palestine towards the slowly emerging societies of the Early and Middle Bronze Age Aegean, later to develop into their palace-based economies and growing complex social structures. My definition of the Aegean is broad; I have included both the west and east shores of the sea, to include what is now mainland Greece, its islands and Crete, but also the western shores of Anatolia, particularly Troy.

From the heartlands of the Harappan Civilisation to the Prehistoric Aegean, starting at the end of the third millennium BC and being curtailed after 1900–1800 BC, objects and commodities were continually on the move within what has been described as a pre-industrial world system and far from being a barrier to contact, the sea was a great highway. This means of exchange and communication as Gregory Possehl asserted, were part of an interregional pattern of third millennium urbanisation that encompasses the Nile valley and the lands from the Mediterranean Sea, east across the Iranian Plateau to the Greater Indus Region.[5]

Recently some scholars have speculated on the evidence of contact between the Harappans and Minoan Crete,[6] particularly following the finding of a Harappan etched carnelian bead at the site of Kolonna on Aegina. What they are all in agreement with, however, is that only a complete study of the objects from the Aegean and the identification of any that originated in India, can help determine the nature of trade and contact. This I have now done and my results are presented here.

After 1800 BC, during a time of decline in the Harappan Civilisation, Possehl suggests that contacts to and from India were greatly reduced from then until around 600 BC, the evidence pointing to only a very limited trade in, for example, cotton fabrics (*sindhu*).[7] Contrary to this view, there is, however, some evidence of a continuation into the later Middle and Late Bronze Ages in the Aegean of the supply of commodities from the Late Harappan and post-Harappan Civilisation cultures that emerged in India in the mid- to late second millennium BC.

The question remains whether in the Aegean, at the western extremity of an extensive pattern of contact and those who lived there knew anything of the origins of the objects and commodities that originated in India; maybe they thought of them as from the Near East or Syro-Palestine or neither, or simply exotica 'from the east' supplied by traders from those two regions.

The Aegean was part of a greater trade network and in this work, I have tried to both evaluate and re-evaluate what evidence and speculation there are for such contacts, particularly for the commodities such as tin and lapis lazuli as well as recently discovered objects. For those whose archaeological research is in Greece and the Aegean, much of what is contained in this article about the archaeology of prehistoric India, its resources, social and economic structures and its interaction with other contemporary societies, will be new. Consequently, I have included a very basic introduction to that civilisation as well as explaining where India and Greece lie chronologically in relation to each other (Table 1).

Since this manuscript was completed, Ludvik *et al.* (2020) has appeared, but it has not been possible to include their conclusions in my text. It re-examines the evidence for long-distance cultural interactions in the mid-third millennium BC, as reflected by the beads found at Kolonna on Aegina. The authors determine that at least 15 carnelian beads can be linked to Indus craft traditions and provides further evidence for my conclusions supporting long-distance interactions between the Aegean, Mesopotamia and the Harappans and strengthens my conclusions as presented in this book.

The reader will from the outset also appreciate that I have challenged some of the accepted views concerning the origin of and trade in many of the Aegean's imported commodities such as tin, gold, lapis lazuli and objects such as carnelian beads. However, the results of my research have meant that I am now able to place the Aegean firmly on the periphery of the late third millennium BC sphere of contact that extended from India to the Eastern Mediterranean.

I am, however, not the first to do this. Some have in the past have also suggested many such connections, but it will quickly become evident that much of the evidence they presented does not stand up to scrutiny. My study is based on more recent and new research, where positive evidence exists and can be substantiated.

Finally, I have examined the period after the end of the Bronze Age to the time of Alexander the Great and particularly the period after the sixth century, when Greeks were now beginning to know a little something about India. Within 200 years India was known to scholar and non-scholar alike, such as those who witnessed the Persian invasions of Greece or who later became Macedonian and Greek foot soldiers.

I offer this study of the evidence as a contribution to our understanding of the place of the Prehistoric Aegean and the Early Greek World as well as the Harappans and their successors into a wider global setting. However, I fully accept that one must not fall into the trap that Klaus Karttunen iderntifies, that sometimes over-optimistic scholars tend to see too many contacts with India, even where the evidence is clearly negative.[8] I hope that I have not done this myself.

Notes

1 In this work, the term 'India' is used in its older (pre-1947) sense, that is the entire sub-continent south of the Hindu Kush Mountains and the Himalayas and is not to be taken as having any other meaning, political, cultural or otherwise. The name *India* is derived from the River Indus (Old Indian *Sindhu)* and its original meaning was the Indian satrapy conquered by King Darius I in 512 BC, when he incorporated Taxila, the lands of The Punjab and Sind up to the River Indus into the Achaemenid Empire. Later, it included other satrapies and soon began to mean the 'lands beyond the Indus'. See Karttunen 1989, 157.

2 Dihle 1987, 47–57; Stoneman 2019, 80–98.

3 Karttunen 1989, 103–108 and further references.

4 The Indus or the Harappan Civilisation has also been named the Indus Valley Civilisation and it is now accepted by many scholars that the term Indus Civilisation is possibly more appropriate, considering the rapidly growing discovery of sites particularly to the east and south of the River Indus. Whilst it is accepted that the use of the term Harappan Civilisation also tends to give undue prominence to one particular but major site, namely Harappa, it goes back to an earlier archaeological convention, established well over a century ago, of naming a culture after the first located and usually principal type-site, such as Mycenae for the Mycenaeans. As much of the chronology that so many scholars of Prehistoric India use, depends upon the stratigraphy of Harappa, I have decided to use the term Harappans and the Harappan Civilisation.

5 Possehl 2002b, 247. See also Lamberg-Karlovsky 1972, 222–229; Ratnagar 2001, 351–379. See also Frank 1993, 390–395, although this theoretical approach is not generally supported by other scholars. As a definition of trade and exchange, Trade in the context of this study, should be understood in its broadest sense, as the traffic, exchange, or movement of materials or goods through peaceful human agency, usually reciprocal. Colin Renfrew has described trade as the procurement of materials from a distance, by whatever mechanism; the crucial point is that goods change hands, with the terms trade and exchange employed interchangeably, see Renfrew 1977, 72.

6 *'Is there any evidence of trade with Egypt and Minoan Crete?'* Comments on Harappan westerly relations, from Randall Law, Mayank Vahia, Dennys Frenez and Massimo Vidale. See the website https://www.harappa.com/answers/there-any-evidence-trade-egypt-and-minoan-crete.

7 Possehl 2012, 769. For cotton see Oppenheim 1964, 94; and Talon 1986, 75–78.

8 Karttunen 2014, 331.

Chapter 1

Prehistory: The Background

The Harappan Civilisation

The Harappan or Indus Civilisation in its Mature Harappan Phase (2600–1900 BC) was the most extensive and sophisticated urban Bronze Age civilisation of its time and is characterised particularly by its great cities.[1] It is contemporary with the later phases of the Early Bronze Age and the earlier part of the Middle Bronze Age in the Aegean.

It covered approximately a million and a half square kilometres, stretching from Kashmir in the north to Gujarat in the south, but with its influence also extending beyond its northern border, into what is now Afghanistan and Central Asia and as far west as the Persian Gulf and Mesopotamia (Fig. 1). The Harappan Civilisation was also the product of two great river systems, the Indus and the Ghaggar-Hakra (or Sarasvatī), the latter now dried up. In prehistory, they ran virtually parallel to each other, creating a vast alluvial plain, the basis for the region's agricultural prosperity.

Its chronology (Table 1) has been largely based on the stratigraphy of Harappa and earlier sites of major importance in our understanding of the cultural development of the civilisation, particularly Mehrgarh.

The Mature Harappan Phase has also been distinguished by the emergence of distinct and large-scale complex features. The civilisation supported nearly 3,000 sites, ranging from village farming communities and small towns, to several fully developed and wealthy major urban centres or cites, such as Harappa, Mohenjo-daro, Rakhigarhi, Ganweriwala and Dholavira, with populations of tens of thousands or possibly even more. These cities featured houses and other structures built from fired bricks, as well as warehouses, massive walls and gateways, public health infrastructures, sophisticated water management for the supply of fresh water and the disposal of sewage and extensive areas for craft and industrial production. This was supported by a rural subsistence economy consisting mainly of large-scale food production and pastoral farming.[2] Additionally, we now see the development of literacy, with the Indus script, finely carved stamp seals and the extensive use of lapidary art, standardised measures, the large-scale use of fired brick, standardised in size, with the ratio of 1:2:4, the most effective for bonding.

The Mature Harappan Phase witnessed a period of rapid urbanisation, which featured the creation of dense and heterogeneous populated cities, which

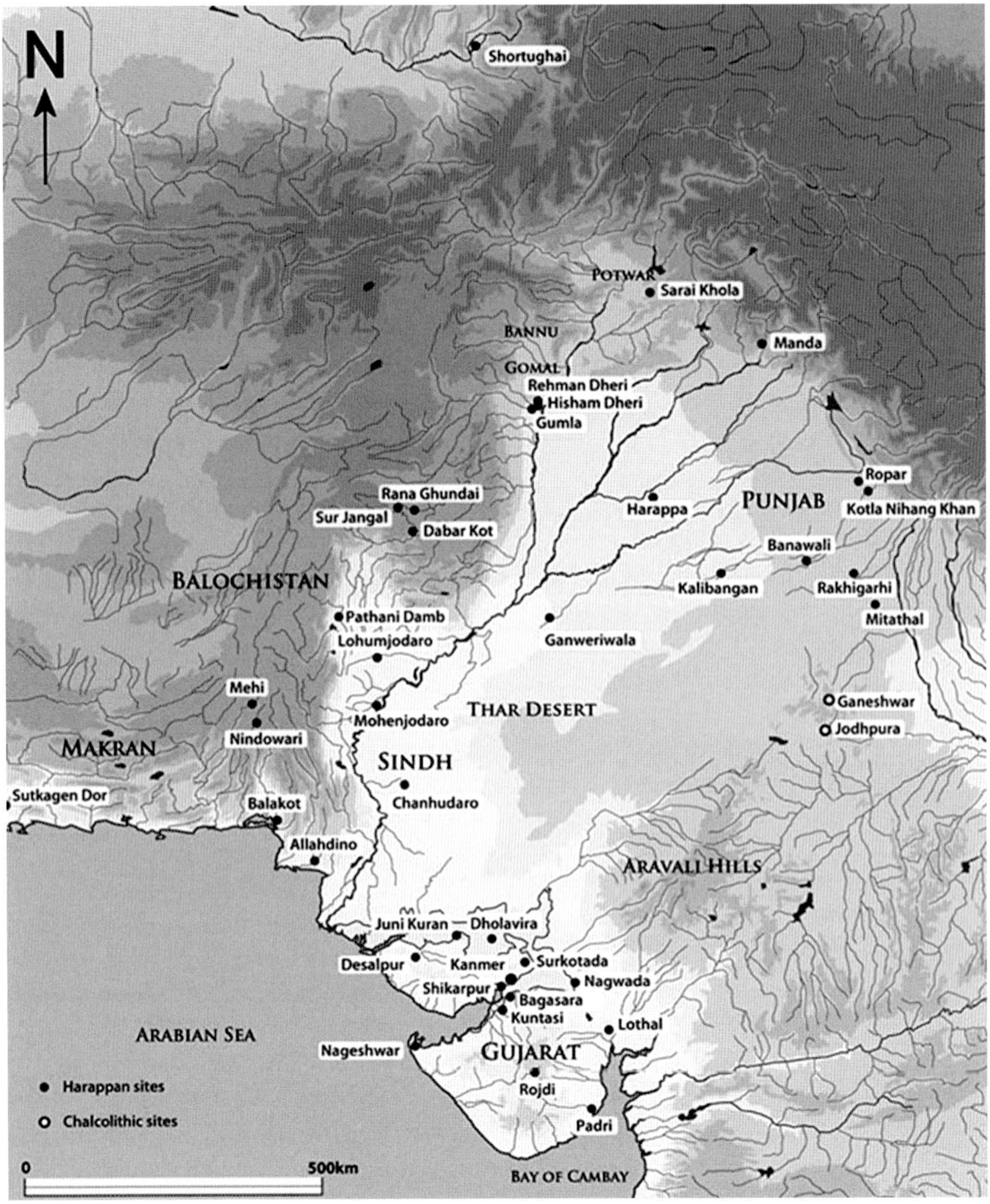

Figure 1. Map of Principal Harappan Sites (After Dr Akinon Uesugi)

Table 1. Chronology of the Harappan Civilisation and Minoan Crete to 1700 BC. The Aegean chronology has been added to as a comparison, not to indicate conscious contact. The Harappan chronology is based on M. Kenoyer, 'Changing perspectives of the Indus Civilization: new discoveries and challenges' Puratattva, 41: 1–18 (2011)

Harappan Civilisation			*Minoan Crete*	*Greek mainland*
Date (BC)	*Phase*	*Sites and events*	*Period*	
	Early Harappan Phase (End)			
2600	Transition Period **Harappa 3A** (2600–2450 BC)	Some settlements destroyed and abandoned New Settlements established Mohenjo-daro founded Expansion of Craft specialisation Emergence of Writing	**Early Minoan IIA**	**Early Helladic II**
	Mature Harappan Phase			
2500	Urban Phase **Harappa 3B** (2450–2200 BC) **Harappa 3C** (2200–1900 BC)	Harappa Mohenjo-daro Mehgarh VIII Lothal (Period A) Kalibangan II External overseas trade expanded Cultural Unity in Indus Region Internal distribution network Towns and Cities and Industrial villages	**Early Minoan IIB** **Early Minoan III** **Middle Minoan IA** **Middle Minoan IB**	**Early Helladic II** **Early Helladic III** **Middle Helladic**
1900	Late Mature/Transitional Phase **Harappa 4**	Lothal (Period B, Phase V) Decline of many towns and cities Flow of River Saraswati reducing Transition to Post-Urban Phase	**Middle Minoan II**	**Middle Helladic**

(Continued)

Table 1. Chronology of the Harappan Civilisation and Minoan Crete to 1700 BC. The Aegean chronology has been added to as a comparison, not to indicate conscious contact. The Harappan chronology is based on M. Kenoyer, 'Changing perspectives of the Indus Civilization: new discoveries and challenges' Puratattva, 41: 1–18 (2011) (Continued)

Harappan Civilisation			*Minoan Crete*	*Greek mainland*
Date (BC)	*Phase*	*Sites and events*	*Period*	
	Late Harappan Phase			
1800	Post-Urban Phase **Harappa 5**	Destruction levels at Harappa and Mohenjo-daro Disintegration of Harappan Polity	**Middle Minoan III**	**Middle Helladic**
170	**Harappa Cemetery H Culture** in The Punjab (1700–1300 BC) Late Harappan in Gujarat	Final end of overseas trade Development of strong regional centres in Gujarat and The Punjab	**Late Minoan IA**	**Late Helladic IA**

become political, economic and ceremonial centres that could offer opportunities unavailable in the rural hinterlands. Technology, production and consumption now had transformed society, where population growth and immigration disrupted the structured settlement pattern. Houses in the core areas of Harappa, for example, often spilled over onto the streets and suburban areas sprang up on low mounds to the west and north-west of its centre.[3]

Supplying the demand for raw materials, food and finished products also required a highly sophisticated infrastructure that integrated the widely dispersed settlements. Many of the specialist products now became standardised through advanced craft specialisation and widely distributed throughout the region. Close similarities in pottery, brick sizes, weights and measures and seals show strong evidence for a shared ideology and the Indus Script, albeit still undeciphered, offers proof of a level of literacy and suggests the existence of a form of an administrative system that oversaw the economy, food production and public health. Some, such as Possehl, believe that the Harappan is also very different from other contemporary societies, as it is a rare example of an early heterarchical prehistoric state, which seemingly developed without any strong and centralised social control or evidence of structural violence.[4]

Some believe that Harappa, Mohenjo-daro and other major Indus urban centres such as Ganweriwala, Dholavira and Rakhigarhi, were multicultural and likely occupied by peoples of different ethnicities and social groupings. Although these centres lacked the temples, palaces and burials that are usually indicative of status, there is evidence that a high degree of social stratification and differentiation did exist and is found in many forms, including possession of, for example, personal adornment, inaccessible to all members of society. Power and social standing could have been created and maintained through control critical resources that included land, livestock and commodities, assisted by ties with kin or clan relations or through interaction with nomadic communities and other migrating ethnic groups.[5]

The rapid appearance of the Harappan Civilisation was originally thought to be the result of cultural diffusion from the Near East. This notion has now been completely discredited by the discovery of a structured subsistence economy and proto urbanisation in the Early Harappan Phase (3300–2600 BC). We now know that it developed directly from the Aceramic Neolithic, which began in the seventh millennium BC in such centres as Mehrgarh and shows a slow and indigenous development of their society and culture.[6] In this Early Harappan Phase, there is also evidence of overland trade contacts with Southern Turkmenistan and with the Iranian plateau, where the Proto-Elamite culture (3200–2600 BC) had spread. This contact may have given the Harappans the impetus to create their own system of writing and literacy.

Discovery

The very existence of this complex urban society that was the Harappan Civilisation, remained largely unknown until the 20 September 1924. It was then that Sir John Marshall, Director-General of Archaeology in India, announced its discovery in the *Illustrated London News*.[7] He named it the Indus Civilisation, because the finds came from two sites in the Upper and Lower Indus Valley, Harappa, near Lahore in The Punjab and Mohenjo-daro in Sindh, 600 km to the south. The discovery struck at the very root of the then prevalent view that the Aryans arrived in India in around 1500 BC and brought with them civilisation.

We are reminded of Marshall's background. Following studying classics at King's College, Cambridge and before his appointment in India, his archaeological career was with the British School at Athens in the early years of the discovery of Minoan Crete, including excavating with David Hogarth at Kato Zakro in the east of the island. He was also strongly influenced by Sir Arthur Evans and his discoveries at Knossos, where he had also worked and the unearthing of the Minoan civilisation. He probably wanted to find his own.[8]

This announcement followed the pioneering excavation campaigns led by the Indian archaeologists R. B. Daya Ram Sahni at Harappa in 1921 (and from 1923 until 1925) and Rakhal Das Banerjee and Madhu Sarup Vats at Mohenjo-daro in 1922–1924 (and to 1925). Since that time, archaeological research both in modern India and Pakistan and even further afield in Afghanistan and the Persian Gulf has been constantly enlarging our knowledge.[9]

The news of the discovery of the Harappan Civilisation quickly came to the attention of scholars working in the Near East. The Assyriologists, the Reverend

A. H. Sayce, C. J. Gadd and Sidney Smith were some of the first to point out the similarities as they saw them between the objects described by Marshall and those recently excavated in Mesopotamia, particularly at Susa in Elam.[10] Ernest Mackay, soon to be drawn to India as the excavator of Chanhu-daro, also saw similarities with the Near East and Mohenjo-daro through the pottery and with a seal depicting a unicorn and Indus Script and especially cylindrical and etched carnelian beads he found beneath an early second millennium BC religious centre at the site of Kish.[11] A tentative chronological framework for dating the Harappan Civilisation was now possible.

The Decline of the Harappans

In approximately 2000–1900 BC, during the Late Harappan Phase, the very first signs of a gradual decline began to emerge and by 1800 BC, many of the major urban centres had been abandoned. Dismissing the notion of Indo-European invaders that destroyed them by force, for which there is no evidence, what we do see is clear evidence of the limited continuity of an identifiable Harappan cultural tradition. While it is accepted that this decline will have led to a major interruption in the overall urban life of the region, elements of the Harappan Civilisation can still be found in later regional cultures that emerged.[12]

More recent archaeological excavations seem to suggest that the decline of the Harappan Civilisation was marked by the final decades of the Late Harappan Phase, with the emergence of the Gandhara Grave (or Swāt) Culture[13] and the final stages of Cemetery H Culture,[14] which some believe may have continued until at least 1200 BC.[15] The period of 1900–1800 BC, also witnessed the eventual withdrawal from its overseas relations, depopulation of urban centres, when settlement was now focused largely in the core areas of the city and was very random. This combined with an indication that the breakdown in authority was likely to be systemic. Eventually there was a new emphasis on agrarian village life and this large-scale depopulation of Indus cities in the Late Harappan Phase seriously weakened Indus society.[16]

Later, we see several Iron Age cultures emerging, such as the Painted Grey Ware Culture (1200–800 BC) followed by the Northern Black Polished Ware Culture (700–300 BC). To what extent they were different from the Late Harappan Phase is not clear. Both are, however, associated with the first use of iron, but the former is also associated with copper hoards, a second millennium BC Bronze Age phenomenon of the Indus-Ganges (or Ganges-Yamuna) Plain with its Ochre Coloured Pottery (OCP).[17]

Whether these later populations can be found to also have been associated with proto-Hindu Indo-European population movements into Northern India, is pure conjecture,[18] although it is accepted that some Vedic texts (possibly excepting the earliest phase of the core of the *Ṛgveda*) are thought to have been written between the twelfth to sixth centuries BC.

The real reasons for the decline and the reduction of trade by the Harappan Civilisation with the west at that time, are ascribed by many to climate change, possibly causing a mixture of floods and a drought, or simply that deforestation or changes in river courses or even the drying-up of some rivers, combined with other environmental factors.[19] Overextended internal economic and political networks may also have been a contributing factor.

Trade and Long-Distance Exchange, Seafaring and Caravans

Any contact, however remote, between the Aegean and India was conducted through the traders of the Near East and Syro-Palestine, either by way of the Persian Gulf sea route, or overland through Iran.[20] As in the Aegean, the Near East and every other early society, trade and gift exchange was important to the wealth and prestige of a society and the Harappan Civilisation, particularly at its height in its Mature Harappan Phase (2500–1900 BC), was no exception.

The start of contacts between Western Asia and the Indus Valley can be traced back to the end of the fourth millennium BC. The eastward expansion of the Proto-Elamite culture started around 3200 BC and reached the Makran coast in what is now Eastern Iran by about 2900 BC. Proto-Elamite pottery, along with compartmented copper seals known widely from the Iranian plateau have been discovered at Mir-i Qalat in Baluchistan. Later layers at this site (2800–2600 BC), various kinds of pottery with motifs such as zebu bulls, leopards and fish now appear that are not unlike pottery motifs in use in the Early Harappan Phase of the Indo-Iranian borderlands.

In the second half of the third millennium BC, the Harappans began to travel farther westwards to Mesopotamia. This was first achieved during the transition from the Early to Mature Harappan Phase (2600–2500 BC), when the Harappans built boats that enabled them to navigate the Indus River and other waterways with large and heavy loads as far as outposts founded by enterprising Harappan seafaring merchants.

The Harappans developed this maritime interest only at the time of the transition between its Early and Mature Harappan Phases; what has been described by Possehl as 'Indus move to the sea' where we now witness a substantial increase in the number of coastal sites, particularly in the Gujarat. We also see a new reliance on the sea as a source of food and some raw materials such as shell and the start of the maritime trading activity with the Arabian Sea and the Persian Gulf.[21] Harappan seals and tablets depict ships with a hut-like cabin and a steersman at the helm with an oar have been found at these sites.

Whilst the inhabitants of the Harappan Civilisation were internally linked by roads, most transport was conducted largely by water on both river and sea-going vessels. Life was to an extent, semi-amphibious; the plain of Sind, the location of Mohenjo-daro, was often a vast lake of water, regardless of the brick flood barrier 7 km to the east which diverted the main flow of the River Indus away from the city. Rivers were mostly navigable for hundreds of miles upriver, encouraging communication.

The sea and river-going vessels are thought to have been small, sea-going flat-bottomed craft with high brows and sterns, built from wood or reeds and equipped with a rear steering oar and a single central mast supporting a sail of woven rushes or cloth,[22] probably canvas made from locally grown hemp. Some vessels would have been larger in order to carry cargoes, such as wood and livestock. Significant developments in water traffic made it possible to transport heavy loads along the rivers and to expand direct sea trade much further afield. There has been discovered what is thought by some to be a dredged canal and a docking facility at the coastal city of Lothal on the southern coast of the Gujarat and an important centre of trade at the time, but that is now disputed.[23]

During their Mature Harappan Phase, the Harappans exported commodities such as timber, gold, copper, tin, steatite, lapis lazuli, agate and ivory as well as finished goods, such as stone beads, including the etched long barrel cylinder-shaped carnelian bead and objects made from shell, faience and steatite, figurines, exotic animals and maybe even slaves. It also probably included agricultural produce, including cotton, silk, jute and textiles made from them, as well as barley, oil, spices and other perishables.[24]

This was particularly remarkable because some of the non-organic commodities, such as tin, agate and lapis lazuli, are to be found in the mountains 1,000 km to the north, not within easy reach of the Harappan heartland and had to be externally resourced and much of it brought southwards overland or by river, facilitated by advances in transport technology. Control of these vital supply and trade routes, especially in commodities and objects of high value, was undertaken by those who also controlled the source of the commodity; in both these cases it was the Harappans that had an economy eventually large enough to support and sustain land and sea trade routes, such as through the Persian Gulf and Mesopotamia and eventually Syro-Palestinian cities such as Ebla, Mari, Ugarit or to a lesser extent and later, Minoan Crete.

The Eastern Mediterranean in the third millennium BC was a period of slowly emerging interregional communication, the start of a system of trade, cultural exchange and communication across a vast area that continued for well over another thousand years. In the Aegean, the Early Bronze Age, particularly the Early Bronze II period, witnessed a slow intensification of this interregional contact, linked to developments mainly in seafaring. Objects of overseas origin now become influential status goods joining locally produced objects made from metal, obsidian and marble, millstones and pottery.

Out of *Meluḫḫa*[25]

For the Harappans, trade with the west, the Persian Gulf and Mesopotamia (Fig. 2), was for the specific export of those commodities that they produced or had control of, which we believe included gold, tin, timber, elephant ivory, lapis lazuli and goods such as carnelian and agate beads, silk, dyes, coloured cotton garments, high quality cotton yarn and leather. Mesopotamia, the centre of any contacts between the Aegean

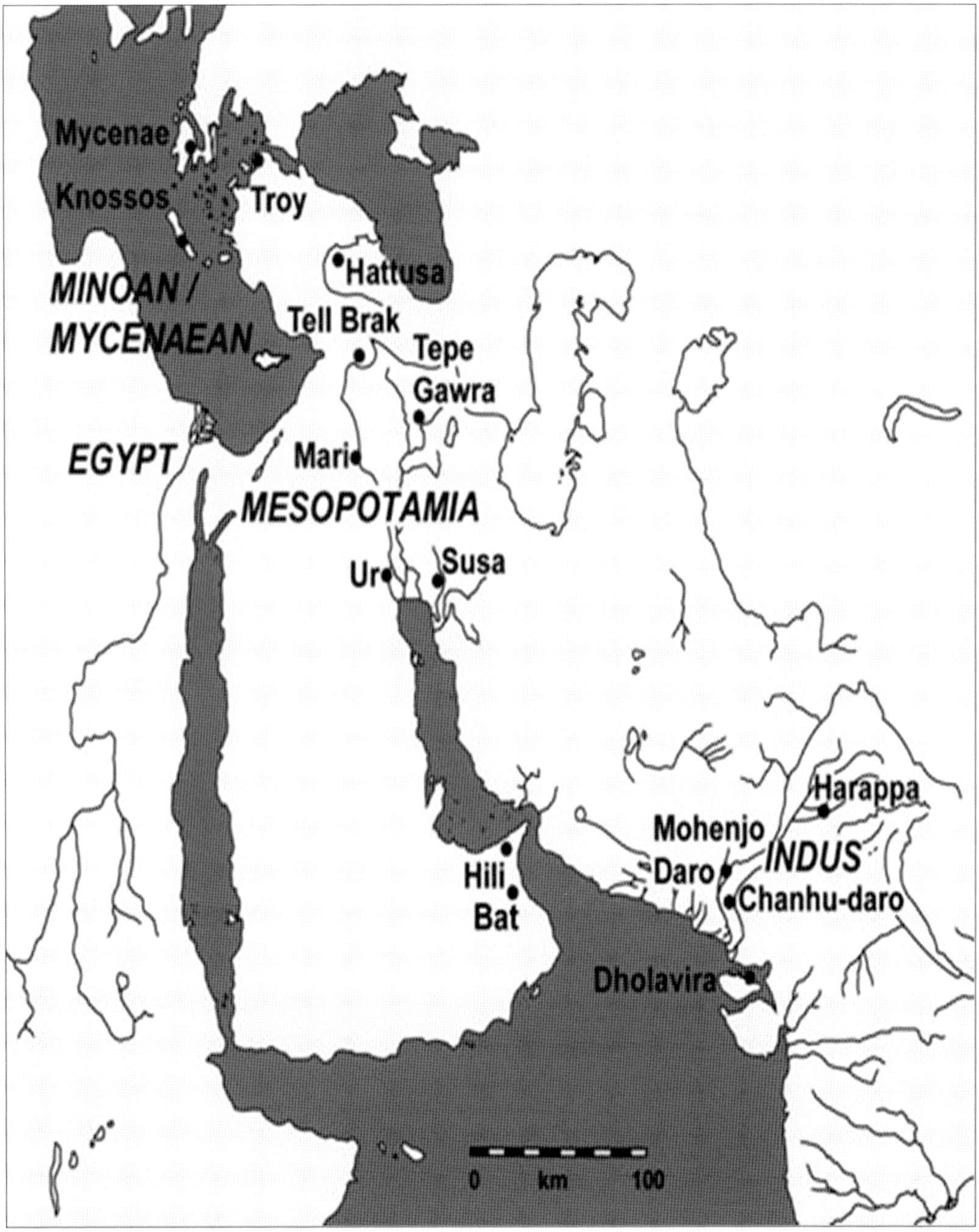

Figure 2. Map of major regions and sites mentioned in the text (From Ludvik et al. *2015, fig. 1)*

and India, is chronologically linked to the Mature Harappan Phase through its Early to Middle Bronze Age, in particular for the Near East, much of the Old Elamite Period (2400–1600 BC) and the later part of the Early Dynastic to Ur III Mesopotamia (2700–2000 BC) and finally in Mesopotamia during the period of rule from Babylon (Old Babylonian Period) up to 1700 BC (Table 1).

In Mesopotamia, the Harappan Civilisation has been identified with the toponym *Meluḫḫa*, which features in the Akkadian texts alongside the cargoes its ships carried.[26] In fact, at least 76 tablets mentioning *Meluḫḫa* bringing to the shores of Mesopotamia, but not specifically by any particular mode of transport, commodities and goods such as carnelian, lapis lazuli, pearls, wood (including *mesa* wood) and plants, fresh dates, animals including a dog and a cat and metals such as copper and gold, together with what have been called '*Meluḫḫan* style' objects: ships, furniture and bird figurines.[27] The first evidence of this direct contact trade with India by Mesopotamians comes from textual evidence of sea-going vessels from India and the Persian Gulf sailing directly as far as the port of Agade or Akkad. An Akkadian text from the time of King Sargon (2334–2279 BC) refers to ships of *Meluḫḫa* (as well as *Magan* and *Dilmun*) docking along its quays.[28]

Additional evidence also points to the period after the end of the Ur III Dynasty after 2004 BC, when we now see merchants meeting in the Persian Gulf to carry out trade and exchange of goods and commodities between Mesopotamia and India, primarily because of its location. They were to become the new middle-men, although we do see Harappan craftsmen establishing an émigré Meluḫḫan Village in Mesopotamia to support their imports.[29] As part of this trade, merchants also came from *Dilmun*, what was for many a mythical paradise in the Sumerian creation myth, now thought to be located on the modern island of Bahrain or possibly the Kuwaiti island of Failaka and from *Magan*, likely to be the Umm an-Nar sites located on the Makran coast of Oman,[30] which also possibly produced copper to supplement existing sources for the Harappan Civilisation and much more for Mesopotamia. This trade is supported by the discovery of over 30 Harappan seals and other objects of the same origin, such as etched carnelian or other forms of beads both in the Persian Gulf and the Near East.[31]

Several south-west Indian coastal settlements like Sotkagen-dor (on the Dasht River, north of Jiwani), Sokhta Koh (on the Shadi River, north of Pasni) and Balkot (near Sonmiani) in the west and Lothal in the east, testify to their role as Harappan Civilisation ports from where the traded objects and commodities started their journey. Other shallow harbours located in the estuary of the River Indus, opening into the sea also would have supported a brisk maritime trade, suggesting the Persian Gulf route as the most plausible for exporting many of the commodities and other goods from India,[32] until the end of the third millennium BC.

This is not to underestimate the likelihood of objects and commodities in the latter half of the third millennium and early second millennium BC, reaching Mesopotamia from areas outside the immediate Harappan heartland, such as in Afghanistan and

Central Asia by a land route, but under Harappan control. This land route westwards would have crossed the northern part of the Iranian plateau, ran along the Elburz mountains and then through the passes of the Zagros mountains on its way to Sumer. Along this trade route were found urban centres such as Tepe Sialk, Tepe Giyan and Tepe Hissar, where finds of lapis lazuli and other objects implicate them in long-distance trade certainly by the beginning of the third millennium BC. At the start of these routes would have been located the Harappan settlements, such as Shortughai, which controlled and managed the supply of these valuable commodities.

It must be emphasised however, that land-trade would also not necessarily have meant direct contact; these goods and commodities would have passed through several middle-men, as a caravan can only carry a restricted amount of merchandise. The sea, however, was the only feasible way of conducting transport on a large scale, but the sea had its problems; very early ships could only carry a little cargo. This and the risks of seafaring itself, including possible piracy, made the long-distance trade a risky business.

In the other direction, no Aegean or Near Eastern material has been located on Harappan Civilisation sites, other than one unique single copper seal, which owes its origins to the Persian Gulf and found at the port town of Lothal.[33] The Harappans were great exporters, but seemingly imported very little, other than possibly copper from the Gulf and those that were organic and no longer have left their mark in the archaeological record. More likely, if any goods were sent in return from Mesopotamia to the Harappan heartland, they have not been recovered archaeologically, but may include wool, incense and other perishable items that are not preserved in the archaeological record.

Further Westwards

The first early indications of sporadic contact between Mesopotamia, Syro-Palestine and the Aegean occurred at a time before seafarers from the Aegean were involved in opening-up this trade route at this end, when extremely infrequent and attenuated long-distance links would have had more of a social impact than the numbers of objects first suggest. Whilst this exchange and trade, starting in the Early Minoan IIB period, was largely contained within the Aegean region itself, we do see a very slow expansion of overseas contact and the beginnings of the appearance in the Aegean of gold, silver, faience, ivory from the Near East and a few Egyptian stone vases.[34]

The cemetery of the Early Minoan site of Mochlos in Eastern Crete, offers examples of elite burials and from the exotic grave goods, an indication that it was these elites that exploited these overseas contacts. However, Near Eastern imports at this time are so rare now, they are better viewed as exotica and are indicative of elite identity, other than evidence for even the most occasional eastern contacts. This would have meant that the few objects and commodities from the India-Mesopotamia trade route, for example, lapis lazuli, agate and carnelian beads, as well as tin ingots, would sooner or later have been passed on through the Near East to the Aegean and other locations in the Eastern Mediterranean.

Regarding Cyprus, the island during the Middle Bronze Age may well have been a stopping point for objects that originated in India by way of the Near East and eventually finding their way to the Aegean, with which it was now beginning to develop contacts. Unfortunately, no specific study has yet been made, there are no reports of objects of Harappan origins having been found in any sites in the Early and Middle Cypriote periods.[35]

The third and early second millennia BC, experienced the development of a system of regional specialisation in the production of goods, set within a system of long-distance contacts which bridged different geographic and cultural areas from India to the Eastern Mediterranean. This system consisted of a series of interconnected and overlapping contacts, interacting among themselves, which were built around a few trading centres. This is evidenced by both the spatial distribution of objects and commodities as well as the different weight shapes and units of measure, which reveal the presence of two distinct, albeit overlapping, exchange networks during this period. The first network was a prominently seaborne network stretching between the Syro-Palestinian coast and the Aegean by way of a maritime route that touched the southern Anatolian coast.

During the Early Bronze Age this network also saw the introduction of luxury items in mid–late Early Minoan Crete. Commodities were passed, as well as ideas and technologies along the southern Anatolian coast; a prime example is provided by the westward spread of metrology and sealing practices in the first part of the Early Bronze Age. It is striking that all these features appear almost exclusively at sites near the coast.

A further exchange network was composed of a bundle of interweaving routes that crossed the Eastern Taurus Mountains at different passes, connecting Northern Syria with central Anatolia and beyond to Mesopotamia and eventually to the Harappans. During the Early Bronze Age, it is marked by the distribution of, for example, Harappan carnelian beads and lapis lazuli artefacts. It is worth assessing the elements of continuity and change between the late third and the early second millennia BC long-distance exchange networks. Among the factors of continuity, one can certainly include the involvement of the same major centres in both periods. Because many sites in the Near East and Anatolia continued to play an important role within these networks, it is also probable that the routes connecting them may have been relatively stable.[36]

It is possible to trace the start of the importation of Indian commodities into Crete from the Near East, to the first use of tin. It first appears at Mochlos, dated by the associated pottery to Middle Minoan IA, in the form of a bronze dagger that was locally made and with a tin content of 4.8%.[37] There are a number of what are thought to be tin-bronzes, dating back to the Early Minoan I–II periods, but these may be the result of local copper ores containing very small amounts of tin and are not intentional alloys.[38] An even more systematic contact began when Minoan seafarers later came into regular contact with the North Syro-Palestinian ports such as Mari and Ugarit from just before 1900 BC onwards. The recipients of this trade and exchange would now have been the earlier palaces in the Aegean that came into existence on Crete during the Middle Minoan IA–B periods, such as Knossos and other such important centres in the Aegean, including Aegina, when Near Eastern and Anatolian trade and cultural exchange was flourishing.

As already pointed out, in 2004 BC, the sacking by the Elamites of Ur (Ur III Period) and the ending of centralised control of trade out of Mesopotamia, meant merchants were no longer promoted by the palace economies which were now denuded of the necessary resources. Mesopotamian traders now only went as far as *Dilmun*, but it had become the centre of commerce in the Persian Gulf, growing rich on the proceeds. Harappan trade with the ports in the Persian Gulf will now have expanded and there were no longer the risks and expense of sailing to Mesopotamia. By the time of King Hammurabi (1792–1750 BC), the trade pattern that had existed for 700 years, came slowly to an end. This decline is particularly true of trade in lapis lazuli, carnelian and agate, to the point where at places outside India, recycled stocks were now the primary source.

By the time that the new ascendant cities of Central and North-Western Mesopotamia had begun to re-establish trade and cultural exchange along the River Euphrates at Mari and into the Syro-Palestinian cities and ports of Ugarit and Ebla, sometime after 1800 BC, the Persian Gulf route formerly controlled by the Harappan Civilisation had now transformed itself back into a predominantly land route, through India, Afghanistan and Iran primarily for commodities. Texts from Mesopotamia no longer refer to the copper sources from *Magan*, but sources from *Alashiya*, identified as Cyprus.[39] However, the trade in tin would have survived, as the demand never diminished.

By 1700 BC, the palatial centre at Mari on the Syro-Palestinian coast had now become the principal market for exotic goods from the east and would have been frequented by foreign merchants from both Mesopotamia and the Eastern Mediterranean. There are records of gifts arriving from the Elamite King of Anshan and from the city of Ugarit, including one talent of tin originally sent from King Hammurabi of Babylon to the court of Aleppo. Tin ingots originating in Afghanistan, no longer under Harappan control, was transported from their source to the Near East and then to Mari and Ugarit, by land and sea, where it was sold to traders from *Kaphtor*, now identified with Crete, who brought with them to these cities goods imported pottery such as Kamares Ware, dated to Middle Minoan IA period and later.[40] This trade continued right through to the Late Bronze Age.

In India, after 1800–1700 BC, the Harappan Civilisation had rapidly begun to decline and the monopoly control of commodities by the Harappans was coming to an end. Cultural homogeneity was breaking up, as was the ability to organise large-scale trade and distribution networks and to control the supply of lapis lazuli and tin. Of course, other factors may have played a part, for example, sea level changes in the Arabian Sea around 2000 BC likely allowed for Sutkager-dor and Sotka Koh to lose their importance. Disruptions in the exchange network had also occurred after 2000 BC, at a time when Mesopotamian trading partners were responding to their own rapid climate change event.[41] At this point, *Magan* and *Dilmun* are mentioned more frequently in Mesopotamian writings, while references to *Meluḫḫa* largely disappear. This is because while their economy up to 1700 BC was still able to maintain an export of commodities, they preferred to use the ports in the Persian Gulf for trading purposes and not sail directly to Mesopotamia.

There is evidence, however, of a few Indian objects largely dated to the very later stages of the Harappan Civilisation in the Late Harappan Phase possibly up to 1500 BC, finding their way westwards for the period. We have the finding of a Harappan seal depicting a humped bull and two signs of Indus Script dated to the early Kassite period (1500 BC) level at Nippur in Mesopotamia,[42] but it may have been an heirloom. There is also, of course, the tenuous evidence of peafowl, which may have been known in Mesopotamia and further west as far back as the third millennium BC onwards.[43] There is a peacock (*Pavo cristatus*) motif at Mitanni, dated to 1500 BC that might suggest East–West contact,[44] or of the introduction of the species of peafowl into the region.

In the succeeding phase of Indian protohistory, however, corresponding to Middle and Late Bronze Ages in the Aegean, we know that the supply of commodities, both organic and inorganic did not completely cease. Any trade routes, however, that then developed or maintained for the remainder of the Near Eastern and Aegean Bronze Ages, would now probably have been dominated by a land route,[45] no longer was the Indian side dominated by one central economy.

The Harappans and Egypt

It is curious that there is very little evidence supporting cross-cultural trade links at the time between the Harappans and Egypt, although proof of trade between Egypt and Mesopotamia does exist. Elam is one of the peripheral regions of the Mesopotamian world and it is from there that the Egyptians imported lapis lazuli.[46] Located immediately west of the Harappan heartland, the Elamites were in close proximity, so it is therefore not surprising that Harappan controlled commodities have been located in Susa, as a testament to their interrelated trading activities.

While the Harappans acted as a core for the Persian Gulf trade route, Egypt acted as the centre of Red Sea trade. Such was the case during the Early Dynastic period of Egypt, when their traders merely ventured out into the Red Sea commercial zone to purchase timber in the Levant and as far as we know, not much further.[47] The rest of their trading activities during this time were conducted along the Nile in Egyptian core hinterland trading activities in Nubia. There is also the relative absence of tin bronzes in Egypt, which is yet another indication of their independence from the exchange networks in the Eastern Mediterranean that linked India, the Near East,

Syro-Palestine, Anatolia and the Aegean in the mid- and late third to early second millennia BC.

Some scholars, however, argue strictly on economic grounds, that the confluence of Mesopotamia and Egypt must have given birth to the world-system sometime in the early or mid-third millennium BC, that is by 2700–2400 BC. This date coincides with the beginning of the Old Kingdom, when Egypt attained its first great cultural peak. Ancient Egypt, however, was not one of the main players in the world-system that formed in the third millennium BC by the most commercially dominant of these forces, the urbanised societies of Mesopotamia, Elam and Harappans through maritime roads in the Persian Gulf and land routes that ran all the way to Turkmenistan and Bactria in 2600–1800 BC.

Archaeological discoveries, however, suggest that this third millennium BC world-system may have included some trade routes leading into East Africa. A copal necklace has been uncovered in a tomb at Tell Asmar and dated to 2500–2400 BC, which likely came from East Africa, more specifically from the vicinity of Zanzibar, now in modern Tanzania.[48] This discovery has forced scholars to rethink the geographic extent of Mesopotamian contacts. If objects such as this copal necklace can be proven with certainty to have made their way into the complex interrelated networks of the Mesopotamian world-system as far as central Mesopotamia, then it could reasonably be assumed that trade links existed between other civilisations and cultures, such as that of the Harappans, but no African objects like these have been discovered so far in the thousands of Harappan archaeological sites.

Iconography

The wall paintings found in Room 6 of Building Complex Beta at Akrotiri, Thera,[49] dating to the period before its destruction in the late seventeenth century BC, depict monkeys that while stylistically Aegean, have hitherto been considered to be closely related to other Egyptian and Ancient Near Eastern monkey paintings. However, the Thera images provide species-specific characteristics and in an attempt to understand their origins, Marie Nicole Pareja and her colleagues compared them with monkeys that originate in the Harappan heartland.[50] They have concluded that the wall paintings of monkeys are not based on the traditional Egyptocentric outlook that has been hitherto accepted by most scholars, as they carry their tails upward in a C- or S-shaped curve. With this distinctive posture, they have identified these primates as likely being grey langurs or Hanuman langurs (*Semnopithecus* sp.), solely indigenous to Nepal, Bhutan and Northern India.

As Pareja points out, these images have iconographic implications for indirect contacts between Aegean and the Harappans and dismisses the monkeys as being the result of a well-established relationship with Egypt. However, she does not argue for live langurs being traded between India and the Aegean; there are no skeletal remains of this type of monkey in the Aegean. The iconography of the animal, however, was likely carried and transmitted as an indicator of status or personal adornment along well-established trade routes that spanned from the Indus to the Aegean.[51]

Monkeys are not indigenous to the Aegean and the Near East and textual evidence indicates their presence in Mesopotamia by way of trade with a location further east. We know that the broader network of Mesopotamian trade and contacts with the Harappans, through objects and commodities, points to Mesopotamia functioning as an intermediary between the east and west. When coupled with the textual and iconographic evidence, an avenue opens through which the transmission of the iconograph, particularly of the Hanuman langur, becoming possible.

An ivory monkey upright seated figurine from an Early Minoan III funerary context in the cave at Trapeza on Crete[52] may also indicate an indirect connection between the Aegean and the Harappan heartland. It preserves a cross-and-chevron motif on its circular base, suggesting it was also used as a seal. The base motif can be found in the Early Harappan Phase at Mehrgarh Periods V–VII (3300–2800 BC),[53] with its use continuing through to the Mature and Late Harappan Phases.

A Late Minoan IA carnelian seal said to be from Prassa on Crete,[54] also bears an iconographic motif that may have originated in India. It depicts a male figure standing beside a monkey that wears a belt or halter, possibly its keeper. Similar domesticated monkeys appear on Near East and Mesopotamian clay tablets that show a male figure who is accompanied by one or two monkeys, often with collars and leashes. This composition may show a scene likely adopted from Elam and with langur monkeys that originated in India; it is possible that this single Aegean example is related to, or perhaps derived from, the scenes from further east. The carnelian is likely to have been re-used from a bead imported during an earlier period. Pareja and Anne Chaplin go on to discuss, also based on iconography, the possibility of the importation of peafowl from India into the Aegean and reinforce the view that there were potential trade and cultural contacts (whether indirect) between the Aegean and the Harappans of south Asia.[55]

Weights and Measures

What is of significance is that for the Harappans, a standardised weight system, with identifiable multiples and fractions of units, was first evident in the third millennium BC. They may have had a common source, with the Harappan Civilisation, Mesopotamia and the Aegean, together with Syro-Palestine sharing a close commonality between their system of weights and measures, based on an intent to facilitate relatively easy inter-conversion.

Standardised weighing systems are particularly significant for trade and exchange, because they emphasise the need to accurately compare material goods that were sourced over large distances. The inter-calculability of the systems that emerged in the third millennium BC also provides an indication of the common acceptance of the need for standardisation and points to similar types of goods being exchanged or imported.

The emergence of the international metals trade must have been the driving force behind the creation of this common weights system, particularly for the areas that metals were becoming central mediators of value, such as in both the Harappan Civilisation and the Aegean.[56]

The spatial distribution of a weight system of measurement and its overlap with others can also provide us with clues about the coexistence and interaction of different trade systems. Therefore, the circulation of commodities between distant shores, including India, the Persian Gulf, Mesopotamia, the Aegean and Anatolia, within a network of long-distance commercial contacts, which started at the beginning of the third millennium BC, created conversion systems that enabled mutual equivalence between different weight systems and which facilitated international trade and exchange.[57]

The use of common metrological standards enables traders to apportion values to commodities which cannot be physically counted, as cattle can be, or measurable in containers, as stones, colour pigments as well as foodstuffs can be. Although no distinctive Harappan cubic stone weights, usually made from chert, have been found in the Aegean, a number of Near Eastern weights have been found both there and in India and some Harappan weights have been found in Mesopotamia.[58]

By 2600 BC, a common system had emerged from the three civilisations as was the use of seals and therefore it is no coincidence that we now see some structured trade and cultural exchange in valuable commodities such as tin, gold, carnelian, agate, lapis lazuli and in objects, such as etched carnelian beads and silver flat disc-shaped beads,[59] common to all three societies. Small standardised weights of imported stone, such as marble, found in some quantities at the site of Kolonna on Aegina (see next chapter), are known in the Central Mediterranean and indicate early standardisation and trading networks at that time.[60]

It is now possible to see that the common use of balance weights, tin bronzes, seals, elite body ornamentation and precious metals are synonymous and are distributed from the Aegean to the Indus, through various spheres of interaction and interlinking of one region with another through trade and cultural exchange. From 2500–2200 BC onwards, metals and many other commodities could now be weighed according to common agreed standards (units of weight) and given proper values. The system would have continued into the early second millennium BC, where evidence now shows that some of the objects and commodities that originated in India continued to arrive in the Aegean in any great quantity and would have required weighing.

Notes

1 For an introduction to the Indus Civilisation and its chronology, see Possehl 2002b; Wright 2010; Kenoyer 2014, 407–432; Coningham and Young 2015; and Possehl 1990, 261–282. Kenoyer 1991a, 334–370, although now slightly outdated, is a good introduction to the results of excavations in the 1970s and 1980s and the social, economic and environmental background to the Mature Harappan Phase. For the Late Harappan Phase and a view of the eclipse of urbanisation,

regionalisation and the paradigm shift in our understanding of this in the last 20 years, see Possehl 1997b, 425–471 and Ratnagar 2002.

2 Meadow 1991, 51–65; 1996, 390–412.

3 Wright 2010, 396–397; Kenoyer 2008b, 183–208.

4 Possehl 1990, 261–282; 1988, 261–291, also see Kenoyer 1992, 79–98; 1998, 126–127.

5 Kenoyer 1989, 183–192; Law 2006, 301–302. For a contradictory view see Schug *et al.* 2012, 136–147; Khan 2016, 1–9.

6 Possehl 2002b, 23–49. Also, within India, there has been identified that several sites located along the new dried-up Saraswati River, such as Jalipur, Bhirrana and Kunal record, like Mehrgarh, continuity and indigenous development from the seventh millennium BC to the Mature Harappan Phase, see Dikshit and Mani 2013, 47–59.

7 Marshall 1924a, 528–534, 548. For his first formal report see Marshall 1924b, 47–51.

8 Gill 2000, 517–526; Lahiri 2005, 33–37. It is interesting to note that Marshall, who had worked at Knossos, wished to emulate a comparative excavation methodology for unearthing a comparable civilisation and noted that cities such as Mohenjo-daro and Harappa required a well organised and comprehensive campaign of excavation conducted on a scale comparable to that at Knossoss, see Guha 2005, 406 n.14.

9 Gregory L. Possehl outlined the recent history and historiography (to 2002) of the archaeology of the Harappan Civilisation, see Possehl 2002a, 1–46.

10 Gadd and Smith 1924, 614–616; Sayce 1924, 566.

11 Marshall 1924b, 48; Mackay 1925, 697–701.

12 A more recent synthesis brings together archaeological and climatic evidence for the end of the Harappans, see Petrie 2017, 43–64.

13 Tusa 1977, 675–695.

14 Kenoyer 1991a, 1–64; 1991b, 29–60; Shaffer 1992, Volume I, 441–464, Volume II, 425–446.

15 Shaffer 1993, 53–67.

16 Mughal 1990, 1–17; Gupta 1993, 51–59.

17 Yule 1985a; 1989, 193–275; Sharma 2002. See also Shaffer and Lichtenstein 1999, 239–260.

18 For a review of the debate concerning the arrival of the Indo-Europeans see Bryant and Patton 2005.

19 Climate change has been suggested as a possible cause for the decline of urban centres of the Harappan Civilisation, see Dixit *et al.* 2014, 339–342 and Ratnagar 2016, 236–252. For the earlier period see also Petrie *et. al.* 2017, 1–30, that shows there is now evidence that the region was directly subject to climate change during the period when the Indus Civilisation was at its height and shows how the Harappans society coped with diverse and varied ecologies and change in their environment. Human settlements in the peripheral zones of the Harappan heartland, such as in the Gujarat, are of considerable importance in our assessment of abrupt climate change, particularly that which occurred towards the end of the Mature Harappan Phase, which is now regarded as one of the major and abrupt arid-events from the palaeoenvironmental record of the period. To date there has been little to prove this, but now evidence from Khirsara in the Gujarat, based on both botanical remains and C-isotopes of soil organic matter ($\delta^{13}C_{SOM}$), show that in around 2000 BC, a major and intentional change in arable farming occurred, substituting barley and wheat for drought-resistant millet, an adaptation in response to deteriorating environmental conditions. The archaeological remains from the site indicate that habitation survived and continued after the 2000 BC dry climatic phase, but with declined economic prosperity. Changing over to millet-based crops would have initially helped inhabitants to avoid immediate collapse due to climatic stresses, but continued aridity and altered cropping pattern would have eventually led to a decline in prosperity levels of inhabitants and eventual abandonment, see Pokharia *et al.* 2017.

20 Textual and archaeological evidence for trade and contact between Mesopotamia, the Persian Gulf and Meluḫḫa in the third and early second millennia BC has been recently extensively reviewed by Steffen Lauresen and Piotr Steinkeller, see Lauresen and Steinkeller 2017. For trade and contact between Mesopotamia and India, see Lauresen and Steinkeller 2017, 79–88. For a review of external trade routes during the Mature Harappan Phase, see also Lahiri 1992, 125–129.

21 Possehl 2012, 758–761.

22 Possehl 2002b, 218. See also Potts 2016, 115–117 for a description of both Mesopotamian and Indian second millennium BC seafaring.

23 For the identification of this feature at Lothal identified as a dockyard, see Rao 1979, 123–136. However, a number of scholars believe otherwise and that it is simply a tank, see Leshnick 1968, 911–922 and Pandya 1977, 99–103; Mathur 2002, 61–67. For Lothal as a centre for trade see Possehl 2002b, 227; Ratnagar 2004, 94–98.

24 Tosi 1991, 111–128. For production of objects and crafts see also Kenoyer 1992, 79–98; 1997, 262–280.

25 For a discussion on Indian relations with the Near East and Iran see Ratnagar 2004; Possehl 2012; Potts 2016. A review (with extensive references), albeit dated, of Mesopotamian-Harappan Civilisation relations but with an interest in the importation of tin from India westwards can be found in James Muhly's authoritative study of the sources of Bronze Age copper and tin, Muhly 1973, 306–319.

26 For a discussion on its location see Legrain 1926, 2–27, no. 41; Parpola *et al.* 1977, 129–165; Edens 1992, 118–139; Franke-Vogt 1993, 72–97; Possehl 1996, 136–137; 1997a, 87–100; 2002b, 215–228; Ratnagar 2004, 98–102; Potts 1993c, 423–440; 2016, 114–116. On the name *Meluḫḫa*, it is that by which the Harappan Civilisation is believed to have been known to the Sumerians (2900–2350 BC) and the Akkadians (2334–2154 BC) in Mesopotamia, see Parpola 2015. *Meluḫḫa* then disappears from the Mesopotamian records at the beginning of the second millennium BC, see Hansman 1973, 564. See also Parpola 1975, 205–238. However, Hansman states that a trace of it in a modified form, as *Baluḫḫu*, was retained in the names of products imported by the Assyrians (911–605 BC), see Hansman 1973, 565 and 1975, 609–610. Romila Thapar also interprets *Meluḫḫa* as a proto-Dravidian term, possibly *mēlukku* and suggests the meaning 'western extremity' (of the Dravidian-speaking regions in the Indian sub-continent). A literal translation into Sanskrit, *aparānta*, was later used to describe the region by the Indo-Europeans, see Thapar 1975, 10.

27 Possehl 2012, 762.

28 University of Pennsylvania Museum inv. no. CBS 13972; Legrain 1926, 2–28, no. 41. See also Potts 2016, 114–116. The location of those regions with which Mesopotamia trades in the third millennium BC have been defined. *Dilmun* includes present-day Kuwait, the eastern province of Saudi Arabia and Bahrain; *Magan* encompasses the present-day United Arab Emirates and Northern Oman and possibly the coastal region of Iran along the Strait of Hurmuz and the western section of Makran/Baluchistan; *Marhaši* roughly corresponds to the Iranian province of Kerman and, of course, *Meluḫḫa* represents the Harappan heartland in the Indus Valley and Gujarat, see Lauresen and Steinkeller 2017, 3.

29 Ratnagar 2004, 51–56, 70–76. See also Lamberg-Karlovsky 1972, 222–229; Parpola 1977, 129–165; Edens 1992, 118–139; Franke-Vogt 1993, 72–97; Potts 1993c, 423–440; Possehl 1997a, 87–100; 2002b, 215–228. The suggestion, however, that there was a Harappan settlement in Southern Babylon in the Girsu/Lagaš province in the Ur III period, founded by Harappan merchants, has now been dismissed, see Lauresen and Steinkeller, 79–82.

30 From Umm an-Nar period sites in Oman there was found Harappan Civilisation pottery, seals, objects like ivory combs, etched carnelian beads and segmented silver beads. For example, the

excavations at Tell Abraq in Umm al-Qaiwain in the Persian Gulf show continuous contact with the Central Asian–Indian area from 2600 BC, at the start of the Umm an-Nar period, see Potts 1990, 93–130; 1994, 615–628; Mery 1996, 167–179; Karttunen 2014, 331. For a more up-to-date review see Potts 2016, 110–114. See also Giardino 2019.

31 Possehl 2002b, 221 and table 12.4; Ratnagar 2004, 256–271.

32 Possehl 2012, 767. There is some suggestion that the port of Suktagen-dor in the Makran may have been used by the Persian Gulf trade for loading or offloading goods and commodities onto small boats headed to and from the River Indus.

33 Possehl 2002b, 226–228. For a review of Mesopotamian and Iranian objects found in the Harappan world see Possehl 2002c, 325–342.

34 For the first Early Bronze Age contacts between the Aegean and the Near East see Klengel 1984, 7–19 and Lambrou-Phillipson 1990, 68 and 73. Elizabeth Shanks argues for Cretan relations with North East Aegean and Anatolia as early as the Early Minoan I–IIA periods as evidenced by pottery from Tomb 140 of the Hagia Photia cemetery, see Shanks 2005, 103–108. See also Aruz 2008, 8. There are many close stylistic links in seals between Lerna and Geraki on the Greek mainland, Crete and Anatolia in Hughes-Brock 2010, 228.

35 In a Late Cypriote context, from Tomb 93 at Enkomi, dated to the Late Cypriote IIC period (1340–1200 BC), comes a necklace with bi-conical bead carnelian spacers separating gold beads of the figure-of-eight form, which seem to be both partly Mycenaean and partly Western Asiatic in origin. Like others, they may have been re-used from an earlier period; see Murray *et al.* 1900, 41, pl. vi, no. 694; Marshall 1911, 35, pl. V, cat. no. 580; Higgins 1981, 175–176, ill. 218. However, there is plenty of evidence for Early Minoan III–Middle Minoan IA contact with Cyprus and the Levant, especially Byblos.

36 Massa and Palmisano 2018a, 78–83.

37 Heraklion Museum inv. no. HM 1560. Seager 1912, 61, fig. 45, no. XI.22; Branigan 1967, 214–215 and n. 44. There are also two small daggers from the Tholos of Krasi on the north coast of Crete, with a tin content of 6% and 10%, originally dated to the Early Minoan I–IIA and Early Minoan I periods, but this dating is uncertain.

38 Rahmstorf 2017, 189–191.

39 Fairservis 1975, 31; Ratnagar 2002, 84–85.

40 Dossin 1970, 97–106.

41 Dixit *et al.* 2014, 339–342. See also Cullen and Demenocal 2000, 853–863; Cullen *et al.* 2002, 315–338; Frahm and Feinberg 2013, 1866–1878. As a background to this climate change, the Harappan Civilisation developed in the context of a semi-arid climate that was pervasive in South Asia for the latter half of the Holocene. It has become increasingly clear, however, that by 2800 BC, aridity levels in the Indus Valley were broadly similar to contemporary levels. This remained until a period of destabilised environment, fluctuating rainfall, increased seasonality and accelerated channel migration began in the Indus Valley region after 2000 BC. From 2200–1700 BC, a significant rapid climate change event in South Asia saw disruptions in monsoon rainfall and significant changes in fluvial dynamics along the Indus Rivers, including the Beas River. Increasing aridity initially occurred in the context of a flourishing interaction sphere that spanned West and South Asia in the third millennium BC, causing problems to social sustainability. See brief review of climate change in Schug *et al.* 2013. For a survey of the events of approximately 2000 BC (including climate change) that affected relations between the Aegean and the Near East at this time, see Wiener 2013, 34–43.

42 Brunswig *et al.* 1983, 102.

43 It may be the multi-coloured bird called in Sumerian DHA.JAMUŠEN which is sometimes identified as a peacock, see Falkenstein 1964, 75. But as Kartunnen points out, there are other multi-coloured birds in India, see Karttunen, 1989, 14 n. 35, but this does not negate the fact that the fowl originated in India. See also reference to the importation of peafowl (or possibly

other multi-coloured exotic birds) from the Harappans to Mesopotamia in the third millennium, see Potts 2007, 123 and Karttunen 2014, 331. Whether any ever reached the Aegean or any other part of the Eastern Mediterranean is not known, but there does not seem to be either iconographical or physical evidence.

44 Brentjes 1981, 145–148; 1988, 163–167; Schmidt 1980, 45. In the annals of King Tiglathpileser III (745–727 BC) for the year 738 BC, there is recorded as being 'birds of heaven with blue wings' among the tributes, which may well be peacocks, see Karttunen 1989, 25.

45 Heskel 1984, 340.

46 Additionally, the blue colour used by the Egyptians is said to have come from Indigo cultivated in India, evidence of which is found at Rojdi, see Zarins 1992, 219–240. A rare single Harappan etched carnelian bead has been found in Egypt, likely imported from Mesopotamia and dated to the Late Middle Kingdom (London, UCL Petrie Museum of Egyptian Archaeology, inv. no. UC30334) and was probably the property of a trader and not an elite object of trade or gift exchange.

47 Demand 2011, 85–86.

48 Meyer *et al.* 1991, 296–297.

49 Doumas 1992, 120–123.

50 Pareja *et al.* 2020, 159–168.

51 Chaplin and Pareja 2020, 220–224; Pareja *et al.* 2020, 159–168.

52 Heraklion Museum, inv. no. HM 1570; Platon 1969, 516, no. 435; Pendlebury 1939, 87 and pl. XII.2.

53 Kenoyer 1998, 45 and fig. 2.21.

54 Precise provenance unknown. Heraklion Museum, inv. no. HM Giam 3438; Müller *et al.* 2007, 540, no. 357.

55 Chaplin and Pareja 2020, 215–226; Pareja *et al.* 2020, 159–168.

56 Wilkinson 2014, 146–147, fig. 4.13a and table 4.1.

57 Massa and Palmisano 2018a, 66–69.

58 Rahmstorf 2010, 94–96. See also Rahmstorf 2006a, 24–28; Potts 2016, 115. The typically Aegean spool weights, a good example coming from Poliochni (Megaron 832, level 2, *c.* 2900–2650 BC), seem to have been a local Aegean innovation and their presence at Tarsus in Cilicia points to a possible maritime route between the Aegean and Cilicia and eventually Syro-Palestine, through the Southern Anatolia during the Early Bronze II period, see Massa and Palmisano 2018a, 66–69.

59 Rahmstorf 2010, 95.

60 Rahmstorf 2006a, 24–28; 2006b, 73–79.

Chapter 2

Prehistory: The Evidence of Objects

One of the aims of this study is to explore the connection between the Early and Middle Bronze Age interregional networks that linked India to the Aegean. I will do so by looking in detail at a range of objects and to achieve this, I will attempt to evaluate this process by assessing the place of manufacture of these objects and address to what extent their spatial distribution is related to one or more trade routes. Although I am using a limited number of classes of object, I shall argue that different patterns of trade and exchange can be traced not only locally, but also at an interregional scale. Therefore, my approach aims at investigating what different trade and exchange patterns, plus economic strategies are responsible for the allocation and distribution of these goods between India and the Aegean materials in the third and second millennia BC.[1]

In the ancient world, objects were transported, traded and exchanged between cultures and civilisations, over both short and long distances. Trade and gift exchange represented more than mere production and use; exchange of goods often led to an exchange of cultural and social experiences. Consequently, the discovery of the sources of objects traded over a distance, often surpass archaeological expectations of trade patterns and geographic distance and can often reveal other factors such as an important technological advance. They can sometimes be the first indicators of acculturation, but much more evidence is needed before that can be substantiated.

As to what all of this means, there is more than one answer. To some it can have significance in cross-cultural contacts, but to others it can mean that a few objects found their way along the trade route and ended up far away at a location where the significance of their origin has been lost, perhaps having been exchanged in taverns by seafarers. However, objects in this category are usually related to gift exchange or were simply keepsakes of individuals. In this case, it is commodities that determine trade and this is quite apparent in the long-distance contacts between India and the Aegean.

I have included in this chapter all objects that are either recognised as having Indian connections or where it is speculated that they do so. For some series of objects, such as pottery kernoi, spiral double-headed pins and bronze weapons, the evidence is at best tenuous and the suggested connections should be largely dismissed and I shall discuss the reasons for this. As for others, such as objects made from carnelian, agate, faience and for flat disc-shaped beads, the evidence strongly supports such a connection.

I have tended to concentrate on beads. This is because they are important if we are to understand relations between the Bronze Age societies of the Old World in the third and second millennia BC. As an artefact type, it represents an important technology used to create ornaments that had symbolic significance in both ritual and social contexts. As Geoffrey Ludwik, Mark Kenoyer and their team remind us, they can also provide information on the structure and organisation of early craft production as well as help trace important trade networks from raw material resource areas to production areas and eventually to the location where a bead was finally used and eventually discarded. Many stone beads were passed down from one generation to another or even collected from earlier periods and reused by later individuals, which can also provide valuable insights into the nature of ancient societies.[2]

Pottery Kernoi

In 1971, B. M. Pande proposed a Harappan Civilisation–Aegean link through the distribution of pottery kernoi, also known as ring or cluster-vases. He described four pottery kernoi from Harappa and Mohenjo-daro, discovered in what the stratigraphy suggests are Mature Harappan Phase contexts (2500–1900 BC).[3] Two fragmentary kernoi were also found at Harappa[4] and two others from Mohenjo-daro.[5] There are a further six, both wheel- and hand-made, reported from more recent excavations at these sites and there is evidence of two more, but whether they are kernoi is uncertain.[6]

These kernoi consist of a circular hollow tube (the largest with a diameter of 15 cm) surmounted by two or more small usually triangular shaped vases set at intervals around the rim. The cups also have a perforated bottom connecting them to the interior tube of the support ring, but their use cannot be exactly determined. It is possible that they were lamps; but within each society they will probably have had a different use.

Kernoi in all their forms have a remarkably wide distribution from the fourth to the second millennia BC, including the Aegean, Cyprus, Syro-Palestine and Mesopotamia. In the Aegean, where they are first found in the Early Bronze Age III period on Crete, the Greek mainland and the Cyclades, roughly contemporary with the Mature Harappan Phase, they tend to be more elaborate and ornate, particularly those made in the Cyclades, likely centred on Melos.[7] There is also evidence of kernoi from Cyprus ranging from the Early Cypriote I–III Periods (2300–1950 BC) to much later, which are more sophisticated.[8]

Of three kernoi similar to the Mohenjo-daro example from the Near East, one comes from Level IXC (Late Uruk Period) of the acropolis at Tepe Gawra in northern Mesopotamia,[9] another from a votive deposit (2400–2300 BC) at Tell Brak in north-east Syria[10] and a contemporary fragment from Eshunua (Tell Asmar), again in

Mesopotamia.[11] They all seem to offer much stronger parallels to the Harappa and Mohenjo-daro examples than those from the Aegean and other locations in the Eastern Mediterranean.

The kernoi from Harappa and Mohenjo-daro are simply made and are essentially small cups attached to a hollow ring, quite unlike the mostly elaborate Aegean examples. An exception is the plain ring kernos with three cups that comes from Mycenae, but since this was found in a much later Late Helladic IIIB context, any connection is unlikely.[12] As the Harappa and Mohenjo-daro examples have a clear Mature Harappan Phase context, if there is to be an Aegean connection, the movement of such vessels between the two regions must have started by the middle to end of the third millennium BC, through Mesopotamia and Northern Syria following traditional early trade routes; however, this seems improbable.

Spiral Double-Headed Pins

The evidence for contact between India and the Aegean from the distribution of dress pins, used to secure clothing to the shoulder,[13] is also not very encouraging. Specifically, these pins have a spiral double-headed decoration, made by splitting the flattened or tubular wire at the top and then delicately splaying and hammering it to form two opposing spirals. Some years ago Stuart Piggott, in his wide-ranging discussion of Harappan Civilisation metallurgical contacts with Central Asia, Northern Iran and the Near East, suggested that these spiral double-headed bronze and copper pins found at Harappan sites, initially dated to the Late Harappan Phases, originated in Central Asia and also that they had connections westwards in Anatolia, the Aegean and as far as the Balkans.[14] He also mistakenly believed it was a sign that a Central Asian population invaded the Indus Valley at the end of the third and the beginning of the second millennia BC. This idea was largely based on earlier work of Gordon Childe with his diffusionist view of the spread of technology and ideas.[15]

Examples of these pins come from several Harappan sites. There is a good Late Harappan silver example from Chanhu-daro (Fig. 3),[16] which Mackay believed, because of its then apparent uniqueness, to be an import. Another silver example, but with a single spiral comes from Mohenjo-daro,[17] although it is likely that this pin, found in a heavily corroded state, once had a double spiral – one side having been broken off.[18] It is, however, thought to be of local manufacture. There is also another but made from copper, from the site of Manda, located in the modern Indian state of Jammu and Kashmir and the most northerly habitation of the Harappan heartland and dated to its lowest occupation level, the Manda IA period (contemporary with the Mature Harappan Phases).[19] Heidi Miller discusses similar finds of pins from other sites including Banawali,[20] Gufkral and Burzahom, all roughly of the same date.[21]

It must be admitted that the Harappan examples are of a type that resemble in many ways similar bronze and gold north-west Anatolian Early Bronze II (Troy IIg) (2600–2250 BC) pins.[22] Several have also been found in Aegean sites such as Tomb 20

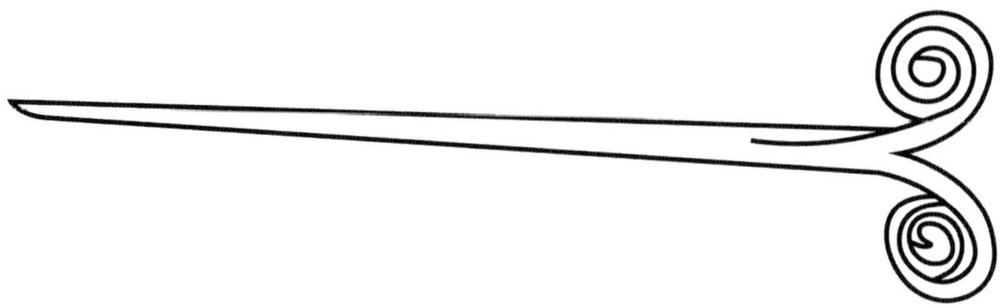

Figure 3. Spiral double-headed pin from Chanhu-daro (After Mackay 1943, 195, pl. LXVIII.9)

at Zygouries in the Peloponnese on the Greek mainland, dated to the Early Helladic II period, but made of silver[23] and another also in silver, comes from Area 28 North at Poliochni on Lemnos, dated to the Early Bronze Age (Phase II, Azzuro/Blue and 2600–2250 BC).[24] Two others from the Cyclades, but this time made from copper/bronze, come from the Early Cycladic II period cemetery of Chalandriani (Tomb 468)[25] and (Tomb 469)[26] on Syros and a third, also in bronze and similarly dated, comes from an unknown location on Naxos.[27]

There are also examples found further to the east; three gold examples, dated to the Early Bronze Age III (Level Va) period have been found at Seyitömer Höyük, located in inland Western Anatolia.[28] From the Central Iranian Plateau has also produced similar pins, such as those from Tepe Sialk (Sialk IV period) and Tepe Hissar (Hissar II–III period).[29] Spiral double-headed pins made from bronze have also been found in Bulgarian Early Bronze Age II period (3000–2000 BC) sites,[30] including Gabarevo, Ruse, Varna, Kabarat, Zavel and Sultan, pointing to a much earlier date.[31]

As these pins were being made at least by 2400 BC in the Balkans, the Aegean and Western Anatolia, Piggott tried to trace a movement of them eastwards over the succeeding centuries through Central Asia, up to the time of the Indian finds which were then dated to late in the Late Harappan Phase, dated to approximately 1800 BC.[32] As effective trade contacts between Mesopotamia, the Persian Gulf and the Indus cannot be seen much earlier than approximately 2300 BC, he believed that they were imports from the west, with an Aegean connection not being impossible.[33]

Like Piggott, Mortimer Wheeler also believed these pins established an indirect link between the Harappans, Northern Iran and Anatolia, as distinct from Mesopotamia where there are no such pins found and suggested that this could be something to do with an overland trade route or route of contact between the Eastern Mediterranean, Anatolia, Iran and India rather than the slightly later sea route through the Persian Gulf.[34]

Proposing a Harappan–Aegean connection between these pins, however, has no meaning, chronological or otherwise. On closer examination, they all have quite major differences, particularly in the metals from which they were made, in the thickness of the shafts and in overall appearance. To confirm this, Miller has now identified the Indian examples as being of an earlier, mostly Mature Harappan Phase date than previously thought and it is now believed that the Indian examples are likely to be a local invention. She has also identified a much earlier copper example with a flattened head found on a mounted platform at Mehrgarh and dated to the Mehrgarh VII period (2800 BC), equating to the Early Harappan Phase[35] and Miller has been able to trace links with these pins within India, between the Bronze Age and Chalcolithic cultures of the period.[36] However, it may have been the transmission of this artistic motif in both form and meaning, that linked these regions.

No evidence, therefore, points to these pins originating outside of the region, as the object of trade or cultural exchange. It is also clear that Piggott mistakenly misrepresented the evidence, influenced as he was by diffusion, partly by his tireless search for Central Asian links and Indo-European invaders.[37] Therefore given their distribution chronologically and geographically, these pins hold no real value in our understanding of Harappan–Aegean connections.

Carnelian Beads

Unlike the previous two categories of objects, the discovery of carnelian beads outside the Harappan heartland has very important implications for our understanding of not only the emergence of ornament technology, but our understanding pf the long-distance interactions between the Eastern Mediterranean, the Near East and India.[38]

Carnelian is a translucent form of chalcedony (microcrystaline quartz) of reddish or reddish-brown colour, due to the presence of oxidised iron, with a hardness and sheen. When imported into the Aegean in the Early and Middle Bronze Ages, it is in the form of a series of manufactured beads. In the Late Bronze Age, it was often used for manufacturing seals, but made from re-used beads imported centuries earlier.

Carnelian seems to have arrived in the Near East and farther westwards, after manufacture as beads in the workshops of India. Gujarat remains the most important source of carnelian in the world and most of the long, barrel-shaped and smaller etched beads that appeared during the late third millennium BC, are without doubt actual products of Harappan craftsmen. The unique colour of some carnelian beads made them highly sought after and in the Near East, some of the rich burials in the Royal Cemetery at Ur contained hundreds of them.

Carnelian was one of the most important semi-precious stones used for making beads and inlay during the third and second millennia BC. It is thought that a symbolic and economic relationship existed between lapis lazuli, carnelian, gold and tin, important if we are to understand the circulation, trade and exchange of these objects and commodities, all of which will have found their way to the Aegean, having what is speculated to be roughly the same source.[39]

Carnelian beads, which originate in India, come in all shapes, but are mostly elongated, biconical, some truncated biconical, like many from the Near East. They are sometimes bleached and very occasionally etched and outside India are distributed over the extensive trade routes that emanated from the Indus Valley to Central Asia, Iran, the Persian Gulf, Mesopotamia[40] and the Aegean, where they were considered both rare and exotic.

The manufacture of carnelian beads is particularly associated with the Harappan city of Chanhu-daro and some centres in the Gujarat, especially the area of Saurashtra, the latter which specialised in making particularly the long bleached and the etched carnelian beads,[41] which we know were exported in both the Mature and the early part of the Late Harappan Phases.[42] There is evidence of the importation into and use of carnelian in the Aegean in two different periods.

Early Bronze Age of the Aegean

The earliest finds of carnelian beads west of Mesopotamia was in Central and Eastern Anatolia and are dated to the Neolithic period, while in the Eastern Balkans and on Cyprus their use is first documented in the Chalcolithic period or earlier.[43] Presumably this carnelian was sourced locally and is not Indian, as it is not of their quality. In the Aegean, carnelian beads first appear in the archaeological record during the latter part of the third millennium BC, in the Early Bronze Age II–III periods.[44] Unlike lapis lazuli, which was transported as a raw commodity, carnelian was traded as manufactured objects, mostly beads, having been made for the Harappans and then exported to Mesopotamia and beyond. This early movement of carnelian offers a key link in the chain of trade and exchange that eventually leads to the consumption of carnelian in Mesopotamia and farther west, particularly at the end of the third and the start of the second millennia BC.[45]

Etched carnelian beads have received most attention. They were decorated with linear patterns by applying plant soda on the surface of the bead and briefly exposing it to heat. This technique, practiced until quite recently, is specific to Western India and it is believed that the etching of such beads originated there. They are quite distinctive and cannot be confused with those made elsewhere, unless they are imitations made in Mesopotamia but by émigré Harappan craftsmen. However, one additional clue to determining that the etched carnelian beads are Harappan, may lie on the fact that their production, imitation and importation ceased with the end of the Harappan Civilisation.[46]

As to the route of the trade in carnelian beads out of India, as with lapis lazuli, tin and possibly some gold, in the early part of the third millennium BC and earlier, it was by the land-routes of Northern or Southern Iran. After the mid-third millennium BC, in the Mature Harappan Phase in India, maritime trade in all forms of beads, by way of the Persian Gulf between India and Mesopotamia emerged, although it is possible that some of the land routes still existed, but under Harappan control until the collapse of circulation of both carnelian and lapis lazuli, which will have happened at the end of the Late Harappan Phase.[47]

While it is safe to emphasise that carnelian is the most persuasive indicator of contact between the Harappan Civilisation and the Aegean in the Early Bronze Age, carnelian beads are still a rarity and are reported from only a few sites, mostly dated to the Early Bronze Age II period. The discovery of carnelian beads together with gold and silver ornaments in hoarded treasures in Troy and on the island of Aegina, suggests that they were also connected to high social status and prestige.[48]

The carnelian beads found on Early Bronze Age sites in the Aegean are generally spherical, long and short biconical or barrel-shaped beads, with some long cylindrical examples as well as one example of an etched bead.[49] Those found so far are:

(1) **Kolonna, Aegina:** In an Early Helladic III period context (Kolonna Phase VI), excavated in 2000, a jewellery and precious object hoard was discovered buried under the floor of House 19 of the fortified coastal settlement of Kolonna on the island of Aegina in the Saronic Gulf. Known as the Aegina Hoard, it consisted of several dozen objects made from precious metals and stones, including gold, silver, carnelian, rock crystal and dentalium shell, that were stored in a small nested bundle, beneath a house floor, presumably safely hidden from intruders. The hoard is clearly a collection of reused or scrap material, as the disk- and ring-shaped beads appear to have originally belonged to much larger jewellery items. The components of the hoard are older than the time of its deposit, dating to the Early Bronze Age II period. Of particular interest is a large golden discoid pendant, a common decorative symbol in the Early Bronze Age north-east Aegean and most likely of Mesopotamian production.[50] In the corner of the bundle were an assortment of beads that had been strung as a necklace onto a very fine silver wire which shows quite an assortment of materials and types, especially those manufactured from gold and silver as well as carnelian and dentalium ring-beads. It is thought that this hoard is a collection of re-used material and that some of the objects, especially the disc- and ring-shaped beads may have belonged to other items of jewellery.[51] The hoard included 19 red carnelian beads and one made from rock crystal.[52]

One of the carnelian beads was an etched short barrel-bead (L. 0.6 cm; D. 1.0 cm) with three groups of two white-on-red concentric circles[53] and 18 others which were plain. One other that was elongated (L. 1.4 cm; D. 0.8 cm), was of an oblong shape, reminiscent of Harappan long biconical beads. The centre channel for the string was drilled from both ends, one of which is broken. Four others have a long biconical shape.[54] The longer beads have tapered conical drillings that do not meet precisely in the middle. These beads would have been imported earlier during the Early Helladic II period, to which many of the finds in the hoard can be stylistically dated, as well as parallels of many carnelian beads elsewhere.[55]

An early analysis of the bead drill holes on four of the beads, one long bicone, one elongated or long barrelled, one short bicone and the one short barrel type with the etched design, indicate that they were made with a Harappan-style constricted stone drill. Although a comparative analysis of the bead shapes and drill-hole measurements with beads from Mesopotamia and from the Harappan heartland are needed to make definite conclusions regarding the precise origin of these beads,[56] a preliminary study by the excavator points to probable links to India through the wide dispersal of these Harappan-style beads.

Kolonna on Aegina is located at the centre of the Saronic Gulf and towards the end of the Early Helladic II–III period (Kolonna Phase VI) and the beginning of the Middle Helladic Period, and controlled the maritime-based trade routes that existed between the Greek mainland, the Cyclades and Crete. Its material culture at that time reflects influences from all these regions and importantly, Kolonna is considered to be the earliest example of a ranked society inthat part of the Aegean and would have been wealthy enough to import prestigious objects through its trade connections eastwards.

Ludvik has undertaken a study of these beads and he also includes an extensive study of their manufacture and internal structures.[57] All were seemingly made from carnelian save one made of rock crystal. The shapes of beads in the hoard were almost all truncated long biconical barrel and short biconical barrel, with only two beads being very short barrel in form. All of the 16 beads identified as being Indus style by Ludvik, were very highly worn and their ends were actually ground down, suggesting that these beads were once longer and were reground at a later date to fit local stylistic preferences.[58]

The first group are the very short barrel beads. One (AK 5)[59] was made of light red slightly translucent carnelian of a high quality, the other (AK 18) was made of clear translucent rock crystal with some cracks. While their raw materials differed, both were around the same size and shape. They were not particularly well made, nor where their shapes symmetrical or standardised in their measurements. The surfaces were both roughly chipped with incomplete fine grinding and a high lustre polish. Ends were roughly chipped, incompletely ground and had a high lustre sheen from wear. Both beads had an identical drill section. Despite the differences in their raw materials, both could easily have been made in the same workshop tradition or at least by craftsmen operating in a similar crafting style given the similarities in their technology of production. Parallels come from contemporary sites around the Eastern Mediterranean, but it is interesting to note for the carnelian example that its fine grinding and raw material matches that of the Indus style beads very closely and suggests that the carnelian example was also produced in an Indus-related workshop tradition, if not indirectly imported from the Harappans.

The second group are the short barrel beads. One (AK 10) was made from mottled opaque dark reddish-brown carnelian with red and lighter coloured bands. Its exterior surface was chipped into a roughly barrel-sectioned form, ground coarsely with striae visible and given a low lustre polish. Ends were roughly chipped, ground incompletely and worn with polish from use.

The third group are the long barrel or elongated carnelian beads. One bead (AK 16) was a stylistically elongated barrel bead, made from a light slightly translucent red orange carnelian with red dots. The bead was well standardised in overall shape but both ends were not well aligned and imprecisely manufactured. Its exterior surface was chipped, coarsely ground with some striae visible and highly polished. Ends were chipped, coarsely ground flat at angles with some striae still visible and well-worn with a high polish. String wear was also evident at both ends. The fourth type are those Indus-type beads with long biconical barrels beads of constricted cylindrical stone, where six examples (AK 2, 7, 11, 12, 13 and 17) were identified. They were made from high quality carnelian of two varieties, both slightly translucent but one more of a dark orangish tan colour and the other, a deep red orange. Regardless of the differences in colour, the material was of exceptional quality, without flaws or inclusions of any kind. Beads were well standardised in shape, though the extent to which the central ridge was defined differed from bead to bead, making some obviously bicones and other more or less barrel-shaped beads with a slight, heavily ground elevation near their centre in section. Excellent parallels in style, technology and proportions come from Tell el-Ajjul, Moza'Illit, Gezer and Azor (Holon), in Syro-Palestine, as well as Mesopotamian sites such as Kish, Mari and the Royal Cemetery at Ur and others in the Indus Valley such as Harappa and Chanhu-daro.

Finally, the fifth group are the Indus short biconical barrel carnelian beads, which are by far the most common type of bead in the Aegina Treasure. Ten beads (AK 1, 3, 4, 6, 8, 9, 14, 15, 20, 21), a full half of the corpus from this site, are in this group. All were made of very similar high-quality carnelian, either light red orange slightly translucent carnelian or deep red orange slightly translucent carnelian. Very few, in fact almost no inclusions or other flaws were noted within these carnelians, a testament to the exception quality of the raw materials used. No two beads looked identical, though they were very clearly made according to the same stylistic template. In each case the section of the bead was more or less defined by the presence of a central ridge. In some beads this was very pronounced with the bead being termed a bicone. But in most cases, the ridge was present but ground down to some extent. The etched bead (AK1) falls within this category. The identical surface modifications also imply a common origin for all 10 of these beads. Each bead was chipped roughly into the biconical-barrel shape, very finely ground off of the central ridge and over it (wearing it down to the desired level) and highly polished with few grinding striae left visible. Ends were chipped, finely ground flat and heavily worn and highly polished. String wear was evident within the drill holes as well.

These beads have their best technological parallels and stylistic parallels at sites such as Harappa, Mohenjo-Daro and Dholavira and other Harappan-related sites throughout the region and into the Persian Gulf and Mesopotamia.[60]

(2) **Mochlos (Eastern Crete):** From Tomb XIX of the Early Minoan cemetery of Mochlos in Eastern Crete, comes a plain drilled cylindrical carnelian bead as part of an Early Minoan II necklace made up of carnelian, steatite, amethyst, shell and crystal beads of various carnelian types and sizes.[61] In terms of production technology, while

the use of stone and bone drills is seen earlier in the Neolithic period on Crete,[62] this bead shows clear Harappan origins.

(3) **Dhaskalio (Keros, Cyclades):** From the settlement of Dhaskalio on the island of Keros, comes two complete carnelian beads, dated to Phase C (2300 BC) in the Early Cycladic II period. The first found in Trench XX, Layer 30 is an elongated, slightly biconical, semi-translucent, polished reddish-orange carnelian bead with light pink spots. It is longitudinally pierced with a straight perforation that is drilled from both ends.[63] Its use is possibly ritual. The second bead was found in Trench XXI East, Layer 9 and is a reddish-orange small, biconical, semi-translucent, polished carnelian bead, longitudinally pierced with a biconical perforation and drilled from both ends.[64]

(4) **Kavos (Keros, Cyclades):** From Special Deposit North, Trench I, Unit 122 of Kavos on Keros, comes a single elongated strongly biconical, polished reddish, semi-translucent carnelian bead, dating to the Early Cycladic II period.[65] This bead is clearly a Harappan import.

(5) **Troy:** A close study of a fragmentary bead (A8.1107) (Fig. 4) dated to the Early Bronze Age (Troy II, 2500–2300 BC),[66] has revealed it as having once belonged to a long biconical carnelian bead, very typical of those found at Harappan sites. The other bead (8710) is dated to Troy III (2300–2200 BC).[67] Additional Early Bronze Age carnelian beads also dated to the Troy III period, now located in the A. S. Pushkin State Museum of Fine Arts in Moscow, from the excavations of Heinrich Schliemann, include one or two that appear to have been made by reshaping Harappan-style long biconical carnelian beads. From Schliemann's Treasure E, dated to the Troy II period (2500–2300 BC), comes a necklace comprised of six truncated carnelian beads of different shapes and mounted on a copper wire, including one elongated example and a single lone elongated bead with a truncated biconical shape.[68] From Schliemann's Treasure L, also dated to the Troy II period, comes four carnelian beads, one a truncated biconical bead with two flat ends with a wire passing through, holding in place two discs with eyelets on each end of the bead, a truncated biconical bead, a lenticular bead with a transverse perforation, and a tubular cylindrical bead, with an off-centre perforation.[69] Both of these Treasures, like at Kolonna, were found associated with large elite dwellings, which may indicate the deliberate burial of wealth in advance of perceived threat, thus suggesting that carnelian beads were of great value. At least four of these carnelian barrel beads seem to precisely parallel Harappan beads.

Bead A8.1107 represents a very different technology than the other beads found at Troy. It is a longitudinally fractured end of a much longer biconical or barrel bead which may have been around 50 mm long.[70] Indus-style elongated biconical carnelian beads are usually between 50 and 70 mm in length and good-quality carnelian nodules suitable for making carnelian beads of this length are known only from Kutch and Gujarat in Western India.[71] This area was part of that occupied by the Harappans and provided raw materials to workshops at the larger sites, such as Dholavira, Chanhu-daro, Mohenjo-daro and Harappa. The shape of the bead can be reconstructed by using comparisons with beads found at Indus sites, such as Mohenjo-daro, Harappa and Chanhu-daro, as well as sites in Mesopotamia. Extremely long biconical or barrel carnelian beads of this type were made at major production centres in the Indus region or possibly by Indus trained craftsmen in Mesopotamia.[72] There are no known production sites for this type of bead in Anatolia or the Mediterranean region, but it is possible that some émigré Indus craftsmen could have worked in Mesopotamian cities to make these beads for the local market.[73] If this were the case, the craftsmen would have had to bring with them when they travelled to Mesopotamia, both their long carnelian nodules and special drills.[74] Also, the carnelian used for this bead has faint banding that is common in beads found at Harappa, Mohenjo-daro and Chanhu-daro. The exterior surface of the bead was finely ground leaving some fine striae visible, but the overall exterior was highly polished to a smooth reflective surface.

During the mid-third millennium BC, constricted cylindrical drills made from ernestite, used to make these sort of beads, were to be found in the workshops that were producing long carnelian biconical beads at Mohenjo-daro, Harappa, Dholavira and Chanhu-daro, as well as some smaller sites such as Shikarpur, Kanmer, Lothal and Khirsara.[75] Troy's location at the land and sea crossroads of Europe and Asia is significant, as the site was undoubtedly constructed and fortified to exploit aspects of the surrounding economic, socio-political and physical environments and involvement in interregional exchange networks as well as the role of the local production of valuable objects.[76] Objects from India were no exception.

The other bead (No. 8710) is an unfinished long barrel bead drilled with a tapered cylindrical stone drill, dating to the Troy III period, manufactured from a deep red-orange carnelian that has a fairly uniform translucent colour with a streak of darker

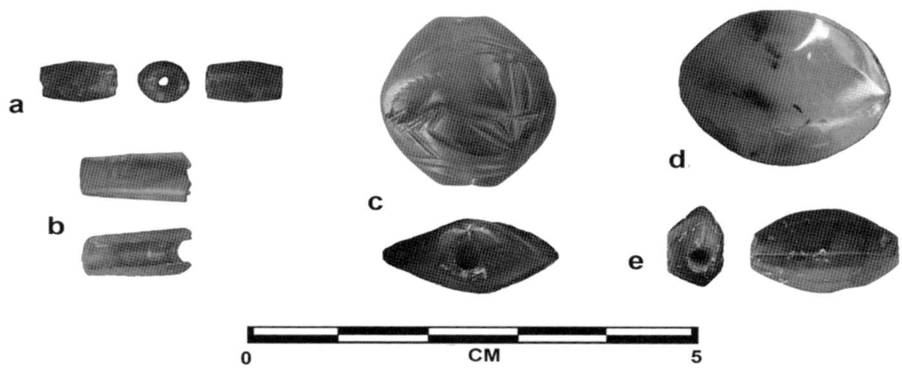

Figure 4. Fragment of Biconical Carnelian Bead from Troy (Troy II) (A8.1107) (From Ludvik et al. *2015, fig. 4b)*

material that may be the result of carbon or other organic stain in one of the cracks in the stone.[77]

(6) **Poliochni (Lemnos):** From Poliochni on Lemnos in the Northern Aegean, comes a necklace comprised of 126 carnelian beads of various shapes, dated to Period Giallo/ Yellow (2200–2100 BC).[78]

(7) **Zygouries:** From Tomb VIIa comes two cylindrical carnelian beads; and from Tomb XX comes one cylindrical carnelian bead, all dated to the Early Helladic II period.[79]

The carnelian beads that have been found in the Aegean in the Early Bronze Age, such as those from Kolonna and Troy, dating to the Early Bronze Age II period in approximately 2300 BC, are certain to have originated in India, when the exports of such beads were at their height during the Mature Harappan Phase and from where there are many parallels. In the Harappan heartland, the etched or elongated carnelian bead was a popular type in use throughout this phase[80] and as already mentioned, close parallels of the Kolonna bead can be found at both Chanhu-daro[81] and Mohenjo-daro,[82] consistent in date to 2400–2300 BC.

So far, however, no specific analyses have been conducted to confirm the geological source of any of the carnelian beads from the Aegean. It has been speculated that both the carnelian etched bead from Kolonna and some others, originated in the Harappan heartland and arrived in the Aegean by way of Egypt.[83] As far as the etched bead found at Kolonna is concerned, the excavator Claus Reinholdt believes that if the carnelian was imported from India, the route could have been through Egypt, Anatolia or the Near East,[84] the Anatolian and the Near Eastern being the most likely.

Susan Sherratt has suggested a more likely Anatolian link at the end of the Early Bronze Age, when Kolonna on Aegina was already playing a role in what she describes as an Anatolian Trade Network linking the overland routes of Anatolia and the Troad in the east with the Saronic Gulf acting as a gateway to Western Asia and beyond. Already Kolonna was a good example of an early ranked society in the Aegean, outside of Crete and a large trading centre located in the Saronic Gulf and a possible entry point to the Argolid. Kolonna in both the Early Helladic II and III periods was an impressive and well-fortified settlement with its corridor houses, consistent with a type of building known at the time, also found at Lerna in the Argolid and Thebes in Boeotia and can be compared with Troy. This Anatolian trade network was now thriving independently from anything that was happening on Crete, when the Minoans were forging links with Cyprus and Syro-Palestine and playing an important role all over the Aegean. This network was in existence during Early Helladic II–III periods and played a significant role in the trade of metal and varying technologies. It would have involved Kolonna, as the site has revealed the presence of, for example, not only monumental structures and Anatolian/ Northern Aegean pottery (Kastri Group/Lefkandi I), but standardised weights of imported stones were found indicating participation in a network with standard measurement units.[85]

The distribution of elongated and etched carnelian beads, such as the Kolonna example, is much wider in the Near East, particularly Mesopotamia, where several similar examples have been located,[86] particularly from Grave PG 55 of the Early Dynastic IIIA period (2600–2300 BC) and the Akkadian period (2350–2150 BC) Royal Cemetery at Ur,[87] where the highest number of these beads has been found, along as well as local imitations. They have also been found at Kish and Tell Asmar, both in an Akkadian context.[88] Of interest is the finding at Tell Asmar in Mesopotamia, of a bead that is a particularly good parallel of the etched Kolonna example.[89] From Iran, Possehl has illustrated the etched carnelian beads found in the region and a picture emerges of a distribution at sites that include Tepe Hissar, Shah Tepe, Kelleh Nissar, Susa, Tepe Yahya, Jalalabad and Marlik.[90]

As has already been pointed out, the Harappans did not necessarily enjoy a monopoly of the physical manufacture of etched carnelian beads and it is now believed that some were made in the Near East supplementing the supply of beads,[91] such as in a local Akkadian workshop, in the hands of émigré Harappan craftsmen. They would, however, be imitating Indian origins and using imported raw carnelian and tools that originated in India, probably from the southern coast of the Gujarat. However, the elongated and white-on-red etched variety, like those found at Kolonna on Aegina and Troy, are seemingly exclusively of Harappan manufacture.[92]

Middle and Late Bronze Ages of the Aegean

Of carnelian beads found in the Middle and Late Bronze Ages, unlike other types, long biconical and long barrel beads are not so common in Minoan, Mycenaean or Northern Aegean contexts. The main exceptions are from the Shaft Graves at Mycenae, from which at least 20 such beads are known, such as in Grave III of Grave Circle A and in Tomb O of Grave Circle B.[93] They are also present in the Aegina Treasure, dated to the Middle Helladic period and now in the British Museum and a few examples are known from later contexts. However, only three out of the over 200 carnelian beads found in the Mycenaean cemetery at Prosymna (Tombs 8, 3 and 44), which date between Late Helladic I and III, are long biconical types.[94] One or two similar examples are known from Crete from Middle Minoan IA to Late Minoan IIIA[95] and from Troy; one bead is dated to the Middle Bronze Age (Troy VI Early, *c.* 1750–1600 BC) and others to the Late Bronze Age (Troy VI Middle to VIIa, 1600–1180 BC). Two others were irregular spherical or oblate carnelian beads, a style typical in the Late Bronze Age in the Aegean.[96]

The importance of carnelian beads of all types as prestige items, persisted throughout the Late Bronze Age when such beads were very often deposited in the graves of mainland Greece and Crete.[97] During the height of the prosperity of the Mycenaean palaces, carnelian beads were still considered a luxury item and are to be found frequently in funerary offerings. In this period globular, irregular, short oblate, short barrel, short cylindrical and short biconical beads were the most common, but other shapes like amygdaloid, 'opium poppy', 'figure-of- eight shield' and 'grain of wheat' also appear.[98] Numerous beads made of carnelian were also found on Rhodes.[99]

We cannot say with any certainty that any of the beads found in Late Bronze Age contexts were imported from India. However, some carnelian beads of Aegean, mostly Cretan manufacture, can be identified as such because of their distinctively local motifs. One of the common hard stone materials used to produce Aegean seals was carnelian and it is not clear if most of the seals produced in the Aegean were made from pieces of raw carnelian. If the seals made from carnelian were originally undecorated amygdaloid, lentoid and other shaped beads and imported and engraved locally, they were probably re-used beads imported much earlier, hence the reason for so few having been found in earlier centuries. The workshops that produced seals and beads, appear to have been located at or near the palaces of major Minoan and Mycenaean sites, such as the Knossos harbour-town at Poros or in Thebes in Boeotia. However, the exact relationship between the administrative elite in the palace and the seal or bead craftsmen is unclear.[100]

Of other carnelian beads dating to the Middle and Late Bronze Ages, in the Aegina Treasure, there are two pairs of gold ornaments, possibly earrings that include grooved cylindrical carnelian beads,[101] three round orange-red translucent carnelian beads, which may be part of a necklace together with three beads of lapis lazuli and five beads of gold,[102] and a necklace which includes 166 carnelian beads of spherical or bi-conical shape, one oval carnelian bead, 15 elongated barrel shaped carnelian beads and three cylindrical etched carnelian beads.[103]

John Younger believes that these beads in the Aegina Treasure cannot be dated any earlier than the Middle Minoan IIB period, when the bow drill was first used in the Aegean for drilling hard stone.[104] That would certainly be the case if the necklace or the individual beads had been made locally and not in India, where such drilling technology had been known for over a thousand years earlier, particularly on the west coast, around the Bay of Cambay.[105] If they are contemporary imports, as it is suspected, and not re-worked, it may even point to a slightly earlier date for the Aegina Treasure than suspected. The carnelian necklace from Eutresis Grave 6, comprised of 11 elongated carnelian beads, but with narrow ends, together with 15 spherical beads, is to be dated to the earlier part of the Middle Helladic period, from the pottery found with them.[106] They may be direct imports.

On Crete in the Middle Minoan III to the Late Minoan IB periods, translucent red carnelian as a commodity may possibly have been imported from India, but more likely, existing objects made from this material were re-used, particularly for making talismanic amygdaloid and red lentoid seals. We know of one such example of the former, but of unknown provenance on Crete[107] and an example of the latter is from the Tholos Tomb at Kazama in the Argolid, dated to the Late Helladic I–II period,[108] but may have been manufactured on Crete, possibly from re-used material.

Regular re-use of carnelian beads originating in India, is identified from several other Aegean Late Bronze Age sites. One is a necklace of spherical carnelian breads from Tomb 67 and a carnelian talismanic seal depicting a two-handled jug and foliage from Tomb 167 in the Late Minoan IIIA–B necropolis of Armenoi in Western Crete,[109] although made in the Middle Minoan III to Late Minoan I periods (1600–1500 BC). From what object the carnelian from Armenoi was re-used is unknown; it may even have been an heirloom.

Carnelian was popular for a very long time in the Aegean for the manufacture of beads and seals from the Early Bronze Age onwards. The use continued through to the Late Bronze Age, many of the beads accumulating value as they built up over the years since they were first imported, a distinguished pedigree of ownership, the manufactured objects originating in India. They will have arrived from India by way of Mesopotamia[110] and many were re-used over time. Olga Krzyszkowska, however, has argued that most carnelian came from India is but pure assumption and that it was only one of the many sources used in both the third and second millennia BC.[111] It is accepted that carnelian has been found in Egypt;[112] coming from the Egyptian Eastern Desert and further south into Nubia which was in use from Predynastic times. Whether these sources were exploited during the Middle to Late Bronze Age Aegean is an unanswered question,[113] but it is of a dull and of inferior quality, quite unlike that used by the Minoans and the Mycenaean elites.

The trade in the Early Bronze Age and early part of the Middle Bronze Age Aegean of Indian carnelian beads by way of Mesopotamia and Syro-Palestine was in sufficient amounts to possibly warrant the term import. But for what it came in trade or exchange, if anything, is unclear.[114] If some carnelian beads from India were still arriving in the Aegean towards the end of the Middle and for the whole of the Late Bronze Age in the Aegean, it will confirm the continuation of the use of some trade routes during the final phases of a post-urban Late Harappan Gujarat (1600–1500 BC) and what succeeded it. Most likely, however, the beads and seals were now being made from re-used Indian beads originally imported through Mesopotamia. This latter idea was suggested in an article by Younger written some years ago, who proposed an Indus Valley origin having been imported as finished beads and then reworked.[115]

To finally answer the question of the source of individual carnelian beads or other objects, preliminary research on the sourcing of carnelian using trace element analysis indicates that it is possible to correlate geological source areas with specific carnelian beads.[116] If similar studies could be undertaken in Anatolia and the Aegean, it might be possible to narrow down the sources of carnelian (and agate) used for making beads.[117]

Agate Seals and Beads

Agate is a very distinct banded form of microcrystaline quartz. The bands are often irregular and ill-defined but are concentric and this makes it an attractive material to use both for seals and body ornamentation, such as beads. It was popular for a considerable period in the Aegean from the Early to Late Bronze Ages and particularly three varieties, one black-and-white banded, one caramel or light-brown coloured with light-brown bands and another clear with occasional spars of clear red or blue colour. Whilst a Mesopotamian, Egyptian or even Anatolian source for the agate cannot be completely ruled out,[118] an Indian source is the most likely and would have been imported in much the same way as lapis lazuli[119] or carnelian.

So far only one agate bead can be attested from the Early Bronze Age. It comes from Grave R22 of the Early Helladic II–III period Round Graves at Steno on the island of Leukas,[120] but we also know that agate was being used for making seals on Crete from the Middle Minoan II period onwards. Younger has suggested, as with carnelian, whilst supporting an Indian origin for the agate used for making seals, that some of the material was imported into the Aegean earlier as finished beads and then reworked.[121] For example, three agate seals from the New Palace Workshop at Thebes, dating to the Late Helladic IIIA–B periods, may also have been made from cut-down Harappan agate beads.[122] In that same New Palace Workshop at Thebes was also found a tear-drop pendant of both an unusual shape and made from a translucent light-brown or caramel coloured agate of Indian type with darker brown veins, for which there are close parallels from sites in the Gujarat at this time.[123] Another example from the Late Helladic IIIB period Thebes is an agate bead; its small size and rarity, with a length of 1.6 cm, undoubtedly means it has been reworked from a larger bead.[124]

Four other Late Bronze Age examples have been found, two Mycenaean, one in Grave 1 of the Barbounas Cemetery at Asine in the Argolid, dated to Late Helladic IIB–IIIA,[125] and one further, of unknown provenance but likely carved by the same Master;[126] and two Minoan examples, one from the Tholos Tomb at Kafkales, Maleme on Crete and dated to the Late Minoan IIIA period,[127] that seems to be a pair with another of unknown provenance[128] and which may come from the same burial. Whether they were made from cut-down Indian agate beads or made from raw agate imported from India is impossible to tell, but the former is more likely.

Flat Disc-Shaped Beads

Within the same hoard (the Aegina Hoard) found on Kolonna on Aegina as the carnelian beads within a context dated to the Early Helladic III period (Kolonna Phase VI), were three silver flat disc-shaped beads (Fig. 5),[129] with a tubular perforation in a raised central midrib (or axial tubular string holes) of a type known from both the Aegean to the Harappan heartland. They were made from two discs, each hammered over a wire running through the centre, aligned and then beaten or soldered together leaving a central tube for stringing.

Although dated to Kolonna Phase VI, as with the carnelian beads, they too are likely to have been imported during the Early Helladic II period, like much of the contents of the hoard. There are good Aegean parallels, but in gold from Troy IIg (2300 BC),[130] and Poliochni (Phase V, Giallo/Yellow, 2200–2100 BC),[131] which may be an extension of the Anatolian–Saronic Gulf links, discussed above. In Mesopotamia of an Early Dynastic III-Akkadian date (2500–2300 BC)[132] they are found at sites all along both the northerly land and Persian Gulf trade routes.[133] From Mohenjo-daro, an example in gold has been found in HR Area below Room 8 of House VIII, Block 2, Sector B (referred to as small globular gold beads), as components of an iconic necklace with the gold beads paper-thin and dispersed with beads of onyx, amazonite, turquoise and agate.[134] It is dated to the Late Harappan Phase (1800 BC), slightly later than the Aegina finds, although it could already have been as much as two to three hundred years older. This necklace and the gold beads are most likely of local manufacture. A similar necklace with gold beads comes from Lothal in the Gujarat (Phase Va), dating to approximately 1900 BC, which may be significant in terms of it being found at a surviving centre for trade with the west at this time.[135] A complete necklace comprised of 26 of the beads has also been found at the Mature Harappan Phase site of Khirsara in the Gujarat.[136]

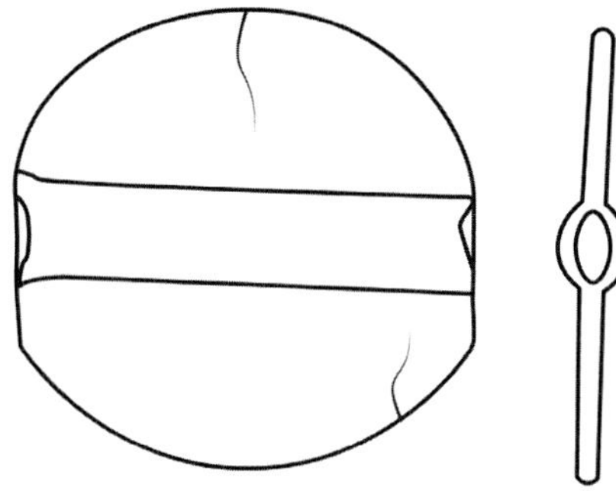

Figure 5. Silver flat disc-shaped bead from Kolonna, Aegina (Silver Bead 030). Aegina, Phase VI (Early Helladic III) (Reproduced with the permission of Professor Dr Claus Reinholdt, University of Salzburg)

For the silver beads from Aegina and other sites where carnelian beads have also been found, a similar trade or cultural exchange pattern eastwards is proposed, with a distribution stretching from the Aegean to India with them being passed on from one centre to another along this route. What it does not prove, however, is that the Aegean examples were made in India. A steatite jeweller's mould from Mari of an Early Dynastic III date includes a hollow for the manufacturing of this type of bead.[137] What this does likely prove is that there was a communality of design and use that stretched through India, the Near East, Iran, Central Asia the Eastern Mediterranean and included the Aegean. Birgitte Musche also offers the distribution of these beads as evidence of the existence of trade routes linking all of these regions.[138]

Other Beads

Stone beads made from materials other than carnelian and agate, found in both India and the Aegean also have a similarity both in shape and form and the material from which they were manufactured.

Faience Segmented Beads

One such bead is the small faience segmented bead,[139] of which a number of white and red or white and brown examples have been found mostly in later levels at

Harappa,[140] at Mohenjo-daro[141] and Chanhu-daro[142] and also in the Harappan IB levels (2200–2000 BC) at Rojdi (Phase B).[143] Identical examples of these beads, but pale blue and green in colour, have also been uncovered in the Temple Repositories at Knossos, dating to the Middle Minoan III period.[144] Spectrographic analysis has shown that two of the segmented beads, one from Knossos and another from Harappa, are identical in manufactured composition,[145] at approximately the same time around 1700–1600 BC during the final part of the Late Harappan Phase.[146] The Knossos and Harappa faience segmented beads are therefore not only contemporary, but are from the same source and this offers additional evidence of indirect contact though prestige jewellery items at a time when the Harappan Civilisation is in its post-urban period, but when there was still enough impetus within the economy to sustain some long-distance trade and contact. We also know that beads can be easily transported over long distances.

Steatite Segmented Beads

Although much of the steatite used in sealstones and in the manufacture of stone vases in Minoan Crete was sourced locally, there were also discovered similar small segmented wafer-like beads made from talcose steatite. Again, they are almost identical in the material from which they are made to the large number of similar beads found in Harappan craft centres, particularly the site of Zekhada in the Gujarat, dated to the Mature and Late Harappan Phases, which was a major site for their manufacture.[147] Like the faience segmented beads, it is quite possible that the examples found in the Aegean may also have had an Indian origin.[148]

Turning to the Near East, to areas that would now have been in contact with the Aegean, a study of seven Early Bronze Age small stone beads, recovered from the site of Tell Fadous-Kfarabida, a small urban settlement located in what is now northern coastal Lebanon, has revealed that six of them are made from fired steatite or synthetic enstatite. As steatite is not a material available locally in Syro-Palestine, these beads must indicate long-distance material and probably technological, exchange. The six beads from Tell Fadous-Kfarabida, can be dated stratigraphically to late in Phase III (2850/2650–2750/2600 BC) (one bead) to Phase IV (2750/2600–2550 BC) (five beads).[149] There is no evidence for on-site bead production, although the required firing technology was certainly available at the time and no steatite debitage or objects needed for bead-making has been found either at this site or at any other in the immediate region. Given this evidence and the relative rarity of steatite as a raw material, we can reasonably assume that these beads were imported in their finished form.[150] The proximity of the Eastern Mediterranean is not lost on us.

Primary sources of steatite from which beads could be made are known in India, central and south-east Anatolia, the Persian Gulf and Egypt and possibly central Mesopotamia. Comparable beads are known from these areas from as early as the fifth millennium BC, but the importance of Tell Fadous-Kfarabida lies in their colour as there is a general correspondence of enstatite bead colour to manufacturing locale, locating white-grey beads to India, but evidence from Anatolia show that a few white examples are also produced there.[151]

The evidence for the foreign connections of Tell Fadous-Kfarabida come from several non-local objects found on site, including pottery, copper and bronze. The relationship between Egypt and the region during the third millennium BC is well attested,[152] as is the value of the Lebanese littoral as a connecting route between Anatolia, Mesopotamia and Egypt. However, finds of metalwork along the Lebanese coast are much more suggestive of connections with Mesopotamia[153] and it is certainly likely that there were open connections to India, even for the earlier periods.[154] There is also evidence of some similar beads having been found at Tell Brak in Northern Syria and dated to no earlier than 3000 BC.[155] It is also possible that these seals and beads made from talcose steatite may also have had some Indian connections.

Bronzes

Bronze Weapons from Lothal

It has been suggested by S. R. Rao, the excavator of Lothal, that the two bronze weapons he found in a Mature Harappan Phase context at the site, one a folded socket spearhead (L. 3.4 cm) and another a triangular dagger with a rivet hole near the tang (L. 8.7 cm), resemble similar weapons from what he described as 'Middle Minoan III Crete'.[156] However, in terms of Aegean chronology, this date would appear to be too late even for Late Harappan Lothal.

A close study of the corpus of Early and Middle Minoan bronzes suggests that the folded socket spearhead should be discounted, but it must be admitted that the triangular dagger does resemble shorter examples from Ayia Triada in Southern Crete, which are dated from the Early Minoan I to Middle Minoan II periods.[157] Rao proposes that the dagger was left behind by a visitor from Crete,[158] but a far more plausible explanation is that if it can be remotely proven that it was manufactured on Crete or any other part of the Aegean, it is again the product of indirect Persian Gulf and Near Eastern contact, like other objects discussed here. However, the assertion that the dagger was Minoan is not repeated in Rao's final and definitive excavation report[159] and an inspection by the author of the bronzes in the Archaeological Museum at Lothal in the State of Gujarat, does not convince one of any Aegean connections.

Other Bronzes[160]

There may well be additional examples of Harappan metalwork, such as weapons, tools or items of body ornamentation, now having found their way into the Aegean and remaining undetected. At present, however, Harappan metal types in Mesopotamian contexts are extremely rare. The only example that can now be identified is that by Mackay, who suggests that a flat copper blade without a midrib from Kish is comparable with one from Mohenjo-daro.[161] Aegean metalwork of the period found further east than Cyprus, is only represented by a Minoan scraper or razor found at Byblos, which conforms to a well-known Cretan type, dating to the Middle Minoan IB–IIB periods.[162] The Harappans traded in metals as commodities, not metal objects, although the importation of tin or tin-bronzes into Mesopotamia may have been by ingots in the form of large rings.[163]

Pottery

From a study of the pottery assemblages from a number of sites in the Aegean, no pottery vessels that originated in India have been located in the Aegean or vice-versa and although there may be some resemblance between coarseware pottery from both regions, this is not of any significance or indicative of contact.

Notes

1 Massa and Palmisano 2018a, 66.
2 Ludvik *et al.* 2015, 1–2.
3 Pande 1971a, 231–233; 1971b, 311–313. A doubtful association of the Harappan kernoi with the Aegean is also made in Davaras 2003, 106.
4 The first example is from the excavations of M. S. Vats at Harappa, Archaeological Survey of India, Central Asian Collection, New Delhi, no. 2348, see Vats 1940, pl. LXXI.76 (illustration only), Great Granary Area. The second example is from the excavations of Mortimer Wheeler, XXIX–30, LXVIII–LXXII, near cemetery R37, Burial 5, unpublished; see Pande 1971b, 311–313.
5 From the excavations at Mohenjo-daro 49.251/2961, unpublished; see Pande 1971b, 311–313.
6 Dales and Kenoyer 1986, 226, 420–421, fig. 92.1–6.
7 Bosanquet 1896–1897, 57–61. For Minoan kernoi (also far more elaborate than the Harappan examples) see Xanthoudides 1905–1906, 9–23; Betancourt 1985, 40, pl. 3k.
8 Pande 1971b, 311–323; Bignasca 2000, 212–213.
9 Tobler 1950, 159, 223, pl. LXXXb; Bignasca 2000, 11, 195, cat. no. O17.
10 Oates 1977, 238, 242, pl. 10a, no. TB45; Bignasca 2000, 11, 195, fig. 2, cat. no. O20.
11 Delougaz 1952, 103, 171, pl. 106.1; Bignasca 2000, 11, 195, fig. 2, cat. no. O19.
12 Athens, National Archaeological Museum, inv. no. NM 5427, Furumark 1972, 69, 618, fig. 20, type 197.1.
13 Higgins 1980, 50.
14 Piggott 1948, 26–40.
15 Childe 1936, 113–119.
16 Chanhu-daro Mound II, Square 8/B, Location 284. Mackay 1943, 195, pl. LXVIII.9. From its find spot below the datum, this example is likely to be dated to the Late Harappan Phase. It was found as part of a corroded metal hoard which included a copper bowl (excavation number 2365) containing a bronze jar, a flat-handled pan, an arrow-head, three heads for staffs or maces, a knife, four spear-heads and two elongated axes or chisels (all Indus Civilisation types) and this pin. However, its find spot was near the surface and its associations were not with other objects of the Mature Harappan Phase and it could be assigned to the Following occupation phase contemporary with the Jhukar Culture or the Sind Late Harappan. See also Yule 1985b, 21, pl. 8, no. 186.
17 Karachi, National Museum of Pakistan; DK Area, Section G, Intermediate Period III, excavation no. DK 5285. Mackay 1938, 539, pl. C, no. 4. See also Yule 1985b, 22, pl. 8, no. 199.

18 Piggott 1948, 26–27. The date is likely not to be Mature Harappan, but from the Late Harappan Phase. However, a good unpublished parallel to the pin originally made with a single spiral comes from Troy (Troy IIg), National Archaeological Museum, Athens, inv. no. NM 4339 (Sophie Schliemann Bequest).

19 Joshi 1978, 100–103; 1980, 19–21 and pl. XIII.B; Yule 1985b, 22, pl. 8, no. 196; Joshi and Bala 1993, 187, pl. 16.2.

20 Bisht 1993, 119, pl. 10.25.

21 For a recent study of Indian spiral double-headed pins, see Miller 2013, 223–238.

22 For parallels of the bronze spiral double-headed bronze pins for Troy IIg, see Branigan 1974, 181–182, cat. nos. 2067 (silver) and 2068 (gold). For the gold pin, Istanbul Archaeological Museums inv. no. 684M, see Şahoğlu and Sotirakopoulou 2011, 281 and 376, cat. no. 167.

23 Blegen 1928, 181, pl. XX, no. 9; Branigan 1974, 181, cat. no. 2069; Kilian-Dirlmeier 1984, 23–25, pl. 1, no. 19, also for discussion of Near Eastern parallels.

24 Bernabò Brea 1964, volume I.1, 220, fig. 320 and volume I.2, pl. LXXXVIe; Branigan 1974, 181, cat. no. 2064.

25 National Archaeological Museum, Athens, inv. no. NM 5212. Tsountas 1899, col. 101, pl. 10, no. 15; Branigan 1974, 181, cat. no. 2066; Hood 1978, 190, pl. 187(A); Şahoğlu and Sotirakopoulou 2011, 243 and 361, cat. no. 25.

26 Tsountas 1899, col. 101, pl. 10, no. 16; Branigan 1974, 181, cat. no. 2065.

27 National Archaeological Museum, Athens, inv. no. NM 12456; Branigan 1974, p. 181, no. 2074 (Type XI); Marangou 1990, 63, no. 36.

28 Kütahya Museum, inv. nos. 13439–13441. Şahoğlu and Sotirakopoulou 2011, 340 and 397, cat. nos. 439–441. For the excavations at Seyitömer Höyük see Bilgen 2015, 218–222.

29 McCowan 1942, 53, table 1; Wheeler 1968, 99, 113–114. For a copper double spiral pendant from Tepe Hissar, dated to the Hissar III period (2500–2000 BC), New York, American Museum of National History, 73-3239, see Aruz 2003, 352, cat. no. 246.

30 Boyadziev 1995, 149–191.

31 Renfrew 1972, 332. For Gabarevo, see Gaul 1948, 192, pl. XXXIV.3; for Ruse, Varna, Kubarat, Zavet, Gaul 1948, 81 and Sultan, Gaul 1948, 129. The tradition of these pins seems to have lasted in the Balkans. What are called Spiral Spectacle-like pins and dated to the Bulgarian Middle-Late Bronze Age (1400–1150 BC) come from a number of sites in Southern Bulgaria such at the Tumulus in Prčevo, Grašica, Latinsko Groblje, Gornia Stražava and Donja Toponika and are what has been described as probably a precursor or served as a model for the spectacle-like fibula known from the Bronze Age in the region. See Luci 2007, 355, fig. 16.

32 Piggott 1948, 29–31, 33 and fig, 3; Childe 1936, 113–119.

33 Two animal-head copper or bronze pins were also found, one from Mohenjo-daro with a stag's head and another well-known example from Harappa, with a stag and a dog intertwined, see Mackay 1938, 539, pl. C, no. 3 and Vats 1940, 390, pl. CXXV, nos. 34, 36. An Aegean parallel to the stag-head pins from Mohenjo-daro and Harappa comes from the Dokathismata cemetery on the Cycladic island of Amorgos, dated to the Early Cycladic II period, but made of silver and surmounted with a ram, National Archaeological Museum, Athens, inv. no. NM 4730, see Tsountas 1898, col. 154, pl. 8, no. 66; Branigan 1974, 182, cat. no. 2078 (Type XIIII); Hood 1978, 190, pl. 187(G). There is a similar gold pin also surmounted by a horned ram from Shaft Grave Circle A at Mycenae (Grave IV) but dated to the very beginning of the Late Bronze Age (*c*. 1500 BC), see Karo 1930–1933, pl. XVIII, no. 245; Hood 1978, 190, pl. 187(F), although it could be an heirloom.

34 Wheeler 1968, 113–114.

35 Excavation numbers EBK 216 and MRK 7c(I) 77.32; Taddei 1979, 528–529, fig. 45.7. It also corresponds to a similarly dated example from Mundigak in Iran, Period IV; Casal 1961, fig. 139.18.

36 Miller 2013, 223–238.
37 Piggott 1950, 248–249.
38 Ludvik *et al.* 2015, 15.
39 Wilkinson 2014, 134. Carnelian is known to have originated in many regions of the ancient world. These are Eastern Iran and South-Western Afghanistan (around the basin of the Helmand River), Bushehr in South-Western Iran, the Elburz Mountains in Northern Iran and in India in the Deccan plateau and the area around Ratnapur in the state of Madhya Pradesh. Carnelian is also reported from the Arabian Peninsula, Bactria, Azerbaijan, Anatolia and Egypt, see Moorey 1994, 97; Wilkinson 2014, 134. However, as the stone is widely found as pebbles in alluvial deposits, it is almost impossible to be specific about the provenance of the raw materials without the aid of archaeological science. The Indian sources are assumed to have been the most important for the third millennium BC and although a detailed examination of the carnelian from Harappa confirms the importance of carnelian from the Gujarat, very little has been done to establish the provenance of carnelian at an inter-regional level, see Wilkinson 2014, 134. It is only by the study of the manufactured objects that we will understand their origins.
40 Ratnagar 2004, 178–185; Kenoyer 1997, 262–280; 1998, 160–162. For discussion of trade in carnelian beads between the Harappan heartland and Mesopotamia, see Peyronel 2015, 217–220.
41 Possehl 2012, 762. For a study of etched carnelian beads, see Possehl 1996, 153–158, which offers parallels to the Aegina beads from Iran, Mesopotamia and the Harappan heartland.
42 Collon 2008, 43–45. She supports the idea that these beads were made on the west coast of India.
43 Ludvik *et al.* 2015, 2. This was local carnelian of inferior quality than that from India. On Cyprus, occasionally the attractive local green-blue picrolite, which became very important in the Chalcolithic period, was used together with carnelian for necklace beads and small ornamental objects such as a little fish from Khirokitia, see Dikaios 1953, 302–304, fig. 107 and pl. 68a:1485 and 1486. Evidence is now emerging of carnelian being found in elite contexts at four sites from Cyprus, dated as early as to the Aceramic Neolithic Period (Pre-Pottery Neolithic B or PPNB, 8200–7900 BC). Although it has not been possible to determine its provenance, the poor quality suggests that it was sourced within the Eastern Mediterranean. See Moutsiou 2021.
44 Alram-Stern 2004, 453–456; Reinholdt 2008, 52–53; and Ludvik *et al.* 2015, 2.
45 Wilkinson 2014, 134.
46 Wilkinson 2014, 134–136.
47 Wilkinson 2014, 136.
48 Colburn 2012, 370–372.
49 Ludvik *et al.* 2015, 2.
50 Reinholdt 2003, 260–261.
51 Felten 2007, 15; 2008, 32–35. The position of Kolonna in the trade networks with the Levant that were beginning to develop at the end of the Early Helladic Period, is best understood by its role in linking the overland routes of Anatolia and the east with the Saronic and Corinthian Gulfs and farther west. This was based on the Gediz and Maeander river routes and another, still more northerly one, on routes leading through Troy. See Sherratt 2010, 81–106.
52 Reinholdt 2003, 260–261.
53 Archaeological Museum of Piraeus (formerly in the Archaeological Museum of Aegina), inv. no MA 6602 (Grave No. Δ 35.8.19); Aruz 2003, 243–244; 2008, 50; Kenoyer 2003, 396–397; Reinholdt 2003, 260–261, cat. no. 166a; 2008, 13, 52–54, 109, pl. 13.1, no. 032. The string side of the beads seems to have been re-cut, suggesting that some of the etched pattern may have been removed for it to be adapted to a local jewellery type.
54 Archaeological Museum of Piraeus (formerly in the Archaeological Museum of Aegina), inv. no. MA 6603 (Grave No. Δ 35.8.22); Aruz 2003, 243–244; 2008, 50; Kenoyer 2003, 396–397; Reinholdt

2003, 260–261, cat. no. 166b; 2008, 13, 52–54, 109, pl. 13.2–3, no. 033; Archaeological Museum of Piraeus (formerly Archaeological Museum of Aegina), inv. no. MA 6604 (Grave No. Δ 35.8, 18, 27, 7.1–7.14; Reinholdt 2008, 13, 52–54, 109–10, pl. 13.2–3, nos. 034–050.

55 Reinholdt 2008, 16 and 52–54, pls. 13.10–3.

56 Ludvik *et al.* 2015, 14–15.

57 Ludvik 2018, 550–567. Ludvik also offers extensive details and illustrations of each bead.

58 Ludvik 2018, 550–567.

59 Numbering of beads is in accord with Ludvik 2018, 550–567.

60 Ludvik 2018, 559.

61 Seager 1912, 72, fig. 41, no. XIX.14. The cleaning of Tomb VI in 1971 produced two more carnelian beads dated to the Early Minoan II period: (a) a cylindrical bead of orange coloured colour, Agios Nikolaos Museum 3110,; and (b) a spherical bead of yellow-red colour, Agios Nikolaos Museum 3111, Davaras 1975, 106, pl. 15b, nos. 2 and 27. Additionally in Tomb 1 was found a carnelian seal, dated by the excavator to the Middle Minoan III period, see Seager 1912, 20, fig. 6 no. 1; Soles 1992, 42–51. Also, in Tomb III was found three small beads of red carnelian, Seager 1912, 39; and in Tomb XII, a three-sided read carnelian seal, see Seager 1912, 75, fig. 30. All three now likely to have been of a Middle Minoan IA date. There is further evidence for contacts between Eastern Crete and the Near East at this time. A silver cylinder seal from Syria has been found at Mochlos, dated to the Early Minoan II period, Heraklion Museum, inv. no. HM 390; Aruz 1984, 186–188; 2008, 40–41, fig. 59, no. 106. From Tomb I (Papoura) at Lebena in Southern Crete was found one carnelian bead, part of a series of beads, possibly from a necklace dated to the Early Minoan II–Middle Minoan IA period, but it is not possible to identify it as an import. See Alexiou and Warren 2004, 35, no. 78.l, not illustrated.

62 Ludvik *et al.* 2015, 2.

63 Haas-Lebegyev and Renfrew 2013, 662–663, fig. 31.20–21, no. 12562.

64 Haas-Lebegyev and Renfrew 2013, 662–663, fig. 31.20–21, no.11017.

65 Birtacha 2007, 363, no. 411, fig. 9.15, 9.16.

66 Ludvik *et al.* 2015, 9–10, fig. 4b. For further study of the Trojan carnelian beads see Ludvik 2018, 571–578.

67 Ludvik *et al.* 2015, 4.

68 Pushkin State Museum of Fine Art, Moscow, inv. no. Aap 120 (П132); Aap 121 (П133); Schmidt 1902, 238, pl. I, cat. nos. 6000–6001; Antonova *et al.* 1996, 111, 211 and cat. nos. 121–122.

69 Pushkin State Museum of Fine Art, Moscow, inv. nos. Aap 218–221 (П128, 130, 126 and 129); Schmidt 1902, 243, cat. nos. 6108–6111; Antonova *et al.* 1996, 172, 211 and cat. no. 218–221.

70 Ludvik *et al.* 2015, 9 and figs 4b and 5b. For complete description and study of this bead see Ludvik *et al.* 2015, 14 and Ludvik 2018, 572–573.

71 Kenoyer *et al.* 1994, 281–306; Ludvik *et al.* 2015, 14.

72 Ludvik 2018, 571–578.

73 Kenoyer 1997, 272–274; 2008a, 19–28.

74 Ludvik *et al.* 2015, 9.

75 Ludvik 2018, 571–578.

76 Ludvik *et al.* 2015, 1.

77 Ludvik 2018, 571–578.

78 Lemnos Museum, Storeroom 643. Bernabò Brea 1976, pls. CCXLVII:d; CCLII:1.

79 Blegen 1928, 47 and 53, pls. xx, nos. 2 and 4; pl. xx. no. 12.

80 For a review of etched carnelian beads from Indian sites also see Reade 1979, 8–23; Possehl 1996, 154–159.

81 Mackay 1943, pl. LXXXIX, no. 11; Reade 1979, 15, fig. 3a (Type C3).

82 Marshall 1931, Volume 2, 515–516 and Volume 3, pls. CXLVI.45; Mackay 1938, 505–506, pl. CXXXV.19G; Reade 1979, 15, fig. 2g (Type C3).

83 Discussed by Hughes-Brock 2011, 108–109. It also includes the remote possibility that these beads arrived through Egypt, see Aston *et al.* 2000, 39–40, although it is unlikely, as Egypt was not part of the regional interconnections that included India, the Persian Gulf, Mesopotamia, Syro-Palestine and eventually the Aegean. For a discussion of the sources of carnelian see Moorey 1994, 97.
84 Reinholdt 2008, 52.
85 Sherratt 2010, 81–106; Sahoglu 2005, 339–361.
86 Reade 1979, 8–23.
87 Woolley 1934, 148–149.
88 Reade 1979, fig. 8.
89 Possehl 1996, fig. 7.
90 Possehl 1996, 153–154.
91 Reade 1979, 24–25.
92 Aruz 2003, 242, fig. 74. For discussion on the trading of beads to Mesopotamia see Reade 1979, 23; Chakrabarti 1993, 265–270. For a study of carnelian in the Ancient Near East see Moorey 1994, 97–98 and 109–111.
93 Ludvik *et al.* 2015, 3.
94 Blegen *et al.* 1958, 90–92 and figs 408,8, 460.12 and 540.2.
95 Effinger 1996, 23–24, 129–130 and 199.
96 Ludvik *et al.* 2015, 4.
97 Hughes-Brock 1998, 3.
98 Hughes-Brock 1999, 277–296.
99 Benzi 1992, 203–204; Ludvik *et al.* 2015, 4.
100 Ludvik *et al.* 2015, 3.
101 British Museum, inv. nos. GR.1892.0520.11–12; GR.1892.0520.13 and 10; Fitton *et al.* 2008, 18–19 and figs 18–19, 20–21.
102 British Museum, inv. nos. GR.1892.0520.106; Fitton *et al.* 2008, 22 and figs 79, 82–84 and 101.
103 British Museum, inv. nos. GR.1892.0520.15 and GR.1914.0725.8–10; Fitton *et al.* 2008, 24 and figs 101, 103.
104 Younger 2010, quoting Platon *et al.* 1969, 109.
105 Collon 2008, 44.
106 Goldman 1931, 200, pl. XX.1. For the Middle Helladic pottery from Grave 6, see fig. 187, no. 4.
107 British Museum, inv. no. GR.1934.1220.9.
108 Pini *et al.* 1975, 460, no. 580.
109 Tomb 67 has produced a necklace (Rethymnon Museum L.2925a); and also, two irregular spherical disc-shaped carnelian beads (Rethymnon Museum L.2925b), one biconical carnelian bead (Rethymnon Museum L.2926) and a Talismanic Seal (Rethymnon Museum S.130). Tomb 35 has produced two further spherical disc-shaped carnelian beads (Rethymnon Museum L.2919a-b). Late Bronze Age carnelian beads, including an amygdaloid bead with two surfaces decorated with grooves parallel to the string-line, dated to the Late Helladic IIIA period and a complete carnelian necklace comprised of spiral beads of different sizes, one an amygdaloid and the others cylindrical, dated to the Late Helladic IIIA–B periods, come from the Aidonia cemetery in Peloponnese; Nemea Museum, inv. nos. 759 and 650, 664, 668, 678, 688, 743, 788, 838; Demakopoulou 1966, 63–64, cat. nos. 48–49.
110 Casanova 1995, 16–17; Inizan 1995, 21–24; Collon 2008, 43–45.
111 Krzyszkowska 2005, 83. Her preferred source of Middle Bronze Age (mostly Middle Minoan) carnelian is not specified. There is only one example of what is thought to be Egyptian carnelian having been found in the Aegean, and it is a rectangular plate seal from Tomb 7 at Kalyvia near Phaestos on Crete dated to the Late Minoan IIIA2 period, Heraklion Museum HM 169, see Younger 1979, 40–44.

112 Hughes-Brock 1999, 284; Aston *et al.* 2000, 27.
113 Aston *et al.* 2000, 26–27.
114 Younger 1979, 40–44.
115 Younger 1979, 40–44.
116 Law *et al.* 2013, 177–184.
117 Ludvik *et al.* 2015, 7.
118 Moorey 1994, 99–100.
119 Yule and Schürmann Yule 1981, 39–46.
120 Athens, National Archaeological Museum, NM 6285; Dörpfeld 1927, 298.
121 Younger 1979, 40–44. He lists in detail the Aegean agate seals he believes may have originated as Harappan beads.
122 Thebes Museum, inv. nos. TM 174, 211, 175. Pini *et al.* 1975, 536, nos. 672, 674–675. See Krzyszkowska 2005, 239, who also believes that agate seals may possibly be trimmed-down beads. As Younger also points out, an Indian origin is also suggested in that the material is different, an opaque, light and dark banded agate. The lumpy shape should point in the same direction as the Indian beads and not surprisingly both stones occur on one necklace from Harappa, dated to the Late Harappan Phase, just before the beginning of the Late Bronze Age in the Aegean, Younger 1979. See also Hughes-Brock with Boardman 2009, 17. Here Hughes-Brock notes that the shape of some seals betrays or suggests origin as beads. She notes that in the Aegean agate is found far more as seals than as beads. Mostly the seal workshops no doubt started with raw material, but in the case of such stones as these they may well have been reworking finished products imported from somewhere like Mari.
123 Arkel 1936, 292–305; Brunel 1972, pl. 3 illustrates a necklace of the same type of agate from Harappa.
124 Symeneoglou 1973, 69, fig. 272 right.
125 Sakellariou 1964, 225, no. 199.
126 Boston Museum of Fine Arts, inv. no. 01.7582, Kenna and Thomas 1974, 34, no. 35.
127 Chania Museum, inv. no. 2055, Pini *et al.* 1975, 235, no. 297.
128 New York, Metropolitan Museum of Art, inv. no. 11.195.1., Kenna and Thomas 1974, 355, no. 263. They are also called Tubular Disc Beads.
129 Archaeological Museum of Piraeus (formerly Archaeological Museum of Aegina), inv. nos. MA 6605 (Grave No. Δ 35.8.17, 25–26); Reinholdt 2003, 260; 2008, 16, 54–61, 108, pl. 12.4, nos. 029–031.
130 Troy: (a) Treasure A (called butterfly or double-winged bead with two flat semi-circular lobes at either end of a central perforation), Pushkin State Museum of Fine Art, Moscow, inv. nos. Aap 77, 79, 82–91 and 93–98; Schliemann 1880, 461, no. 712; Schmidt 1902, 235–236, no. 5956 (Type D4); Antonova *et al.* 1996, 84–94, 210–211, cat nos. 78, 80, 83–92 and 94–99. (b) Unpublished, Istanbul Museum, inv. no. 5554; Kenoyer 2003, 398, no. 167; Musche 1992, 121–122, pl. XLI.3. Gold beads, numbering 252, were found in Room 253 during the 1932–1938 excavations, also dated to the Troy IIg period, see Blegen *et al.* 1950, 356–357, pl. 357, no. 37–712. For discussion on manufacture see Reinholdt 2008, 59, pl. 15.
131 Lemnos Museum, Storeroom 643; Branigan 1974, 193, pl. 24, cat. no. 3072 (Type III); Bernabò Brea 1976, 199, pl. CCLII.14–17.
132 Maxwell-Hyslop 1971, 10, type no. 16 and pl. 17a. (Type 16 – discoid); from examples in gold from Ur see Woolley 1934, 366, fig. 70.16; Possehl 1996, 161, fig. 15 above.
133 For a general view of the distribution of these beads in the mid- to late third millennium BC, see Possehl 1996, 161 and Aruz 2003, 240 and fig. 74 (distribution map). Other than those identified from Troy, Poliochni and Mesopotamia (see text above), we have the following examples: (a) an unusually larger example (L. 10.1 cm) in silver from Tomb 1 (a royal tomb) at the site of Tuba (Tell Un el-Marra) in Syria, National Museum, Aleppo, inv. no. 11679-1-2; the size may reflect

a local tradition, see Aruz 2003, 182–183, cat. no. 120; (b) an example in gold from the Burial 1 in the cemetery at Novosvobodnaya in the North Caucasus, dating to the Kurgan I culture (mid-third millennium BC), National Museum of Adygeya, Maikop, Russian Federation, see Aruz 2003, 296, cat. no. 197; (c) in red gold from an Umm an-Nar type tomb from Sharjah, Tell Abraq in the Persian Gulf, Sharjah Archaeological Museum, United Aran Emirates, see Aruz 2003, 314, cat. no. 211a–b; (d) another in gold from Altyn-depe, see Masson 1988, pl. 22:2 and Possehl 1996, 161 (where he refers to them as 'beads the Harappan type'); (e) in gold from Tepe Hissar, see Schmidt 1937, fig. 138, pl. 66, inv. no. H2360; McCown 1942, table I.4 ('gold-sheet beads with tubs'); and (f) in gold from Tell Brak, part of a necklace; FS Hoard 1957, TB15073; Museum of Deir ez-Zor, Syria, inv. no. 13248, Aruz 2003, 231–232, cat. no. 158 a–c. For other sites in the Near East, Iran and Turkmenistan, see Antonova *et al.* 1996, 210–211.

134 Mohenjo-daro Museum, inv. no. 1369, Marshall 1931, Volume 2, 522–523 and Volume 3, pls. CXLIX.7 and CXLVI.34 (no. HR 4212A); Wheeler 1968, 99–100, fig. XXVI; Kenoyer 1998, 140, 201, fig. 7.34, no. 56. Wheeler 1968, 99, also speculates about what he calls segmented faience beads having a wide distribution, also including the later levels of Mature Harappan Phase Mohenjo-daro, Harappa and Chanhu-daro to Middle Minoan III period at Knossos (1700 BC), although they may have been manufactured earlier.

135 Rao 1973, 102, pl. XXIX.B; Possehl 1996, 161, fig. 15 below.

136 Nath and Kumaran 2017, 541–555. For details of all Flat Disc-Shaped Beads see Appendix to Jablonka 2018, 139–166.

137 Vats 1940, pl. 133.3.

138 Musche 1992, 122.

139 Possehl 1996, 158–159.

140 Beck in Vats 1940, 405–406. For later excavations by Mortimer Wheeler see Wheeler 1947, 123, pl. LI, nos. 21–22.

141 Mackay 1938, 511.

142 Mackay 1943, 205.

143 Possehl 1996, 158; Stone 1949, 201–205.

144 Evans 1921, 486–494, fig. 352.13–14. Similar beads have been found in the Mace Bearer's Tomb at Knossos, dated later to the Late Minoan IIIA period, Evans 1921, fig. 352.15–17. Evans could not have associated the beads with India as the Indus Civilisation was not known to him at the time of writing; he thought them to be Egyptian. See also Pendlebury 1939, 165–167, 173. The use and possible production of faience was introduced to Crete by the Early Minoan IIA period, either from the Levant or Egypt. Faience beads have also been found in a third millennium BC context at Mochlos where they are likely to have been imported.

145 Stone 1949, 201–205. For the spectrographic analysis see Ritchie 1935, now believed lost owing to enemy action during the London Blitz of 1940–1941.

146 Stone 1949, 203–204; Wheeler 1968, 99–100, 114 and fig. 16.10–11.

147 For the manufacturing process, see Hegde *et al.* 1993, 239–244. See also Hegde 1983, 68, 70 and 72. In fact, steatite disc beads are so common that their presence alone could almost be considered a marker of the Harappan character of a site or as a Harappan export, see Vidale 1989, 29.

148 Hughes-Brock 1995, 106–107.

149 Damick and Woodworth 2015, 603–614.

150 Damick and Woodworth 2015, 611–614.

151 Bar-Yosef *et al.* 2004, 493–502; Pickard and Schoop 2011, 14–32.

152 Wright 1988, 143–161; Sowada and Grave 2009.

153 Gernez 2007, 119–134.

154 Bar-Yosef *et al.* 2004, 500.

155 Mallowan 1947, 254.
156 Rao 1973, 82; and for excavation context see Rao 1979, 530–531, fig. 109.1–3.
157 Branigan 1974, 157, cat. no. 79 (Type Va). If the Lothal dagger does originate on Crete, an Early Minoan I–Middle Minoan II date would be more acceptable. Daggers with a long tang (an eastern design found at Byblos) appear both in Cyprus and Crete in Middle Minoan I–II, at a time Late Harappan Lothal was still functioning. See Branigan 1966, 123–126.
158 Rao 1973, 82.
159 Rao 1979, 530 (spearhead) and 530–531 (dagger), both unillustrated. There are possible parallels to the spearhead, clearly locally manufactured from Chanhu-daro, see Mackay 1943, 390, pl. CXXV, nos. 65–77.
160 New scientific techniques point to the ability in the future to determine the origins of tin using tin isotopes. The science as well as the earliest work and results in this field has been described by Rahmstorf, see Rahmstorf 2017, 197.
161 Possehl 1996, 170; Mackay 1929, pl. 39.3.4; Wheeler 1947, 80, citing Vats 1940, 122.6.
162 Dunand 1937, 254, fig. 222, no. 3707; Branigan 1967, 120.
163 Rahmstorf 2017, 197.

Chapter 3

Prehistory: The Evidence of Commodities

The middle of the third to the middle of the second millennia BC witnessed the Eastern Mediterranean, the Near East and Central and South Asia being drawn together by a network of connectivity. There were several prime movers behind this network building, but the principal one was the demand for commodities by the consuming elites of the emergent Bronze Age societies, particularly in the Near East and towards the end of this period, in the Aegean. Crete lacks virtually all metal resources: metal ores such as gold, silver, the copper and tin to make bronze, all had to be imported from the start of Cretan metallurgy.

In prehistory, complex societies in the Near East and the Eastern Mediterranean, consumed both labour and commodities for the benefit of their elites, their social and political structures and for military expansion. Commodities such as tin were greatly in demand, for the making of bronze tools and weapons, as well as others that adorned the elites or exhibited their status and wealth, such as lapis lazuli and gold. Such demand ensured that trading networks were ever expanding and the flow of materials from the east ever increasing. This meant that new routes developed, importing these commodities from Central Asia, Afghanistan and India.

Many of the commodities that were so valued, originated in Iran and Afghanistan and in the fourth millennium BC, the cities of the Iranian plateau owed their wealth to their ability at that time, to control the raw materials increasingly in demand father westwards. For example, by the end of that millennium, there is evidence of east–west trade at Godin Tepe, a town lying towards the northerly end of the Zagros Mountains and many of the other settlements in that region show similar evidence for trade or manufacture.

At first, it is thought that this trade was carried out overland to Mesopotamia by caravan, but by the mid-third millennium BC, it will have been under the control of the Harappans, the new dominant political and trading power east of Iran. An active maritime trade now began, linking territories from the head of the Persian Gulf to the coasts of Arabia and India and much of it would have passed through the Harappan heartland before being exported. The importance of any commodity was more significant and important than the occasional object and is much more indicative of patterns of contact.

We are reminded that a number of Akkadian tablets mention ships from *Meluḫḫa* bringing to the shores of Mesopotamia commodities and goods, which included carnelian beads, lapis lazuli, pearls, rare woods and plants, fresh dates, fabrics, fragrancies, livestock and metals, such as copper, tin and gold,[1] that the elites required in order to maintain their social structure, The movement of some of these commodities eventually into the Aegean, however, will have been by way of Mesopotamia and then Syro-Palestine; no distinction would likely have been made by Eastern Mediterranean traders as to their origins, be it Mesopotamia, Syro-Palestine, India or anywhere else.

Determining the route by which commodities would be shipped westwards by sea or land, would have been an important consideration for traders in the third millennium BC. It can be argued that long-distance trade, such as in tin and perhaps cotton, leather and other bulkier or heavier items would have been considered uneconomic and time-consuming to be conducted overland. With advances in technology, navigation and organisation, sea transport would have become more profitable. Some commodity shipments in small amounts, however, will have continued to be passed westwards directly from their source in north-west Afghanistan through the settlement at Shortughai, but under Harappan control.

Trade networks served to link the Bronze Age societies of Mesopotamia and the Indus Valley to societies in the Levant, Egypt, the Arabian Peninsula, the Iranian Plateau, Central Asia as well as Anatolia and the Aegean. The intensity of exchange gained momentum starting in the earlier part of the second millennium BC and then into the Late Bronze Age. During these periods, bronze was produced across Europe and Asia and urban societies developed a rapidly growing interest in exotic goods, including plant and animal products.

The Role of Shortughai

The importance of commodities to the Harappans and the geographical extent of the resources available to it, implies that both raw commodities and manufactured objects were being produced and traded to keep the major urban centres supplied and the economy buoyant. Playing an important role in their control process was the small town of Shortughai.

The River Kokcha rises in the central highlands of Badakhshan in north-east Afghanistan, a tributary of the River Oxus,[2] which then eventually flows into the Aral Sea, deep in central Asia. Around the confluence of the Rivers Kokcha and the Amu Darya lies a relatively small agricultural area, the Plain of Khunum, where were located seven Harappan settlements, although Shortughai is the only one that has so far been excavated. Founded in around 2000 BC, it thrived during the period immediately afterwards when trade with the west expanded. The settlement consists of two hills, one the town proper and the other, the citadel; both of which were approximately 2 ha in size. The finding of both a ploughed field with remains of flax seeds, which points to dry land farming and of irrigation canals which were dug to bring water from the River Kokcha, almost 25 km away, points to huge efforts to support their agriculture and source of food. Only the Harappans would have possessed the resources for such hydro-engineering.

Shortughai (Period I, 2000–1750 BC), exhibits all the features of a Mature Harappan Phase habitation, including the local processing of raw lapis lazuli, carnelian and steatite. Typical Harappan finds from the site include a sealstone depicting a rhinoceros (not known in the region) and an inscription in Indus script, clay models of cattle with wheeled carts, copper-bronze objects, gold pieces, lapis lazuli beads and many other types of stone beads, drill heads and shell bangles. Also of significance was a pottery assemblage dominated by Mature Harappan Phase heavy red wares, some decorated in a painted black on red slip style.[3] Bricks found at the site had the typical standard Harappan measurements. It is significant that the finds exhibit strictly Harappan types and for the pottery types and decoration; nothing can be attributed to influences from other cultures, local or otherwise. In fact, not one of the standard characteristics of a Harappan cultural complex is missing. Even the plant remains found within the settlement, mostly foodstuffs, such as barley, wheat, panicum millet, lentils, peas, almonds, pistachios, grapes and linseed/flax seeds are all very familiar from Harappan sites located between 800 (Harappa) and 1100 km (Mohenjo-daro) to the south.

The location of this apparently isolated Mature Harappan Phase site, at the modern border between Afghanistan and Tajikistan is highly significant. It was where it had both access to and control of the source of lapis lazuli, which can be approached mainly up the valley of the River Kokcha and the local Badakhshan sources of tin as well as gold. However, it has also been proposed that the rise of the Oxus Civilisation or Bactro-Margiana Culture (BMAC) of Central Asia was based on their trade in tin and that they supplied the Harappans at their trading centre at Shortughai with some of their stock. The contact between them is attested by the finding of kidney-shaped stone vases and pipal motifs and imitations of the Harappan seals at BMAC sites, while BMAC seals, pins, mirrors, sceptres and ceramics are attested in Harappan sites or on the fringes of their homeland.[4]

Shortughai would also have been particularly well placed to maintain close links with its neighbours, to the east and west, with the southern geographical extremities of China as well as other locations in Central Asia. Access to Shortughai was not easy and required knowledge of the passes through the Hindu Kush Mountains and the plains to the south. Regardless of the terrain, the inhabitants and their Harappan kinsmen must have maintained an overland caravan route into the Harappan heartland if commodities were to pass this way southbound. Some of it, however, passed westwards on the overland caravan route to Iran, Mesopotamia and beyond,[5] eventually under Harappan control.

Shortughai was undoubtedly an important Harappan trading colony mediating trade between their heartland and Central Asia and specialising in the sourcing of lapis lazuli, tin, gold and possibly even Bactrian camels.[6] Its importance came to an end just before 1700 BC (Shortughai Period II), when Harappan control of the town ended and it was gradually absorbed into the local BMAC material culture.[7]

Organic Commodities

It was not always high-value inorganic commodities that were transported very long distances; some non-perishable organic ones would have similarly travelled and have equally secured added value and thus become very desirable and goods such as these would also have contributed to the establishment of trade and exchange networks.

The organic imports from the Harappans to the Eastern Mediterranean and the Aegean by way of the Near East, was also the result of a chain of short-distance transactions, that we have seen with, for example, carnelian beads, where the eventual destination of the goods is not known at the point of origin. Transport systems were now capable of carrying quantities of bulk goods by sea or overland and with this capacity, the trade in perishable goods, such as grain and textiles for example, from one region to another, becomes economically viable. Other non-perishable commodities may have included wood, leather and perhaps some non-perishable foodstuffs. In the Eastern Mediterranean and the Aegean, there was access to food from distant locations, including South Asia, and such goods were likely consumed as oils, dried fruits and spices. These insights force us to rethink the complexity and intensity of Indo-Mediterranean trade during the Bronze Age.

Spices

Of the organic commodities in use in the Aegean throughout the Bronze Age that are believed to have had Indian origins, one such example is the imported dried herb and condiment sweet rush or ginger grass (*Andropogon schoenanthus* L.) identified by John Chadwick as the word *ko-no* (and variations) in Mycenaean Greek on Linear B tablets from Late Bronze Age Knossos (tablet KN Ge 953+955), Pylos (tablet PY Ga 953+955) and Mycenae (tablets MY Ge 602+, MY Ge 603+ and MY Ge 606 [as *ko-i-no*]).[8] This plant produces aromatic oil that can be used in the manufacture of perfumes or as medicines. Chadwick understood it to originate in India (it is indigenous to north-west India), being spread along the same trade routes as in the earlier periods, through the Persian Gulf and the Syro-Palestinian coast and eventually locally cultivated. Another example of a herb that is believed to have originated in India and found its way to the Aegean by way of the Near East, was cardamom (*Cardamontum ssp.*),[9] also identified as *Lepidium sativum* L. or garden cress and as *ka-da-mi-ja* in a Linear B tablet from Mycenae (tablet MY Ge 604).[10] The seeds contain a delicate spicy essence and have use as a condiment, a component of medicines and in cooking.[11]

An additional plant that is thought to have originated in India was sesame (*Sesamum indicum* L.). There are records of remains of this herb from the middle of the third millennium BC site of Abu Salabikh in Mesopotamia and of it also being found at Harappa a millennium earlier.[12] It is understood to be native to India and was likely exported starting in the Early Harappan Phase and like the other plants, subsequently grown locally. Commonly used in the Aegean from at least the second millennium BC, sesame was cultivated throughout the Eastern Mediterranean for its edible seeds and its oil. It is recorded in its seed form in the Linear B spice tablets from Mycenae as *sa-sa-ma* (tablets MY Ge 602+, MY Ge 603+, MY Ge 604+, MY Ge 605+605a+607[+]*fr*, MY Ge 606),[13] sometimes abbreviated by means of the syllabogram SA, its use as referred to in the tablets, however, is uncertain. The minuteness of the quantities recorded seem to eliminate industrial utilisation, leaving either medicinal or culinary use as a flavouring as the probable explanation. Finally, it has been suggested that it is possible to attribute the condiments cinnamon (*Cinnamomum cassia* Blume) and black pepper (*Piper nigrum* L.), so ubiquitously in use through the Eastern Mediterranean in the Bronze Age and later, to an Indian origin.[14]

Evidence for a long-distance trade in spices involving India also can be found at the site of Terqa (Tell Ashara) located on the banks of the Middle Euphrates in Southern Syria and dated to approximately 1700 BC, where in the House of Puzarum, kernels of cloves (*Syzygium aromaticum* L.) have been found in a kitchen jar.[15] This spice was not known in the west much before the Romans and more significantly, it originates in the Molucca (Maluka) Islands of the East Indies (now Indonesia) and was then the result of long distance trade, having been first imported through India. Like the other spices featured here, there is no reason as to why it could not also have found its way to the Aegean.

It is just possible that some non-perishable foodstuffs that originated in India also found their way to the Aegean. For the second millennium BC Mycenaeans, with their growing population density and an expanding economy, the importation from outside the Aegean of agricultural produce as well as herbs and spices for the kitchen and medicine was a prerequisite to the stability of its palace economies.

Timber

Although there are very few archaeobotanical remains of wood in the Aegean, it is possible that wood such as Indian sandalwood may also have been exported from India to the Near East[16] and some found its way further west into the Aegean. Indian sandalwood is the common name of a class of highly fragrant woods that are made from trees (*Santalum album* L.), which are evergreens and range in size from tall shrubs up to fully-grown trees. Both the wood and the oil produced from it, offers a distinctive fragrance that has been highly valued in antiquity, widely used for religious and medicinal purposes and was a prime source of incense and perfumes. Its exact origin is not known, but it was, like cloves, probably originally native to the islands in the East Indies. Some believe that it comes from South India, but it is now thought that it was introduced to northern India in earlier prehistory. Traded by the Harappans, it will have been imported from the south by sea into ports such as Lothal. In the Late

Bronze Age, a great deal of trade was being conducted between the Mycenaeans and the Near East through cities of North Syria, such as Ugarit and Mari and we know it included commodities such as sandalwood.

Foreign woods were imported into Mesopotamia by sea. In around 2500 BC, King Ur-Nanshe of Lagash boasted that ships of *Dilmun* brought timber from foreign lands. We have no real idea what type of timber may have been involved, but it is likely to have been a higher-grade wood than that which was available locally and thought to have originated in India. As with the tin trade, the fact that the cuneiform texts record *Dilmun* as the source of the timber imported by King Ur-Nanshe, does not lead one to think that it was local timber grown on what is now Bahrain. *Dilmun* was likely to have been transhipping timber from further east.

Other woods, such as blackwood, what is known as Ceylon ebony (*Diospyros ebenum* L.) seems also to have been imported by the Harappans from South India and traded westwards. This wood from *Meluḫḫa* was apparently in use in the temple at Lagaš dated to the Ur III period.[17] There is also a possibility that it may have been teak or *kusabku* (seawood) or (*Tectona grandis* L.), native to most of India. Whatever type of wood it was, it would have been imported and used for building houses and boats.[18] *Mesu* wood, or sisso or rosewood (*Dalbergia sissoo* Roxb.) is another likely export. Common in the lower slopes of the Himalayas in Northern India, its distribution extends far into the North Indian plain, following the principal river systems. It was much appreciated for its hardness, resistance and dark brown colour. Archaeological and textual evidence exists of it being used in Mesopotamia (Sumerian ^{giš}*mes.má-gan-na*), originating in India and there is evidence of it being found at Harappa and Mohenjo-daro and in the Persian Gulf as early as 2200 BC. It can be used in construction and for the manufacture of furniture, tools, carts and boats.[19]

Ivory

Although it is believed that the Harappans exported elephant ivory to the Near East that came from the Asian (or Indian) elephant (*Elephas maximus*),[20] there is no evidence to suggest that any of it reached the Aegean or anywhere else in the Eastern Mediterranean in the third and second millennia BC. Although a single molar of an Asian elephant has been identified as far as Ugarit and dated to the Late Bronze Age,[21] this is an exeption and may well have been a keepsake or talisman belonging to a trader or a seafarer. It is likely that if any ivory did originate from Syro-Palestine or Mesopotamia, it would have been the consequences of hunting of what is now known as the Syrian Elephant, which is believed to have roamed wild in North Syria, the Zagros Mountains and Southern Mesopotamia at the time but may have died out by the Early Iron Age.[22]

Textiles

Textiles have a universal use and display a high diversity in production. They are not just used for keeping warm; they are also a means of displaying wealth, status and identity. They also can be relatively long-lived and can provide years of service to the owner. However, their study is handicapped by the fact that so little survives in most archaeological records of the Eastern Mediterranean, the Near East, India and the Aegean.

Archaeological evidence points to the Harappan heartland as having a high level of technological sophistication in textile manufacture and use, together with the ability to have available as part of this process, particularly cotton. It is thought that the Harappan textile industry of the third millennium BC would have been a large operation and centred on the major urban settlements such as those of Harappa and Mohenjo-daro.[23] It is also speculated that for the Harappans, part of their overseas trade would have been in manufactured textiles and textile products that used cotton (*Gossypium arboretum* L.),[24] silk (from the silkworm *Bombyx mori* L.),[25] jute (*Corchorus capsularis* L.),[26] as well as manufactured dyes. These products would have included coloured cotton garments and high-quality yarn, again mainly cotton. Even after the end of the Late Harappan Phase, the evidence points to a continuation of a limited trade in cotton (*sindhu*) and probably cotton fabrics.[27]

Whilst there is no textual evidence for the importation of textiles into the Aegean, we have a little evidence of silk use at the site of Akrotiri on Thera, dating to the period before its destruction in the late seventeenth century BC.[28] It is thought by those who studied the evidence to be of a cocoon found in a deposit located in a building east of the House of the Ladies, of a silk-moth that produced wild silk. Hitherto, there is no evidence for imported silk anywhere in the Aegean before the fifth century BC, but there is a possibility that either Harappan silk or imported silkworms may have found their way to the Aegean at some point in the Bronze Age and produced some of the garments depicted in Minoan, Cycladic and Mycenaean frescos. However, the iconographic and textual (Linear B) evidence of what has been thought to have been silk moths is rather speculative.

Inorganic Commodities

Most major Bronze Age civilisations in the third and second millennia BC, developed in the lowland shadow of large rivers that sustained a high and growing population through intensive agricultural production. These heartlands were almost always devoid of strategically important metals such as copper, tin and gold, which could often only be resourced in remote mountainous regions.

The mode of transportation of inorganic commodities within the Harappan Civilisation, from their source or place of storage prior to trade, would have been varied. It has been generally accepted that within the Harappan heartland itself, much of it would have taken place by rivercraft. Whilst no actual physical remains of such craft have been found, there are three depictions from Mohenjo-daro,[29] which may also have been used for coastal navigation as far as the Gulf and even Mesopotamia. However, within the plains and plateaus of the greater Indus Valley region during the third and late second millennia BC, the primary mode of transport would have been by zebu or humped cattle (*Bos taurus* or *Bos taurus indicus*), either carrying an individual load or, more likely, pulling a cart, and small terracotta models of such carts have been found in huge numbers at most Harappan sites.[30] However, zebu cattle would not have fared well on the steep, rocky trails and slopes of the mountains to the north, where most of the valuable elite commodities found at Harappan sites for the control of their export are located.

We do not yet know how commodities were transported from their highland sources to the points where they could be loaded onto zebu carts or rivercraft. Randal Law has suggested the use of sheep or goats as pack animals, which can move across landscapes inaccessible to other animals; a single large goat can only carry a few dozen kilograms at most but an entire herd could potentially move much more.[31] Law has also pointed out that human porterage should also be considered, as single porters transporting goods in the mountains reportedly could carry anywhere from 30–100 kg on their heads or backs.[32] The Harappans would have journeyed to regions far outside of their heartland to obtain vital commodities and their outpost of Shortughai is clearly representative of this. However, to procure these commodities, Harappans would have needed both the sanction and the assistance of the local central Asian population. It has been suggested that the primary procurer and initial carrier of commodities that were to end up in the Harappan heartland would have been transhumant pastoralists, who as seasons change, are compelled to move where their herds can find adequate water and pastures.[33] In the ancient world, semi-precious stones were powerful status symbols, particularly when used in jewellery, inlays and in the manufacture of cylinder seals. For the most part, the exotic semi-precious stones most favoured in the Near East and the Eastern Mediterranean came from the east.

Lapis Lazuli: An Indian Commodity

Even before the time of the emergence of the major urban centres in both India and the Near East, there was sufficient demand for high-value commodities such as lapis lazuli for them to travel over vast distances to be procured. It is a metamorphic rock, which contains various minerals hence the varied colour, such as aluminium silicate, iron pyrites, magnesium, potash and calcite; but it is the dark blue variety that lends itself particularly to the manufacture of seals and articles for personal adornment and for the indication of elite status.

In the ancient world, lapis lazuli was used to make beads, cylinder seals, amulets, ritual-use stone axes and as an inlay and other objects such as figurines, musical instruments, jewellery and stone-bowls. Its consumption was driven by two factors; the first was its value brought about by the distance of trade and the difficulty of access at its place of origin. Secondly, it is thought that it had some magical properties. However, throughout the whole of the Bronze Age, it was the lapis lazuli bead, with its variations for which it is most frequently associated.[34] A pigment made from crushed lapis lazuli and made into clear glass ingots which are then crushed and suspended in

Figure 6. Badakhshan, in north-east Afghanistan, source of lapis lazuli (Public Domain)

a colour medium, can also be used for the blue colour in wall painting. For whatever purpose it was used, it was only available to the elites.

Source

Evidence from the third and second millennia suggests that a major natural and exploited source was located above Sar-i Sang, located by the Kokcha River in Badakhshan in the Hindu Kush Mountains of modern north-east Afghanistan (Fig. 6),[35] where it was extremely hazardous to extract,[36] but can with confidence, be identified as the source of lapis lazuli for the Early and Middle Bronze Age Near East. There is thought to also have been a source of lapis lazuli in the Chaghai Mountains of Baluchistan and although of lesser importance, it may have remained active to some lesser degree throughout prehistory and later, but this is now questioned.[37] Other potential, albeit presently unconfirmed, sources are the Pamir deposits in Tajikistan, approximately 130 km from Sar-i Sang.[38]

Although routes out of Badakhshan were neither direct nor easy, well before the time of the Mature Harappan Phase of the Harappan Civilisation, lapis lazuli began arriving in the Near East, starting in the late Al Ubaid Period (3800–3500 BC) and appearing at Tepe Gawra as early as Gawra XI.[39] However, it is unlikely that in any period, trading expeditions set out to make the trek all the way to Badakhshan, but that it was by way of peddlers, caravans or trading families, that lapis lazuli reached the elite of the Near East.

The Demand for Lapis Lazuli

In around the mid-third millennium BC, there emerged in Mesopotamia increased demand and the need to acquire it in much larger quantities. In the third and second millennia BC, the main concentration of worked lapis lazuli is to be found in Mesopotamia (approximately 89%) and not in regions close by the source of the stone.[40] At the end of the third and the beginning of the second millennia BC, texts from Ur, Lagaš and Mari identify several places, including the Persian Gulf and *Meluḫḫa* as the regions through which lapis lazuli was acquired by Mesopotamian merchants. Most of the Early and Middle Bronze Age lapis lazuli objects were shaped as beads (74%), inlays (17%), pieces of composite objects (8%) and seals (0.7%); the extreme rarity of larger artefacts (0.3%) is probably related with the thin tabular nature of the lapis lazuli deposits and the corresponding difficulty in carving substantial three-dimensional objects. Direct archaeological evidence for lapis lazuli production, in the form of drill bits, working debris and unfinished artefacts, is abundant in Afghanistan, the Harappan homeland and Iran. In the Near East, unworked lapis lazuli nodules are found at several sites, including in the Early Bronze Age, Jebel Aruda, Susa, Ur and Ebla and in the Middle Bronze Age, Kaneš. Several textual references also indicate the procurement of raw nodules from Mari, Larsa and Lagaš between the late third and early second millennia BC, as raw materials for local manufacture.[41]

The chronology of this growing trade is based on it coinciding with the introduction into Mesopotamia of the stone stamp seal that combined features from the two major trading areas, a disc form from *Dilmun* or *Tilman* and the motif of the short-horned bull from the Harappan Civilisation.[42] These stamp seals have been recovered in large numbers at Ur and all along the maritime trading corridor from Mesopotamia, the Persian Gulf and the Harappan Civilisation and point to the expansion of these trade routes at the time for trade in lapis lazuli and other commodities.

By the mid-third millennium BC, in its Mature Harappan Phase, the Harappans will have taken control of the supply and distribution of this valuable commodity through the medium of their local trading colony of Shortughai. From there it was then either exported directly to Mesopotamia by an overland caravan route through Southern Turkmenistan, Elam, Egypt, Syro-Palestine and Anatolia,[43] or to the Harappan homeland and then as a secondary export to Mesopotamia by the sea route through the Persian Gulf. This model is supported by Daniel Potts who has also suggested that many commodities such as lapis lazuli not being found in their natural state in the Harappan heartland were sent southwards either to be worked, or as raw commodities and then transhipped further afield from Harappan seaports such as Lothal[44] or those on the Arabian Gulf. Both at Chanhu-daro in the Harappan

Civilisation heartland and in other regions under Harappan influence, we find lapidary tools and drills for polishing and cutting, holders for beads and containers filled with semi-processed lapis lazuli,[45] as it appears that here lapis lazuli was partly refined on-site and then exported.

In India, the first use of lapis lazuli is reported from the Pre-Harappan Phase at Mehrgarh (Mehrgarh Period III–IV, 4300–3300 BC).[46] Later, however, during the Mature Harappan Phase, it appears there was not a great deal of it used locally for personal adornment or for making seals, because it would have been far more lucrative to export the material to markets in the west than to retain it in any quantity for local use. This can explain its virtual absence in sites in Sind, the Gujarat and at Mohenjo-daro. Consequently, the manufacture and extensive use of faience in the Harappan Civilisation may be a substitute.[47] Alternatively, it is possible that lapis lazuli did not have the same symbolic or even magical value for the population of the Indus as it did the Mesopotamians and elsewhere.[48]

With control by the middle of the third millennium of the source and supply of lapis lazuli from Afghanistan now in the hands of the Harappans, it confirms what we know of its supply together with carnelian beads, both of which are referred to as coming from the land of *Meluḫḫa* in cuneiform texts of this period, such as for example, the *Hymn to Ninurta*.[49] There are many other references to trade in lapis lazuli from India to the Persian Gulf and this would explain the occurrence of lapis lazuli in *Dilmun* or *Tilman*. Whatever the method of export of lapis lazuli, whether to the Indus Valley and thence by ship to Mesopotamia by way of the Persian Gulf or overland by caravan, during the period 2600–1900 BC, it was controlled by the Harappans and was essentially an Indian commodity.

This control mechanism is best described by Shereen Ratnagar who has concluded that the trade of lapis lazuli out of Badakhshan takes different patterns in two successive periods. In the earlier period, at Shahr-i Sokhta, located between Afghanistan and the land trade route into Iran (Periods II–III, 2600–2450 BC), there was a major working centre in the material, both for local consumption and for export, particularly in the preparation of the raw material, such as the removal of impurities, but not for the manufacturing of objects.

In the period immediately succeeding the Shahr-i Sokhta Periods II–III, after 2450 BC, contemporary with the beginning of the Mature Harappan Phase, lapis lazuli processing in Iran seems to have ceased and the unworked stones were now being taken directly to the Harappan heartland for working and export.[50] At this time, we are reminded that we see the establishment of Phase I of the Harappan colony at Shortughai, where from the very start of its occupation, lapis lazuli working is clearly in evidence, with workshops identified through the evidence of chipped lapis lazuli debris, together with workshops for gold and some copper. It is believed that the Harappans from this location controlled the procurement of and trade in lapis lazuli from Badakhshan, for some very limited domestic use, but primarily intended for the transit trade to the markets in Mesopotamia and beyond, including only in the case of lapis lazuli, Egypt. Lapis lazuli became common in Egypt during the Naqada period and the First Dynasty, but after the apparent disruption of lapis lazuli exchanges in the early third millennium, witnessed in both Egypt and Mesopotamia, lapis lazuli returned to popularity for the remainder of the Early Bronze Age and in parallel with the trend in Mesopotamia, considerable amounts of lapis lazuli are found in Egypt in contexts at this time, with Byblos possibly funnelling lapis lazuli further south to Egypt via a maritime route.[51]

The exportation of lapis lazuli westwards from India into the Eastern Mediterranean continued spasmodically into the Late Bronze Age, when a much-limited supply through the Persian Gulf and overland likely remained open,[52] but as one suspects with a great deal of re-use of the material from much earlier imports.

Lapis Lazuli in the Aegean

The long-distance supply by India to the Aegean of lapis lazuli, as an extension of contacts between India and the Near East, only started at the very beginning of the Aegean Middle Bronze Age, at the time towards the end of the Mature Harappan Phase. Of evidence of earlier importation there is one bead and a cylinder seal found at Troy in Troy IIg levels (2600–2250 BC)[53] but was probably made in the Near East as also was a highly polished ritual carved lapis lazuli hammer-axe found with three unique jade examples in Schliemann's Treasure L and similarly dated.[54] This lapis lazuli axe from Schliemann's Treasure L at Troy, represents an astonishing and unique find. At 1.3 kg in weight and measuring 28 × 7 cm in size, it is one of the largest lapis lazuli artefacts ever recovered in the Bronze Age. It is a witness to the importance of Troy as an interregional commercial centre, able to attract and funnel a large range of luxury products circulating within different trade circuits. In the third millennium BC from Crete, we only have a single bead from Koumasa, dated to the Early Minoan II period, although the Aegean remained largely outside the lapis lazuli trade network until the Middle and Late Bronze Ages and only then spasmodically, with only a small number of objects retrieved.

During the Middle Bronze Age, lapis lazuli trade seems to have witnessed a significant contraction and became extremely rare, a phenomenon possibly at least in part connected with the collapse of maritime contacts with the Harappans. From the Aegean Middle Bronze Age, there are, however, several surviving examples of its importation. There are little over 18 Minoan seals made from lapis lazuli (five of which are enhanced by gold mountings), which can be dated to as early as the Middle Minoan IB–IIB periods.[55] However, some of these spotted with white calcite inclusions are of lesser quality. Additionally, there is a lapis lazuli gemstone from Pertras, date to the Middle Minoan IA–IB Period, an amulet from Aghia Triada, dated to the Middle Minoan I Period, a cylinder seal from Archanes, dated to the Middle Minoan IB Period and from the end of the Middle Minoan Period, a seal from Palaikastro.[56]

Lapis lazuli was used in rings and beads found in the Aegina Treasure, which shows distinct Minoan influences, if not manufacture.[57] However, in the Aegean in this period, it is likely that a few of the objects were re-cycled imports, possibly from an earlier period. It is not thought that any objects of lapis lazuli for export were manufactured in India, other than possibly the bead from Troy.

During the Late Bronze Age in the Aegean there is some evidence that the material continued to be imported from India through North Syrian traders, where it is mentioned in the Amarna Letters between King Burna-Buriaš II of Babylonia (1349–1323 BC) and Pharaoh Amenhotep IV (or Akhenaten) of Egypt (1350–1334 BC).[58] The route would have been from Afghanistan to Mesopotamia by way of the Persian Gulf or by land over the Zagros Mountains[59] and then from Babylon westwards.

Of the use of lapis lazuli in the Late Bronze Age of the Aegean, like the earlier periods, it again remains relatively rare.[60] A good example is a lentoid seal with rather splendid decoration that comes from the South House at Knossos, dated to the Late Minoan IB period.[61] From the Greek mainland in the Late Bronze Age there have been discovered at least 10 local seals made from lapis lazuli, although it is reported that the material is, like its Middle Minoan predecessors, of poor quality with calcite inclusions.[62] One thing is apparent: that re-worked imports account for most of the lapis lazuli in the Aegean in this later period.[63]

Included in the cache of 33 lapis lazuli cylinder seals, some of the later ones re-worked from much earlier imported material, in a context dating to the Late Helladic IIIB period, within the Treasure Room of the Later Palace (New Kadmeion) at Thebes in Boeotia are seven seals of various Mesopotamian styles dating to the Early Dynastic III or the Old Babylonian Periods (2500–1700 BC) and 12 Kassite seals from Babylonia (mid-thirteenth century BC), of which 17 are made from lapis lazuli, the earlier ones made at a time when the Harappans controlled the trade in the material. When these seals arrived in Boeotia is unknown, but it was certainly much later than when they were manufactured and whether they were a royal gift or not, the Indian origins of the material from which these seals were made is not in doubt,[64] although they were manufactured in the Near East. Other than these seals, nearby from where they were found, was also found a hoard of over 75 finished and unfinished beads and inlays made from lapis lazuli.[65] They were found in a partially excavated workshop that belonged to the New Palace at Thebes, destroyed by fire at the end of Late Helladic IIIB period.

Of other uses in the Late Bronze Age for example, two rather poor beads and a pendant made from lapis lazuli come from Room 19 (Room of the Idols) of the Cult Centre at Mycenae,[66] dating to the end of the Late Helladic IIIB period, possibly as the result of itinerant trade and two very similar pendants come from a workshop in the Later Palace (New Kadmeion) at Thebes, but dated earlier to the Late Helladic IIIA period,[67] where the additional fragments were found. From the style, it is also clear that all these beads and pendants are of local manufacture. It has been suggested that lapis lazuli was imported into the Aegean by way of Egypt, but there is no direct evidence. For the lapis lazuli used in the Aegean, while originating in Afghanistan, we cannot determine at which point during the journey from its origins the raw lapis lazuli was converted into finished goods. We must also remind ourselves that much of the lapis lazuli available in the Late Bronze Age may well have been re-used from earlier objects. Although in comparison to the Near East little lapis lazuli was imported into the Aegean, it was seemingly highly sought after and treasured. Whether on Crete and the Greek mainland it had any of the status and likely ritual associations as it possessed in the Near East and Syro-Palestine, is unknown, but unlikely.

Jade

Among the semi-precious materials recovered from Mohenjo-daro are examples of beads made from what has been described as jade,[68] which is either nephrite, an extremely tough calcium-magnesium-aluminium-silicate, or possibly jadeite, a pyroxene. Heinrich Schliemann during his excavations at Troy in 1890 uncovered three highly polished ceremonial carved hammer-axes also either made from nephrite or jadeite in a hoard (Treasure L), which has been dated to the Early Bronze Age Troy IIg period.[69] In an earlier excavation, he also found four jade hand-axes, one of which is made from jadeite and the other three nephrite and dated to the Early Bronze Age Troy I period.[70] An attempt has been made to associate the importation of jade to Troad by a route that involves the Black Sea region,[71] or with a possible source for at least the jadeite in Anatolia.[72] A close association with the lapis lazuli trade route has also been suspected, as one of the Trojan hammer-axes found in the same hoard, is made of that material[73] and there is no reason to doubt that the lapis lazuli from which it was made did come by way of that link.

Placing doubt on an Indian origin of jade, Roger Moorey examined objects from the Near East made from what he called greenstone and concluded that it was sourced within that region.[74] Some years ago, Colin Renfrew also suggested that the Trojan axes were of greenstone and that the raw material could have been sourced in the Central Alps or even on the Cycladic island of Syros;[75] but none of these suggestions has been confirmed. Green jade or nephrite (and jadeite) is widespread in Central Asia and was greatly valued in China since the fourth millennium BC, although Schliemann wrongly suggested the origins of the Troy jade as far away as Lake Baikal in Siberia, a source in history of much of Chinese jade. The Harappans likely imported their jade from a source in Eastern Turkmenistan,[76] or possibly south-west China beyond the Karakoram Mountains and then traded down through the passes into Northern India to their heartland, with perhaps a little finding its way westwards.

Gold: Also an Indian Commodity?

The question arises as to whether the Aegean could have imported any gold that originated in India or areas under control of the Harappans. There is clearly a lack of evidence for the source of gold within the Aegean from the Early Bronze Age II period onwards and this has led to seeking a source outside the Aegean, especially when one has in mind the quantity of gold found, for example, in the Shaft Graves of Mycenae in the Middle Helladic and Late Helladic I periods. It has long been thought that this and other gold originated in Egypt, Anatolia or the Balkans. The basic answer to the question is that we just simply do not know.[77] On this basis, we cannot rule out India as a possible source at least for some of the gold in use, especially in earlier prehistory.

Sources of gold in India from the time of the Harappans are well known.[78] Some was obtained by panning from the sands of the upper Indus River or its tributaries and another alluvial source was from the River Kokcha, near the confluence with the River Oxus, which was relatively pure. This latter source is located near to Shortughai, where tin and lapis lazuli was also sourced and traces of gold working has been found in workshops located in the town, which comprises fragments of gold found in association with charcoal and fire seared pebbles.[79] This source may well have been adequate to have supplied the Harappan heartland and any of its export needs.

Like the Aegean, the evidence for the source of gold in Mesopotamia is also quite obscure and imprecise. Particularly at Lagaš, gold has a special connection with *Meluḫḫa* with cuneiform texts referring to 'gold in the dust' as coming from that location and the trade with *Dilmun* or *Tilman* in the later third and early second millennia BC, indicates that some gold was now still reaching Ur from the Persian Gulf.[80] There is good reason to suppose that at least some gold in the Aegean may have originated in India, having made the long and tortuous journey through Mesopotamia and Syro-Palestine.

The earliest evidence for large-scale use of gold in the Aegean appears on Crete in the Pyrgos deposit (12 objects) dating to Early Minoan I–IIA and in Tombs XIX and VI at Mochlos (160 objects), dating to the Early Minoan II period. There are also a few items from the lower levels of Tholos A at Platanos (eight objects) and a single bead from a deposit at Maronia, both similarly dated. All objects appear to have been locally made on Crete, with the gold being imported as a commodity. What is of interest, is that the carnelian bead from Mochlos was also found in Tomb XIX and a Harappan link is already established for that burial and period.

Tin: Another Indian Commodity

The other metal that became in the Bronze Age of increasing major importance was tin. From about 3000 BC onwards, it was used for alloying with copper to produce bronze, which is better suited to the manufacture of tools and weapons. Tin occurs in its oxide form as cassiterite, a distinctively heavy mineral which can be mined or panned from alluvial deposits. It is rarely found in Europe or the Near East but is reasonably prolific in Afghanistan and these sources must have supplied much of the Near East. It has long been pointed out that the main sources of tin for Mesopotamia in the Bronze Age were in Central Asia.[81]

The prodigious mineral wealth of North-East Afghanistan may, at least in part, account for the prosperous urban culture that developed in south-east Iran by 2000 BC, concentrated on the towns of Shahr-i Sokhta, Shahdad, Tepe Yahya and Khinaman. The region occupied a central position between resource-rich Afghanistan and the consuming states of Elam and Mesopotamia beyond; it also lay comparatively close to the Makran Coast of the Arabian Sea, which by now had become part of the sphere of influence of the Harappans, which helped their control of the trade.

Towards the end of the third millennium BC, tin was beginning to be in use in most early Bronze Age societies for the making of tin-bronze. For the Aegean and the rest of the Eastern Mediterranean in that period, tin was not locally available, so this meant that the trade routes that extended eastwards beyond Mesopotamia, Iran and the Persian Gulf to the Harappans at the time, may have been partly created by the search for a supply of this valuable commodity. For the Harappans, metallurgical technology first developed in the Early Harappan Phase and the first use of tin bronzes brought an understanding of the importance of tin not only locally but as a highly valuable export commodity.[82]

Source

The location of the sources of tin in the Near East in the Early Bronze Age has been the subject of considerable debate,[83] but evidence now conclusively points to

Figure 7. A valley in Badakhshan Province, Afghanistan, source of tin (© Zack Knowles, https://commons.wikimedia.org/wiki/File:A_valley_in_Badakhshan_Province,_Afghanistan_-a.jpg. Licensed under the Creative Commons Attribution-Share Alike 3.0 Unported license)

Badakhshan in North-East Afghanistan (Fig. 7), where Shortughai was located, in order to control the mining and gathering operation, which had by the end of the millennium emerged as a major source for the Near East, Anatolia and the Eastern Mediterranean.[84] Here it was being sourced in its natural pre-smelted form from alluvial deposits of cassiterite and then either taken to *Meluḫḫa* for re-exportation westwards as tin ingots or even possibly tin-bronze ingots by sea or exported directly overland from its source, but from quite an early stage, under the control of the Harappans.

There may have been other sources of tin. Recent discoveries of Early and Mature Harappan Phase artefacts (including pottery, animal figurines, steatite and carnelian beads), tin slag, furnaces and crucibles, together with geological evidence of tin deposits in the Tosham area of Bhiwani District in the Indian State of Haryana offers evidence for sources of tin and the use of tin bronzes. Excavations at the site of Khanak in Haryana during 2014 and 2016, also revealed ample evidence for metallurgical activity through the finding of slag, ores as well as evidence of ashes and furnace fragments, together with bronze objects. This clearly points to mining and metallurgy of local polymetallic tin. The extent of the area as a tin source for the Harappans or as a source for exports, is still unknown and will be the subject of future excavation and survey.[85]

Early Bronze Age of the Near East and the Aegean

The Harappans preferred to develop their own mining and distribution of tin rather than reply on alliances with such places as Mundigak or Shahar-i Sokhtra.[86] The region where tin was sourced is also rich in other minerals such as alluvial gold and also in lapis lazuli, so as Toby Wilkinson reminds us, the aura and physical properties of tin, gold and lapis lazuli are strongly interrelated and in at least the Mesopotamian imagination, if their use in personal adornment and statuary is anything to go by.[87] There is a text on a clay cylinder from the time of King Gudea of Lagaš (2150–2111 BC), which refers to the importation of copper, tin (presumably for making bronze) and lapis lazuli from *Meluḫḫa* into the region which is also believed to have locally hosted a Harappan settler community or colony.[88] It provides a clue to the origin of Mesopotamian tin as well as lapis lazuli, used in his extensive building programme. It reads (Cylinder B, column XIV, lines 10–13): '[copp]er (and) tin, blocks of lapis lazuli... bright carnelian from (the land of) *Meluḫḫa*'.[89] This is the only direct reference to tin from *Meluḫḫa*, but the passage from Lagaš does also associate it with trade that also involves copper, lapis lazuli and carnelian beads. The metalworkers in Sumer seemingly did their own alloying of bronze, but it is suspected that tin from India moved westwards either as ingots (possibly bun ingots), having been smelted *in situ* to enhance its value as a commodity. Tin for the Harappans, like lapis lazuli, was for export. It was not used extensively in the Harappan heartland, other than for some local bronze making.[90] The copper referred to in the text was sourced in the Persian Gulf and was not an import from India.

Whichever way tin was transported, it would have been under the control of the Harappans by way of one of the two potential routes from the source in Afghanistan to Mesopotamia and further westwards. We are reminded that the sea route ran from the Harappan homeland along the coast of the Arabian Sea to the Persian Gulf, which brought many other products of *Meluḫḫa* to the west. The land route would have crossed the northern part of the Iranian plateau, ran along the Elburz mountains and then through the passes of the Zagros mountains on it way to Sumer. Along this latter route were found urban centres such as Tepe Sialk, Tepe Giyan and Tepe Hissar, where we know that finds of lapis lazuli implicate them in late third millennium BC long distance trade to Mesopotamia.

Tin first appeared in the Near East at the beginning of the third millennium and it is mentioned in the texts of Ebla during the Akkadian period. It is at the end of the third and beginning of the second millennium that the use of tin became more regular as shown by analyses on objects, for example, from Susa, and it is then that cuneiform texts attest the most of its value and, more generally, of an intense circulation of commodities, goods and people. Clay tablets discovered in Mesopotamia at the time of the Third Dynasty of Ur show that maritime trade now existed with *Magan*, not only because it was their main copper source area, but also because it was a transit centre for goods coming from *Meluḫḫa*. At the same time, Susa had established relations with *Dilmun,* which became, during the following Isin-Larsa period, one of the main centres of Persian Gulf trade for the Harappans.[91]

From Mesopotamia, the route was by way of Syro-Palestine or Anatolia. Textual evidence points to the Middle Bronze Age I (2000–1900 BC) city of Kültepe in Central Anatolia and other cities of North Syria and Cilicia beginning a period of intense commercial activity, trading in metals such as gold, silver and particularly tin (known in Old Babylonian as *annaku*).[92] Timothy Potts has also suggested that the distribution of tin to late third and early second millennia BC Western Asia, was controlled by *Meluḫḫa*.[93] This view is based upon the pattern of early tin-bronze use in the region and particularly its dearth in highland Iran, which Potts sees as reflecting differential access to maritime trade through the Persian Gulf.

If tin was in fact coming to Mesopotamia from the Harappans, we must imagine that it was either not traded through Central and Eastern Iran, or that when it was, none was utilised in local metal industries. A southern tin and tin-bronze trade through the Persian Gulf is particularly supported by Potts, as such a trade route could explain the known distribution of tin-bronze in Southern Mesopotamia and at Susa. He stresses the importance of Anatolia; once tin and tin-bronze reached Mesopotamia, they could have been further dispersed to the west to the Troad and the Aegean via overland trade through Syro-Palestine or Anatolia. The higher tin-bronze frequency in the Troad, rather than in Central Anatolia is not a significant stumbling block to an overland trade hypothesis, if one regards the trade as directed more towards some consumers than others, rather than being simple down-the-line exchange.[94]

Lorenz Rahmstorf supports the view that the evidence points to the Afghan region as the only possible origin of the tin that supported its demand in the Aegean and the Eastern Mediterranean in the early and middle part of the third millennium BC and that it was traded westwards from India, controlled by the Harappans, as tin or as tin-bronzes.[95] In his review of the manufacture and use of Eurasian bronze objects in the early and middle third millennium BC (to 2200 BC), he has discussed at length the use and the sources of tin. He notes that tin deposits are very rare and Europe is well supplied with them, but in the Aegean, Eastern Mediterranean and the Near East, no significant deposits are known that would support them being a source of tin at this time.[96] Known or reputed tin sources, such as those in Anatolia at Kestel and Göltepe have been dismissed and the possible source at Deh Hosein in the Central-Eastern part of the Zagros Mountains in Western Iran has now also been dismissed as to be of a later date and it is safe to also dismiss any tin sources in Europe at this time.[97]

The evidence for tin-bronzes at this time in the Near East, the Persian Gulf and Oman, corroborated by texts, shows that tin is no longer quite such a rarity and that the trade in both tin bronzes and tin was flourishing, with the tin being imported from the Harappans. Lead-isotope analysis of tin bronzes found in the Persian Gulf and the Aegean, suggests that they originate from the same source, namely *Meluḫḫa*.[98] In the Harappan heartland, it is difficult to judge the role that tin-bronzes played, as they are quite scarce; only eight sites have yielded them, including Harappa and Mohenjo-daro,[99] but like lapis lazuli, tin will have been for trade not local consumption.

Of significance is the result of the study of lead-isotope ratios of metal objects from sites in *Magan* or *Makkan* in the Persian Gulf. It appears that these ratios are very similar to those from Early Bronze Age I–II sites in the Aegean, such as Kastri on Syros, Thermi on Lesbos, Poliochni on Lemnos and Troy, as well as some Balkan and North Caucasian sites. This points to either tin or tin-bronze (already as an alloy) having been imported into these regions. Since the tin-bronzes from the Persian Gulf are primarily small rings or fragments of small rings, it is possible that it may have been imported in the form of bronze rings as ingots, which in the expanse from the Aegean to the Harappan heartland are frequently encountered in the shape of rings.[100] The textual evidence also suggests that the metal was stored and transported in a ring of some kind.[101]

Pure tin may have been imported in the same way. While there is a tin bangle from Thermi in Lesbos, dated to the Early Helladic II period, it is worthwhile determining whether tin in the Eastern Mediterranean, the Aegean and Anatolia was used as ingots for trade as they are by the Harappans.

Middle and Late Bronze Ages of the Near East and the Aegean

Tin is a commodity that if used to make bronze is, of course, not re-usable and there will have been a need to import fresh supplies on a regular basis. Into the second millennium BC, Afghanistan would have continued to be exploited for its sources of tin, carrying the resources westwards, following the same pattern as for lapis lazuli.

After 1800–1700 BC in the Middle and Late Bronze Ages, the sourcing of tin from Afghanistan was no longer centrally controlled by the Harappans and its supply was now being undertaken directly from source. There was now an element of control by palatial centres such as that at Mari, which had become a major market for exotic goods and important commodities moving from east to west and tin was one such commodity. For example, details of Mari's tin inventory include gifts of tin from the Elamite king of Anshan, including one talent of tin originally sent from King Hammurabi of Babylon to the court of Aleppo. Two collections of cuneiform texts from Kültepe and from Mari (the Mari Tablets) dating to the nineteenth and early eighteenth centuries BC have references to the tin trade, which documents this trade moving exclusively from east to west. The pattern of the tin trade talks of movement from Mari to Ugarit and then to the Keftiu. Arriving in Mesopotamia from the east, post-smelted tin, possibly in the form of rings, was transhipped up the Euphrates to Mari, or overland to Assur. From Assur, the tin, probably in addition to Babylonian textiles, was transported overland via caravan to various Assyrian trading colonies such as Kaneš/Kültepe in Anatolia, where it was traded for exotic manufactured goods. From Mari, the tin was traded further west to sites in Syria and Palestine and then to the Aegean.[102]

For the Aegean, tin was a vital commodity and by the early Middle Bronze Age, we see it as the only other metal that was alloyed with copper to make bronze. The trade link between Western Asia and the Aegean can now be traced. From Mari and Ugarit and other Syro-Palestinian centres, it was sold to traders from, amongst others, *Kaphtor*, which is now identified as Minoan Crete, characterised by the finding along the coast of imported Kamares Ware pottery, dated mostly to the Middle Minoan IA period. One tin inventory at Mari lists the sites to which tin was distributed and another inventory mentions the route by which Mari received tin from the east by way of the town of Shauna, located in Mesopotamia on the River Tigris, with access to the trade routes from India.[103]

By the Middle Minoan II period, Crete was now establishing a relationship with North Syria that included Ugarit, Byblos and Qatna with less secure evidence from as far inland as Mari. Located at the closest point between Cyprus and the coast of Syria, it linked the river traffic of the Euphrates with the coast of the Mediterranean. The major factor for this development was their growing bronze industry.[104] The best textual evidence for trade between Crete and the Levant in this period in tin from the east, is contained in a group of Mari tablets from the palace of King Zimri-Lim, dated to approximately 1780–1760 BC, roughly contemporary with the second half of the Middle Minoan IIB period. One important text, a tin inventory,[105] refers to an allocation of tin to a merchant from Minoan Crete or Caphtor and also to the interpreter of their Chief Merchant, both resident in Ugarit (Table 2). From this text, we learn that a group of Minoan merchants was resident in Ugarit in the early eighteenth century BC and that they were probably structured hierarchically, which suggests probable palatial control. We also learn, owing to the value of tin, that it seems to have been used as a form of primitive currency.

Later in the second millennium BC, there is also evidence of larger tin ingots being traded in the East Mediterranean with a likely destination of the palaces and workshops of the Mycenaeans. Within the cargoes of several shipwrecks of the period can be found tin ingots; one such example is the Uluburun shipwreck, dated to 1300 BC which carried approximately 40 such ingots, supplied from the Syro-Palestinian coast, which were approximately one metric ton in total weight. Many of the ingots were in the ox-hide form as used for copper, although there were a few that were in other forms such as bun ingots and rectangular slab ingots. These ingots were seemingly cut into smaller pieces before loading and probably represent an assemblage that was cut up for distribution and use (Fig. 8). It is likely that the ore was smelted and the ingots were first cast at sites east of Mesopotamia,[106] probably Afghanistan or Central Asia, where the ore was first sourced, long after the Harappan control ceased.

James Muhly is of the view that the Harappans mined or imported only enough tin for their own consumption[107] and one cannot see any reason as to why the amount exported was limited in any way. In some Mesopotamian texts of this period, tin is often mentioned together with lapis lazuli and carnelian[108] and some have taken this to mean that there is a common origin for all three commodities to the east.[109] Lapis lazuli, tin and carnelian are often referred, collectively as it appears, of coming from the land of *Meluḫḫa*, now identified with the Harappan heartland.[110]

Figure 8. Tin ingots from, the Uluburun Shipwreck. c. 1300 BC (Bodrum Museum of Underwater Archaeology)

We know, however, that there were very limited tin deposits in the Harappan heartland itself,[111] but before 1800 BC, an Indian origin of some tin in the Near

Table 2. Text from Mari allocating tin to a Minoan and his interpreter

Line	*Transliteration*	*Translation*
1	1+ x/3 MA.NA AN.NA a-na kap-ta-ra-i-im	1+x/3 minas of tin to the merchant from Caphtor
2	1/3 MA.NA AN.NA a-na ^{LÚ} ta-ar-ga-ma-an-nim	1/3 mina of tin to the interpreter
3	UGULA [DAM.GÀ]R k[a]p-ta'-ra-i	(of the) Chief Merchant of the merchant from Caphtor
4	i-na ú-ga-ri-ti KI	in Ugarit

East and the Aegean can be explained by centralised Harappan control of the limited Afghanistan (and possibly other) sources available to them as well as other commodities such as lapis lazuli. The evidence of geology, archaeology and texts points to an Afghan and Indian source for the tin trade in both the third and second millennia BC.[112] A source in the region around Troy or elsewhere in Anatolia has been ruled out by geologists, and others, such as the Western Arabian peninsula or European sources that clearly did not supply the Aegean or the rest of the Eastern Mediterranean at this time.[113] In fact, geology and lead-isotope analysis also seems to support the idea that Afghanistan was the source for tin as used in Aegean tin-bronzes.[114]

Notes

1 Possehl 2002b, 219–220; 2012, 762.

2 Dupree 1981, 103–115; Francfort 1984, 301–310; 1989. See also Possehl 1999, 57–70.

3 Possehl 2002b, 235.

4 Lyonnet 2005, 191–200.

5 The location also gave them the opportunity to source turquoise, jadeite and probably other commodities from the neighbouring Namazga Culture in the Kopet Dagh area of Southern Turkmenia, where Indus Civilisation material, such as etched carnelian beads, seals, ivory rods and dice has been found at their principal site of Altyn-depe, see Masson 1988.

6 For camels see Shaffer 1987, 1315–1328.

7 Francfort 1989, 337–340.

8 Wylock 1972, 125–129; Ventris and Chadwick 1973, 226–228, 308–309, 441–442, 555; Hiller and Panagl 1976, 172, they refer to it as *Cymbbopogon schoenanthus v. Acorus calamus* L. See also Cline 1994, 131 (E.24); Duhoux 2008, 284. For discussion of *ko-in-o* or *ko-no* see Sarpaki 2001, 212–214. For a study of foodstuffs and spices imported from India into the Ancient Near East (and possibly the Aegean) see Scott *et al.* 2021.

9 Sarpaki 2001, 206.

10 Wylock 1972, 118–125. See also Ventris and Chadwick 1973, 549.

11 Sarpaki 2001, 206.

12 Serpico and White 2000, 397. For a discussion of sesame, see Sarpaki 2001, 226–227.

13 Ventris and Chadwick 1973, 135, 227–228 229–231, 441, 581–582; Hiller and Panagl 1976, 172; Wylock 1972, 115–118. It has been argued that it was imported through the Near East, as the word appears to have Semitic origins, see Cline 1994, 128 (E.3) (and references).

14 van de Mieroop 2007, 46. However, there is a view that black pepper was imported into India well after the Bronze Age. See Lawler 2012, 288. For cinnamon see Sarpaki 2001, 209–210.

15 Buccellati and Kelly-Buccellati 1983, 47–67. There is a suggestion that the contents of three juglets from the Canaanite site of Megiddo, dated to 1600–1500 BC, subjected to organic residue analysis (GC-MS), produced evidence of what is thought to have been the chemical components of vanilla, the product of aromatic vanilla orchids. If it is vanilla, India is the most likely source. There is an element of scepticism, but if proven right it would give further evidence of Near Eastern contacts between India, this time southern India and the Near East, at the end of the Middle Bronze Age, where some vestiges of the Late Harrapan Phase still existed. We now need to find vanilla in the Aegean to complete the link. Lawler 2018, 980–981.

16 Possehl 2012, 763. See also Witzel 2000, 497–508, for his discussion on the wood trade between the Harappans and the Near East.

17 There is a reference to the 'blackwood of Meluḫḫa' being imported into Lagaš, which is likely to have been ebony, see Leemans 1960, 122; Falkenstein 1966, 48; Potts 1993a, 1456–1459.

18 Falkenstein 1966.

19 Possehl 2012, 762; Tenberg and Potts 1999, 129–133 (with references); Maxwell-Hyslop 1983, 67–72. A well-known text from the middle of the third millennium BC, records the boast of Ur-Nanshe, king of the city-state of Lagash, that ships from *Dilmun* brought him timber qualified as being 'from foreign lands', see Sollberger and Kupper 1971, (IC3C), 12–17. This inscription might have been alluding to timber from the Indian sub-continent, such as (a) Indian cedar, reportedly discovered at Borsippa in Iraq, see Potts 2007, 122–130; (b) teak, 'two rough logs' of which were said to have been found in the Nanna-Ningal temple complex at Ur; and (c) *sisso* (see text), all of which could have come from there or from further afield, in Baluchistan or the Indus River region, by ship, see Heimpel 1987, 22–91; and Potts 2017, 134–135.

20 For general discussion on the ivory trade between India and the Near East, see Massa and Palmisano 2018a, 69–73. Indian ivory may have been traded in Mesopotamia at least between 2500–1900 BC. While exploitation of the elephant populations living along the banks of the River Euphrates seems very probable, a flourishing trade in raw and worked elephant ivory between Southern Mesopotamia and the Indus valley is also well documented. An Early Dynastic III period text from Lagaš and an Akkadian text from Girsu, mentions the receipt of tusks from unknown locations, while several Ur III period texts from Ur refer to raw and manufactured ivory being shipped from Meluḫḫa through the Persian Gulf. During the ensuing Middle Bronze Age, ivory exchange networks seem to have witnessed a radical reconfiguration. With the disruption of the trade connections with India by way of the Persian Gulf, in Mesopotamia archaeological evidence for ivory becomes sparse. See also Potts 1993a, 1456–1459; and Leemans 1960, 161, who also refers to several texts from the end of the Ur III Dynasty, which mentions objects carved out of ivory (*zú-am-si*) from Meluḫḫa. In addition to timber and carnelian, the Indus Valley and possibly Central Asia, was a source of ivory; Heimpel 1987, 22–91; Potts 2017, 135. Ivory carving was a well-developed craft in India as well. In the late third millennium BC, ivory objects from *Meluḫḫa*, conventionally identified with the Harappans, were being imported at Ur in Southern Mesopotamia via *Magan*. Among the objects recorded are ivory birds of *Meluḫḫa* analogous to an ivory tufted duck (*Aythya fuligula*) on a carved base found from a collective tomb at Tell Abraq, a site in the Persian Gulf, datable to approximately 2100–2000 BC, see Potts 2000, 131. Also found in the tomb were over a dozen ivory combs, which are presumed to have come from the Indus Valley, while the examples with incised tulips, find close iconographic parallels with softstone flasks from the site of Gonur Depe in Turkmenistan, Potts 1993b, 591–596; 1994, 615–628.

21 Hooijer 1978, 187–188.

22 Colburn 2008, 206; Krzyszkowska 1988, 227–229; 1990, 15; Pfälzner 2013, 112–131. The fact is that elephant ivory, whether African or West Asian varieties, apparently were unknown as a material in the Aegean until the late Middle Bronze Age and was quite rare in Syro-Palestine before around 2000 BC. Elephants themselves cannot be documented in Syro-Palestine before that date.

23 Ratnagar 2004, 108. Looking for evidence of trade in textiles can be based upon an examination of the different types of wild and domesticated species of bast-fibre plants, such as flax, cotton trees and bushes that exist in a particular area and which suggests that they were used for making fabrics. This then gives a broad indication of the movement of textiles to regions where the identified fibre is either absent, limited or that there is no evidence that they were harvested and used, see Wilkinson 2014, 247–248.

24 Cotton is a soft, staple fibre that grows in a form known as a boll around the seeds of the cotton plant, a shrub native to tropical and subtropical regions around the world, including

South Asia. The fibre is spun into yarn or thread and used to make a soft, breathable textile, which is the most widely used natural-fibre fabric in clothing. Evidence suggests that it was first cultivated 7,000 years ago in the Early Harappan Phase and a fragment of woven cotton cloth has been found at Mohenjo-daro and is the earliest evidence in the world of the growing of cotton, see Possehl 2002b, 64. See also Fuller 2008, 1–26.

25 Of interest is the recent microscopic analysis of archaeological thread fragments found inside copper-alloy ornaments from Harappa and steatite beads from Chanhu-daro, used for threading the beads. These have been identified as silk fibres, dating to approximately 2450–2000 BC, see Good *et al.* 2009, 457–466; Wilkinson 2014, 247–248. For a study of the origins of Harappan silk production see Dayalan 2019.

26 Wright *et al.* 2012, 137–143. See also Wilkinson 2014, 244–246.

27 Possehl 2012, 769. For cotton see Oppenheim 1964, 94; Talon 1986, 75–78; Wilkinson 2014, 246.

28 [28] Panagiotakopulu *et al.* 1997, 420–429.

29 One on an unfired seal, Mackay 1938, pl. LXXXIII.30 (see front cover); one as graffiti on a potsherd, Mackay 1938, pl. LXIX.4; and another on a terracotta tablet, Dales 1968, 39. These depictions feature high-prowed, flat-bottomed boats similar in appearance to the ones still used on portions of the lower Indus River today. Evidence for seagoing vessels is indirectly provided by the existence of sites like Lothal, Dholavira, Sotka Koh and Sutkagen Dor, that are located along what would be important coastal trade routes and, in the case of Lothal, have port facilities and ample evidence of trade with cultures across the Arabian Sea and the Persian Gulf. One complete and four fragmentary terracotta models of boats were also found at Lothal, see Rao 1985, 505.

30 Law 2006, 307.

31 Law 2006, 307–308.

32 Law 2006, 308.

33 Shaffer 1978, 153.

34 Wilkinson 2014, 125–127.

35 [35] Hermann 1968, 22–27. For an overview of Near Eastern lapis lazuli see Moorey 1994, 85–92; Casanova 2013, 203–208. With the current knowledge, out of 13 deposits known worldwide, the Badakhshan mines in Afghanistan, particularly Sar-i Sang, are the only ones that have been with some confidence identified as a source of lapis lazuli for the Early to Middle Bronze Age Near East. Other potential, albeit presently unconfirmed, sources are the Pamir deposits in Tajikistan, approximately 130 km from Sar-i Sang, see Massa and Palmisano 2018a, 76–78.

36 Ratnagar 2004, 186–187.

37 Delmas and Casanova 1990, 493–505; Casanova 1999, 191–193; 2013, 208–209. However, a further study has proven that this source is a myth, see Law 2014, 419–429.

38 Massa and Palmisano 2018a, 76–78.

39 Sarianidi and Kowalski 1971, 12–15. There is a model of early and pre-Harappan controlled overland caravan routes, carrying lapis lazuli to the Near East. The first is a northern one which led through Hissar and Sialk in Iran; and secondly, a southern one, running through Mundigark and Shahr-i Sokhta, either to the Arabian Sea or by land through Anshan and Susa to the Persian Gulf. This would have created three links, one the centre of production; the second the cities in Iran, acting as the intermediaries and small sales markets; and thirdly the markets of cities of Elam and Southern Mesopotamia, intermediaries for buyers from the west, such as Syro-Palestine and Egypt and eventually the Aegean. Neither of the two proposed caravan routes undermines the suggestion of Indus Civilisation control, particularly the second where there is ample evidence of Indus Civilisation presence and until towards the end of and after the Late Harappan Phase when centralised control would have ceased, see

Tosi 1974, 3–22. There is a suggestion that lapis lazuli was traded between Egypt and Byblos in the earlier part of the third millennium BC. This points to the trade in the commodity being earlier than originally thought, see Pinnock 1988, 110.

40 Wilkinson 2014, 129.

41 Massa and Palmisano 2018a, 76–78.

42 Aruz 2003, 246–247, 411–412; Casanova 2013, 215.

43 An understanding of these trade routes is based on the find-spots of the regions mentioned, see Sarianidi and Kowalski 1971, 12–15. See also Wilkinson 2014, 129 for discussion on trade routes for lapis lazuli. Lapis lazuli became common in Egypt during the Naqada period and the First Dynasty, but after the apparent disruption of lapis lazuli exchanges in the early third millennium, witnessed in both Egypt and Mesopotamia, lapis lazuli returned to be popular for the remainder of the Early Bronze Age and in parallel with the trend in Mesopotamia, considerable amounts of lapis lazuli are found in Egypt in contexts at this time, with Byblos possibly funnelling lapis lazuli further south to Egypt via a maritime route.

44 Potts 1993a, 1456–1459.

45 Mackay 1937, 1–15; Tosi 1969, 371–374; Piperno and Tosi 1975, 186–197. For a study of Harappan drills and drilling see Menon 2014, 127–141.

46 Chakrabati 1978, 51–58; Tosi and Vidale 1990, 89–99.

47 Foster 1979, 33.

48 Ratnagar 2004, 190–191.

49 Cohen 1975, 22–36; Ratnagar 2004, 125–126.

50 Ratnagar 2004, 185–193, for discussion of Indian and Mesopotamian lapis lazuli and its trade. In an analysis of the third millennia BC textiles found at Shahr-I Sokhta, it has been speculated that some of the fabric netting or string-based made from sheep or goat's wool or sunn-hemp (*Crotalaria juncea* L.), which originated in India, may have been used as the rough packaging for imported products or products in transit on their way from India on their way westwards, such as lapis lazuli. See Good 2006, 202–203.

51 Massa and Palmisano 2018a, 76–78.

52 Olijdam 1997, 119–125.

53 For bead see Blegen *et al.* 1950, pl. 297, inv no. 37–30. This might suggest that the trade began earlier than 1900–1800 BC, but land contacts across Anatolia may be the origin of this find. For cylinder seal see Schliemann 1880, fig. 502.

54 Pushkin State Museum of Fine Art, Moscow, inv. no. Aap 169 (П523), Antonova *et al.* 1996, 152 and 219–222, cat. no. 169.

55 For example, there are two examples of lapis lazuli seals. One is a re-carved Syrian cylinder seal from Archanes found in an Early Minoan III–Middle Minoan IA level, possibly imported and embellished locally. The other is a rectangular Middle Minoan II stamp seal from Palaikastro with distinctive floral patterns on two faces; Heraklion Museum inv, no. HM 1678. Aruz 2008, 272, fig. 197, no. 110. For the others see Platon 1969, 424, no. 286. See also Krzyszkowska 2003, 201, n.18. Since then only one more seal has been published and an old fragmentary one republished, see Hughes-Brock 2011, 99. See also for discussion of some lapis lazuli objects found on Crete and whether the objects made from it were manufactured locally or elsewhere and their significance. Lapis lazuli is also reported from Tholos Tomb B at Koumasa, dated to the Early Minoan IA–Middle Minoan IA periods, see Xanthoudides 1924, 3–5.

56 Massa and Palmisano 2018b.

57 Fitton *et al.* 2008, 22–23. For Minoan lapis lazuli see Hughes-Brock 2011, 99–114, n.98.

58 Amarna Letter EA7.49–62, Moran 1992, 12–16 and n.18; Amarna Letter EA13, Moran 1992, 24–27; Cline 1994, 25.

59 Cline 1994, 25.

60 Aruz 2008, 96.
61 Krzyszkowska 2003, 204–205; Platon and Pini 1984, 27, no. 24.
62 Krzyszkowska 2005, 237, n.22.
63 Krzyszkowska 2005, 239.
64 Thebes Museum, inv. nos. TM 176–179, 180–183, 186–187, 191–194, 197–199, 200–203, 205–208, 212–215, 226, Porada 1981–1982, 1–70; Cline 2007, 190–200. In the second millennium BC, there is good evidence of the continued importation of lapis lazuli into Kassite Babylonia from Badakhshan by the land route via Marḫarsu and Elam, long after the disappearance of the Harappans, see Clayden 2019. However, there is a suggestion that the Mesopotamians favoured 'purplish blue' lapis lazuli, whilst the Mycenaeans favoured the 'pure royal blue' colour, see Porada 1981–1982, 6–7 and 77–78. Some of the cylinder seals found at Thebes in a Late Helladic IIIB1–2 context, are Kassite and points to Kassite objects being found on the Greek mainland at the end of a trade pattern, an extension of the lapis lazuli supply from South Asia to the Aegean.
65 Symeneoglou 1973, 63–71.
66 Unpublished. Mycenae Museum, inv. nos. MM 1471–1472 (two beads), MM 1473 (pendant); Taylour 1981, 47–48.
67 Thebes Archaeological Museum, inv. no. TM 227. Touloupa 1965, 230, pl. 276β; Demakopoulou 1988, 116, cat. no. 51.
68 For example, there are some jade barrel-shaped beads found from the earlier excavations, see Marshall 1931, Volume 2, 683–684 and Volume 3, pls. CXLVIII.A.6 and CL. Some of these beads (excavation no, DK 11337, g, h, u and t) have also been found in a jewellery hoard and some small jade balls and cones (perhaps toys) have also been found, see Mackay 1938, 498, 527, 565, 571 and pls. CXXXV.19 and CXXXIX.7. For examples of very early jade at the Neolithic levels at Burzahom see Allchin and Allchin 1982, 116 and on jade in the Mature Harappan Phase see Allchin and Allchin 1982, 186.
69 Pushkin State Museum of Fine Art, Moscow, inv. no. Aap 165 (П521, 166 (П520) and 167 (П522), are recorded as being made from nephrite and Aap 166 is recorded as being made from jadeite. Another Aap 168 (П523) is from lapis lazuli, see Treister 1996, 197–234 and Antonova *et al.* 1996, 148–151, 219–222 (and for additional references).
70 Schliemann 1880, 238–239, with illustration of nos. 86–89, nos. 86, 87 and 89 are made from nephrite and no. 88 is made from jadeite. For references to the nature and sources of the stone see pp. 86–89.
71 Hiebert 2000, 11–20, which illustrates the Borodino Hoard from Moldova that also contains ceremonial axes of jade/nephrite and dated contemporary with the Troy examples. See also Antonova *et al.* 1996, 220–222. They also discuss other likely parallels from the Near East and Prehistoric Europe.
72 Antonova *et al.* 1996, 220.
73 Pushkin State Museum of Fine Art, Moscow, inv. no. Aap 168.
74 Moorey 1994, 83.
75 Renfrew 1972, 445–446.
76 Thapar 1993, 9, 11.
77 Muhly 1983, 1–14. It is certain that most of the gold in the Aegean originated in Egypt or Nubia, where it is found in some abundance, or Syria, where there is to be found alluvial gold. There are also limited gold sources in the north-east Aegean and in the Balkans. It is notable, however, that the Greek word for gold, χρυσός, which occurs in Mycenaean Greek, is of Semitic derivation, see Colburn 2008, 206.
78 Major gold sources are known from the modern Indian state of Karnataka and South India, but it is unknown whether these resources were utilised by the Harappans. Small alluvial

gold nodules (gold dust) are widespread and are reported from the Upper Indus, Baluchistan and Uttar Pradesh, see Allchin 1962, 195–211; Kenoyer and Miller 1999, 119–120; Wright 2010, 197–198. Ratnagar has reviewed the extensive evidence for the sourcing of gold in India, its availability as a commodity to the Indus Civilisation and how it was used internally and as an instrument of exchange and trade. She concludes that it is not impossible that the Indus Civilisation exported gold to Mesopotamia, see Ratnagar 2004, 154–159.

79 Stech and Pigott 1986, 39–64; Ratnagar 2004, 155; Wright 2010, 197–198; Francfort 1989, 136, 207.

80 For example, Gudea *Statute* B, VI.38–40, see Falkenstein 1966, 48. For reference to Meluḫ̮ḫ̮a gold (ships from Meluḫ̮ḫ̮a bringing gold as well as silver and lapis lazuli to Lagaš) in the text *Enki and the World Order*, see Falkenstein 1964, 67 (lines 126–127). See also Moorey 1994, 220; Oppenheim 1954, 7; Leemans 1960, 120–121.

81 Lyonnet 2005, 191–200.

82 For a review of Harappan copper and bronze metallurgy, see Hoffman and Miller 2014, 697–727. The small amount of copper and bronze objects found at Harappan sites were, probably due to their scarcity and as a symbol of wealth and status, passed down from one generation to another. Copper alloying although common in the Near East, from those copper objects found in the Harappan heartland, only 30% of the copper and bronze objects from Harappa and Mohenjo-daro that have been studied, show the use of tin, arsenic, nickel or lead alloying, with tin the most common, which ranged from 1–12%. This may have been because of several reasons; no less the need to conserve tin for export, see Massa and Palmisano 2018a, 76–78.

83 Dayton 1971, 49–70; 2003, 165–170; Muhly 1973; Stech and Pigott 1986, 39–64.

84 There is a suggestion of another source of tin. In Southern Afghanistan, the tin deposits at Mesgaran (with the ores containing >6.6% tin), Herat and on the modern Iranian–Afghan–Pakistan border area would have been a more convenient source for the Harappans.

85 Kochhar *et al.* 1999, 115–118; Singh and Singh 2016, 847–856.

86 Kenoyer and Miller 1999, 118.

87 Wilkinson 2014, 162.

88 Cleuziou and Berthold 1982, 14–19. A tin source from Anatolia has now been effectively discounted, see Hall and Steadman 1991, 217–234. At the end of the third millennium, evidence has how emerged of the establishment of an Indus Civilisation settlement in Mesopotamia. Called Guabba in Lagaš, it was an inland harbour town, dating from the Ur III period (2113–2004 BC). Parpola *et al.* 1977, 129–165; Potts 1993a, 1456–1459; Vermaak 2008, 553–570. It may well have been the centre for trade between Mesopotamia and India. Unfortunately, no tin ingots have yet been found at any Indus Civilisation site to emphasise that the trade was in the hands of officials from that civilisation. For comprehensive discussion of the alternative sources of tin see Wilkinson 2014, 163–165, but the evidence for any source other than Afghanistan is inconclusive.

89 Falkenstein 1966, 14 and 48; Muhly 1973, 306–307; Wilson 1996.

90 Kenoyer and Miller 1999, 118. A pre-Sargonic text from Lagash and described as a Sumerian merchant's account of the *Dilmun* or *Tilman* trade, mentions obtaining from the region 27.5 minas (*c.* 14 kg) of *an-na zabar*, a phrase literally translated as tin bronze. The fact that the isotopic characteristics of the Aegean tin-bronzes are similar to those from the Persian Gulf, adds further weight to the hypothesis of an eastern source for these early alloys and their components, see Foster 1997, 59.

91 Lyonnet 2005, 191–200.

92 Özgüç 1968, 53–58; Ratnagar 2004, 124. For *annaku*, Roth 1968, 127–129.

93 Potts 2016.

94 Potts 1994, 281. Regarding tin supplies to Egypt, copper, mostly mined and smelted in the Eastern Desert and the Sinai, was the most common metal used for tools and weapons. A great deal of it contained natural arsenic, which would have hardened the copper to make arsenical bronzes. There are already a few bronze objects known from the Second Dynasty and there are also some well-known bronze objects from the Middle Kingdom (2025–1700 BC), bronze is only in general use from the New Kingdom (1550–1069 BC) onwards. There are occurrences of tin in Egypt, but there are no signs that these deposits were mined in dynastic times. It is thought that tin was imported through Crete and Cyprus, after approximately 1350 BC (Jacke Phillips, personal communication, 2017) and presumably was of Afghan origins.

95 Rahmstorf 2017, 198.

96 Rahmstorf 2017, 184–185.

97 Rahmstorf 2017, 197–199.

98 Rahmstorf 2017, 196.

99 Rahmstorf 2017, 196–197.

100 Rahmstorf 2017, 197.

101 Rahmstorf 2017, 197.

102 Dossin 1970, 97–106; Malamat 1971, 38; Muhly 1985, 282; Cline 1994, 25. For the place of Mari in the tin trade see Montero Fenollós 2019, 125. From the textual and archaeological evidence excavated from the site, it is possible to determine that the tin trade occupied a very prominent place in its economy. Some metals, such as tin, were of high value due to its scarcity and the enormous effort used in importing it from very distant lands. Tin was an exotic product requested by the oriental elites to reinforce their social position and possessing it was a symbol of prestige and power from the beginning of the third millennium BC.

103 Dossin 1970; Cleuziou and Berthold 1982, 14–19.

104 Astour 1973, 20–21.

105 Strange 1980, 90–91 (33); Cline 1994, 126 (D.2).

106 Dossin 1970, 97–106; Pulak 2001, 12–61.

107 Muhly 1985, 281–283. It is likely that the Afghan source served India as well. For a discussion on possible tin sources within the Indian Sub-Continent see Chakrabarti and Lahiri 1996, 25–26.

108 Weeks 1999, 51; Ratnagar 2004, 1850–193.

109 Hermann 1968, 21–57; Potts 1994, 155.

110 Muhly 1973, 307; Ratnagar 2004, 125–126.

111 Stech and Pigott 1986, 44–45; Moorey 1994, 299–300.

112 Weeks 2004, 180–181. See also Penhallurick 1986, 21–32. This raises the issue of Indian tin being resourced within what are the accepted boundaries of the Indus Civilisation, whilst accepting that the copper for their bronzes is local, he generally supports the contention that the tin was in the third millennium BC, sourced from Afghanistan and traded westwards as a commodity, some if it appearing in the Aegean in the Early Bronze II period.

113 Weeks 2004, 180–181. There has also been some speculation about tin sources in other locations in Central Asia, see Cierny and Weisgerber 2003, 23–31. For further speculation about tin sources in the Near East and the Aegean see the other papers in this volume, but none of it is entirely convincing.

114 Pernicka *et al.* 1990, 290; Pernicka 1995, 108.

Chapter 4

Prehistory: A Conclusion

Earlier Work

Rakhal Das Banerji, the first excavator in 1922 of Mohenjo-daro, chose to compare the painted pottery and the inscribed seals he found with Minoan parallels. The palace-based, civilisation of the Minoans at Knossos, would have presented to Banerji sources for comparison with his finds from Mohenjo-daro. Both yielded inscribed tablets, knowledge of metal technology and a complex social organisation, and like Mohenjo-daro, presented no apparent clues on the nature of government. Marshall, with his experience of working on Crete, rejected the resemblances he proposed, as being too intangible to warrant any inferences being drawn as to a cultural connection between the two regions.[1]

There has been much previously written about other contacts between the Aegean and India in prehistory, but none of it is supported by any real evidence. The first to have examined the possibility of such relations was Heinz Mode.[2] While he objectively discussed relations between the Harappans and the Near East, based on knowledge at that time, his views about relations with Greece and the Aegean in the same period, like so many others since, were based on rather wild speculation.

Inez During Caspers also discussed Harappan contacts with the Aegean, but in reality she mostly theorises about an unproven trade link through Egypt.[3] She also suggested that the three-sided prism-shaped stamp seals found on Crete, which are mostly made of local steatite (and not faience as she states) and dated to the Early Minoan III–Middle Minoan IIB periods,[4] are very similar to four-sided steatite prisms drilled lengthways and found at Mohenjo-daro and Harappa.[5] However, all the Cretan examples are clearly Minoan and locally made and none have been found outside the Aegean, therefore this trade or cultural exchange scenario is unlikely.

In his 2003 book and in a paper published two years earlier, Costis Davaras attempted to examine the parallels as he saw them of affinities between the Minoans and the Harappans. An eminent and highly respected archaeologist renowned for his work in Eastern Crete and recognising the archaeological realities of the third millennium BC, he cautiously prefaced his remarks with the following comments:

> Whilst there are no possibilities that the two areas, Minoan Crete and the Harappan Indus Valley, had any direct relationship during the second millennium BC or earlier, it is possible that their inhabitants mingled in Mesopotamia, where at least an Indian presence was known.[6]

He properly understood that similarities between objects may simply be coincidental and many of the parallels he makes are, in his own words, speculative and he does not offer evidence for anything that would pass archaeological scrutiny and be regarded as conclusive.

One example of this coincidence is that bull leaping in Minoan Crete and bull grappling sports in the Harappan Civilisation are very similar and some have therefore thought that this may be the result of contact in the third millennium BC. Two clay amulet sealings from Mohenjo-daro, show possible Harappan bull or a zebu, leaping or grappling.[7] Other sealings from Mohenjo-daro, a terracotta sealing and a twisted clay sealing,[8] show bull sacrifice to, presumably, a deity. While one is greatly struck by the similarity between the activities of both bull grappling and bull sacrifice depicted in both Minoan and Harappan iconography, there is clearly no evidence to support any connection between the two.

There has even been a bewildering attempt at associating Mycenaean place and population group names with those found in the second to first millennium BC *Ṛgveda* and in Indian myth.[9] While a remote Indo-European connection is not lost on us, the argument is based on a number of sweeping and rather doubtful assumptions, including a naïve association of Homer with the Mycenaeans of centuries earlier, an acceptance of the now entirely discredited theory of Aryan Invasion during the second millennium BC and a complete disregard for well-known onomastic and other evidence in the Linear B tablets and recent scholarship. None of it can be taken seriously.

Summary of the Evidence

In this work, my focus has been on an analysis of trade routes westwards from India during the third to first millennia BC. While I have adopted a methodology based on the identification of specific commodities and objects, utilised by cultures in different periods, I recognise that such an empirical study requires a theoretical framework. In this framework, the term trade, for example, has not been used without understanding and specifying the parameters and often its interchangeably with exchange. The term trade denotes a wide range of exchange relationships from hand-to-hand 'trickle-down trade' to redistribution, as well as long-distance organised trade. Trade was, in the ancient world, risk-taking, profit-motivated, entrepreneurial behaviour, although professional trade and commerce were largely absent in prehistoric communities, though certain commodities and objects could acquire commercial value. It is then obvious that the term trade cannot be used indiscriminately in the context of diverse archaeological cultures and I have recognised the importance of exchange networks rather than to demarcate trade-routes merely by the availability of commodities.

New evidence and the revaluation of the existing evidence now points to a form of very indirect or what might be called 'trickle-down' contact between the Aegean and India in prehistory. They can be placed into three categories: (a) the importation of objects manufactured in India or from Indian commodities in the Near East, which eventually found their way to the Aegean at the end of the third and the beginning of the second millennium BC and have parallels at Indian sites, such as carnelian beads; (b) the importation of inorganic commodities such as agate, tin, possibly some gold and lapis lazuli, exported from under Harappan control, but where it has been used to make objects either locally or in the Near East, Anatolia or even Egypt on their way to the Aegean; and (c) the importation of non-perishable organic commodities.

While all three are indicators of trade and remotely possible cultural exchange, it must be stressed that it does not testify to direct cultural and trade links and geographical knowledge between the Harappans and the prehistoric Aegean. In many ways, it was just the natural extension of trade between the Near East and India. No goods or commodities arrived directly from India; they accumulated added value in the Near East and Syro-Palestine.

The third and early second millennia BC experienced the development of a system of regional specialisation in the production of goods, set within a system of long-distance contacts which bridged different geographic and cultural areas from India to the Eastern Mediterranean. The Aegean was at the periphery of this system. It consisted of a series of interconnected and overlapping contacts, interacting among themselves, which were built around a few trading centres. This is evidenced by both the spatial distribution of objects and commodities as well as the different weight shapes and units of measure, which reveal the presence of at least two distinct, albeit overlapping, exchange networks during this period.

Various models of exchange have been proposed for the movement of goods between the Harappans and Mesopotamia, a distance of 2500 km, that include indirect overland trade through Baluchistan and Iran, direct trade by seas between the major cities in both regions, through the Persian Gulf, using middle-men in the Persian Gulf region as the main traders.

One network was a prominently seaborne one stretching between the Syro-Palestinian coast and the Aegean by way of a maritime route that touched the southern Anatolian coast. During the Early Bronze Age this network saw the origins of luxury items in mid–late Early Minoan Crete. Along this route, commodities, such as bronze and tin were exchanged, as ideas and technologies certainly travelled along the southern Anatolian coast; a prime example is provided by the westward spread of metrology and sealing practices in the first part of the Early Bronze Age. It is striking that all these features appear almost exclusively at sites near the coast.

Another exchange network is composed of a bundle of interweaving routes that crossed the eastern Taurus Mountains at different passes, connecting Northern Syria with central Anatolia and beyond to Mesopotamia and eventually to the Harappans. During the Early Bronze Age, it is marked by the distribution of, for example, Harappan carnelian beads and lapis lazuli artefacts. It is worth assessing the elements of continuity and change between the late third and the early second millennia BC long-distance exchange networks. Among the factors of continuity, one can certainly include the involvement of the same major centres in both periods. Because many sites in the Near East and Anatolia continued to play an important role within these networks, it is also probable that the routes connecting them may have been relatively stable.[10]

It also was unlikely to have been a two-way trade of objects and commodities. This long-distance trade appears to be quite one-sided, with little going from the Near East to India at the time,[11] other than possibly some copper from the Gulf. The question must be asked, however, how did the tin, the lapis lazuli and other commodities sent by ship through the Persian Gulf or by land over Iran enhance the Harappan economy? The answer is that we do not know. One thing we can be sure of is that although the Harappans will have appreciated the economic benefits of this trade, it was of little importance to the evolution of their cultural complexity and identity.

The Harappans from *Meluḫḫa*, during their Mature Harappan Phase, must surely be considered the largest and, in some ways, the most advanced of the great Bronze Age societies of its time. It held in its grasp many of the natural resources of Afghanistan, Central Asia and Northern Iran and considered its trade and relations with these local societies, as well as the Persian Gulf (*Magan* and *Dilmun*) and Mesopotamia and possibly Egypt on the periphery an even possibly Western China, to be of the highest importance. We also cannot lose sight, however, of the principal relations outside this sphere that the Harappan Civilisation would likely have had with the rest of the Indian Sub-Continent and even China, South-East Asia and East Africa.

By the third millennium BC, both the Persian Gulf and the earlier trade routes that crossed between Mesopotamia and the Indus Valley by way of the Iranian plateau will have involved, other than trade exchange, a range of early diplomatic exchanges, elite marriages, cultural hegemony, political connections and war. The trade and exchange system itself involved the importation into Mesopotamia of tin, timber, copper, semi-precious stones, beads and possibly textiles. Precious commodities can be itemised as gold, ivory, carnelian beads, dice, bird and monkey figurines, conch shells and lapis lazuli. In return, the Mesopotamians would have probably exported to the Harappans several products, including food, silver and even copper. Steatite vases were also traded, both as trade items in themselves, but also as containers of other luxury goods. Therefore, little or no pottery became part of trade and exchange; it is heavy if carried by caravan or even by small ships, rendering containers made from textiles or reeds more economical.

In about 2200 BC in the Mature Harappan Phase we see ships from *Meluḫḫa* sailing into the ports of Akkad (Agade) and Sumer and trading in goods and commodities that were sourced and controlled by the Harappans. This included specifically lapis lazuli, carnelian, tin and gold, for which we have evidence from Akkadian and Sumerian texts. Just after 2000 BC, for many reasons, which include the possible effects of climatic change and a transformation in the political and economic structures within Mesopotamia with the emergence of Ur III Dynasty, traders from *Meluḫḫa* seem to have ceased to use Mesopotamian ports and instead used as intermediaries the traders from *Magan* or *Makkan* and *Dilmun* or *Tilman* located in the Persian Gulf. This was also for reasons of time, maritime security and cost.

Clay tablets, discovered in Central Anatolia, show the existence of a trade route emanating from Assur. One of their most important items of trade was tin, bought 'in the east' of Assur and sold in Kanis Karumu at a much higher price in exchange of gold and silver. It has been suggested that about 80 tons of tin circulated between Assur and Kanis Karumu, which together with some other centres in Anatolia, arranged for tin and other commodities be sent to Egypt (through the Levant), the rest of Anatolia and Crete.[12] Later sites like Assur and Susa, were providers of tin and lapis lazuli for the Near East as shown by the texts from Mari, which shows the redistribution of these commodities from these centres to different places mainly in northern Syria, but also as far south as Hazor in Palestine and as far west as Ugarit. It is here that we first see merchants from Crete and the establishing of commercial relations with them.[13]

This period of economic prosperity for the Harappans lasted for approximately 200 years until approximately 1900 to 1800 BC, in the time of the Old Babylonian Period in Mesopotamia. Now we begin to witness the start of a decline of their economy and, consequently, trade began to slow and eventually almost completely ceased. What is left for the rest of the second millennium BC is likely to be restricted to trade in cotton and cotton garments and a slow but continual supply of tin and possibly a little lapis lazuli, but which is now undertaken through the hazardous overland route from Afghanistan, avoiding India. Trade and contact only fully resumed in the first millennium BC.

The great diminishing of this trade structure at the end of the Mature Harappan Phase, generated by the manufacturing potential and consumption of an urban society and dominated by a mercantile elite, may well have seriously damaged the Harappan economy and made some significant changes to the social fabric of society as unemployed urban dwellers stayed unemployed in the cities and towns or returned to the countryside and hastened its end.

Relations between India and the Aegean can only be seen in the context of contact and trade between India and Mesopotamia. On its way farther west, little in terms of cultural contact, such as manufactured objects, reached the Aegean and when it did, it certainly places the Early and Middle Bronze Age Aegean within the sphere of trade and connections of its time, which some refer to as a world system. The effect was quite an expansion of trade and the possibility that objects and commodities were now reaching the Eastern Mediterranean, including the Aegean, is now a reality. The latter was also stimulated in the Middle Minoan I–II periods by Minoan traders being more active in the ports of the region.

By this time, the Aegean with its early palace societies on Crete and later the Greek mainland, were just emerging and could never compete with its mightier neighbours or those who existed a continent away; they were never on a par. The fact is that we may never know the absolute truth about what happened and we are reminded of the remarks of Cyprian Broodbank that for the Early Bronze Age in the Aegean:

> It cannot, of course, be denied that over a period of some five hundred years a few Aegean canoes might have paddled far into the sunrise, or occasional eastern traders entered the Aegean, given that by this time Sumerian ships were ranging as far as Oman and the Indus.[14]

What we do allow ourselves is to have a vision of seafarers and caravan drovers from different parts of the Near East and even India, starting in the latter part of the third millennium BC, mingling in the taverns of Mesopotamian and Persian Gulf cites and seaports, exchanging objects, telling tales and much else and finally these objects coming into the possession of similar seafarers from or with experience of the Eastern Mediterranean.

Although a few objects and some commodities were making their way westwards by the time of the Early Bronze Age in the Aegean, controlled as they were by the Harappans, by the time that the Minoans on Crete and subsequently the Mycenaeans were building their first palaces, the greatness of Harappa and Mohenjo-daro with their economy and expansive trade and cultural exchange links and were beginning to decline. Trade links continued for a time, but this was now the time of the expansion of Minoan seafaring and the more systematic contact with the Near East began when Minoan seafarers first came readily into contact with the North Syro-Palestinian ports.

Some centuries later in the Late Bronze Age, the Uluburun and Cape Gelidonya shipwrecks show evidence of a well-established Eastern Mediterranean trade route that likely ran primarily anticlockwise from Crete down to Libya and along to Egypt, up the Levantine coast, over to Cyprus and along the south coast of Anatolia into the Aegean, based on gold from Egypt, silver from Anatolia, copper from Cyprus, dyed woollen clothes and perfumed oil from the Aegean. But they still needed tin acquired from Afghanistan.

Trade expeditions were commissioned by Aegean palace officials, who also needed to learn the more advanced skills on how to make better bronze from copper and tin ingots – the copper coming from Cyprus and the tin from farther east, from India. Along the route in all centuries under consideration, the ships and caravans would have picked up several random and exotic items, such as beads to sweeten the heavy bartering that would have occurred at every port of call.

As for later Indian imports in the Late Bronze Age, while the last remnants of post-urban Late Harappan Phase society had by all accounts now largely disappeared, there is a little evidence that trade in a few commodities would have continued and this offers witness to Mesopotamian and Syro-Palestinian trade and influence in the second millennium BC and links that would endure to 1100 BC, when the Late Bronze Age in the Eastern Mediterranean came to an end.[15] In reality, however, this says nothing much about the Aegean as they were largely only on the receiving end of these contacts.

We are finally reminded that an echo of the Harappans was known to the Graeco-Roman world nearly 2,000 years later. In AD 23 in his *Geographica*, Strabo wrote:

> when he [Aristobulus] was sent upon a mission [to India] he saw more than a thousand cities, together with villages, that had been deserted because a great river had once abandoned its proper bed.[16] (trans. Author)

This is perhaps a short but fitting epitaph to a great and important civilisation with which the prehistoric Aegean was in contact, unknowingly and certainly at a very long distance.

Notes

1 Marshall 1924a, 548.
2 Mode 1944; 1959, 59–70; 1961, 7–11. See also David 1956, 56–65, for additional fantasies regarding Indo-Aegean relations based on putative closer affinities between Mesopotamia and the Aegean and the now discredited view that the Near East was largely or even partly responsible for the diffusion that created the Indus Civilisation and it was not an indigenous cultural development.
3 During Caspers 1985, 435–452.
4 Illustrated in Boardman 1970, 29, pl. 3–5; Krzyszkowska 2005, 92–95. For recent study of these seals, see Anastasiadou 2011, 56–58. She does not even consider the option offered by During Caspers.
5 Mackay 1938, pls. LXXXI, nos. 1–2, XC, no. 13; XCI, nos. 4, 20; XCII, nos. 11, 12; CI, nos. 7, 12; Vats 1940, pl. XCV, no. 386. Mackay in his synthesis of Indus Civilisation expressed a view that it was doubtful if India had any direct trading connection with the Aegean. He did point out that some motifs found on Northern Greek and Cretan seals have also been found at Mohenjo-daro, dated 'to very early times', but was unspecific, although he believed that the motifs originated there, see Mackay 1948, 149–150.
6 Davaras 2003, 30; 2005, 126.
7 The first, Mackay 1938, 337, 361, 659–660, Volume II, pls. CII.5 and CIII.8, excavation number DK9281; and the second, Mackay 1938, 386, no. 510, pl. XCVI, excavation number DK8321. See also Fábri 1937, 93–101, fig. 3. There is also a steatite seal from the Middle Harappan Phase Period II levels at Banawali, (excavation number BNL5683) that shows an acrobat leaping over a bull, see Umesao 2000, 88, cat. no. 335. See also, Duff 2012.
8 Mackay 1938, 358–359, Volume II, pl. XCII.11, excavation number DK8120, p. 359, pl. XCII.12, excavation number DK4547; Fábri 1937, fig. 6.
9 Srinivasan 2005, 1–24.
10 Massa and Palmisano 2018a, 78–83. Peter Jablonka has produced a series of 26 archaeological distribution maps of third millennium BC finds from the Aegean to the Indus, using exploratory data analysis to discover which of these regions have common finds and which of these finds occur together. His results indicate a globally connected world, caused by overlapping distribution of finds in similar areas. Direct exchange mainly occurred between adjacent regions. Jablonka 2018, 139–166.
11 Some scholars, however, believe that Mesopotamian elements (but not Aegean) can be identified in the Indus Civilisation, such as carved stone boxes, dice, faience, wheeled vehicles, shaft-hole axes, some objects depicting religious motifs and the 'ram style' sculptural motif as examples, see Wenke and Olszewski 2007, 425, but this remains unclear.
12 Lyonnet 2005, 191–200.

13 Guichard 1999, 165–177.
14 Broodbank 2000, 286.
15 There is evidence of the continuation of this external trade as Late Harappan Phase seals have been found in mid-second millennium BC Kassite levels at Nippur and Failaka, see Chakrabarti 1995, 138–139. As proof of the continuation of the Persian Gulf trade well after the end of the second millennium BC, as late as the seventh century BC, the Neo-Assyrian King Esarhaddon of Assyria and Babylon, who reigned from 681–669 BC, prided himself on being 'king of the kings of *Dilmun*, *Magan* and *Meluhha*'. See Potts 1993a, 1452.
16 Strabo, *Geographica*, xv.1.19.

Chapter 5

From the Iron Age to Alexander the Great

The Late Bronze Age to Iron Age Transition

If one is to look for potential long-distance contacts between India and the Protogeometric to the Early Archaic Aegean, as with previous millennia, one must again make a starting point an examination of India's contacts with Mesopotamia and other parts of the Ancient Near East as a stepping-stone. Possehl has argued that trade activity westwards and specifically contacts to and from India after 1700 BC were much reduced and it was not until around 600 BC that it changed significantly. For over 1,000 years in between, he believed that the evidence pointed only to a very limited trade in cotton yarn (*sindhu*) and probably cotton fabrics.[1] Other than the likely continued export from India of commodities westwards after 1700 BC, particularly tin, it does appear that direct evidence for any contact for the rest of the millennium is extremely limited, restricted to the occasional piece of evidence, for example, the finding of a Harappan seal depicting a humped bull and two signs of Indus Script dated to the early Kassite period (*c*. 1500 BC) level at Nippur in Mesopotamia,[2] which may have been an heirloom

There is also some speculation that in the later part of the second millennium BC, the Mitanni, who ruled a Bronze Age Hurrian speaking state located in northern Syria and south-east Anatolia from *c*. 1500–1300 BC[3] and whose ruling elite, if it is believed had strong Indo-Aryan roots, may have maintained some connections. Although defining the ethnicity of the Mitanni has been problematic, a Hittite treatise on chariot horses contains several Aryan glosses[4] and the names of members of the Mitanni elite can also be identified as having Indo-Aryan origins. However, it is the names of their deities that show more specific roots, such as the Vedic gods *Mitra*, *Varuna*, *Indra* and *Nasatya*. Whether these ethnic connections with the Indo-Aryans which were at this time slowly moving into Northern India and which had been separated well before this migration started, would have facilitated material contact is another question; so far there is only speculation.[5] There is also the tenuous evidence of peafowl, which may have been known in Mesopotamia and further west from the third millennium BC onwards.[6] There is a peacock motif at Mitanni, dated to *c*. 1500 BC that might also point to East–West contact at this time.[7] The alternative theory is that they were bred locally for 800 years.

As an indication of possibly some continuity from the Bronze into the later part of the Iron Age, we do also have the inscription of the Neo-Assyrian King Esarhaddon of Assyria and Babylon (*c*. 681–669 BC), priding himself on being 'king of the kings of *Dilmun*, *Magan* and *Meluḫḫa*'[8] but what this means we are unsure. It had been originally speculated that the name *Meluḫḫa* had already been lost, but this throws some doubt on this suggestion.

Finally, a tentative example of post-Bronze Age contacts is the so-called Black Obelisk of King Shalmaneser III of Assyria (*c*. 859–824 BC) found at his palace at Nimrud (or Calah or Kalhu),[9] erected in 825 BC and depicting his military achievements. It shows in relief tributes brought from Musri; a small ancient kingdom now located in the Kurdish areas of northern Iraq. They number a honed animal, probably a rhinoceros, a long-tailed monkey, a Bactrian camel and an Indian elephant. Whether they are of Indian origin, it is quite possible, but the monkeys and the camel may suggest contacts with the east.

What we do know is that by 900 BC, much had changed in the Eastern Mediterranean and the Near East. There may be evidence of Phoenician contacts with the Near East and India in the tenth century BC, through trade routes beyond the Euphrates, where they would have had indirect access to resources of Mesopotamia and beyond. These great seafarers and explorers from the north Syro-Palestinian coast were now exploiting some of the same trade routes that existed in the previous millennia. Biblical evidence shows that starting in the late tenth century BC, they travelled between the Near East and what is believed to be Western India, by way of the Red Sea and the Horn of Africa, reputedly bringing back with them exotic commodities such as silver, gold, beads of carnelian and agate, elephant ivory, apes and peafowl and possibly re-establishing, albeit tenuously, those lines of communication between India and the Near East that existed before the end of the Bronze Age; but it was never on the same scale.

Ophir in India?

Daniel Potts recounts that in the tenth century BC, kings of Israel mounted seaborne expeditions in search of wealth.[10] There is an account of the fitting out of an Israelite sea-borne expedition, but equipped with Phoenician crews, which was in reality a joint expedition of King Solomon (961–922 BC) and the Phoenician King Hiron I (971–939 BC), sailing from the Red Sea port of Ezion-geber (now modern Eilat in the Gulf of Aqaba) in Edom and then heading south and east to Ophir,[11] with a view to bringing back with them gold, silver, ivory, apes and peafowl.[12] This points to it being India, at the end of the southern trade route by way of the Red Sea, the Horn of Africa and the Arabian Sea, an event that is reputed to have occurred every three years. Other texts refer additionally to bringing back precious stones and sandalwood (*almg*).[13] It is thought that the expedition was much needed because King Solomon was facing mounting debt as the result of his building programmes, particularly of the first Temple.[14]

The actual location of Ophir has been open to speculation and Edward Lipiński has produced a wide-ranging review.[15] Arguments have been made for sites in Ethiopia, south-west Arabia and the Horn of Africa, but in view of the nature of the return cargo, the west coast of India, nearby the mouth of the River Indus is the more likely location.[16] Richard Barnett made a convincing argument for the location of Ophir in India based on linguistic evidence,[17] although Klaus Karttunen is emphatic that it is not and like Barnett bases his views on purely etymological. Neither has any persuasive archaeological arguments either way.[18]

We do, however, know that Ophir existed through later evidence of contact. The inscription *[z]hb 'prl-Byt Ḥrn* on the ostrakon found in a level dated to the eighth to the early seventh century BC, at the site of Tell Qasile on the Palestine coast, refers to the arrival of gold from Ophir.[19] Originally a Philistine urban settlement found on the outskirts of the modern city of Tel Aviv, Tell Qasile was re-occupied now by the Phoenicians. This not only indicates that Orphir was not a Biblical fantasy,[20] but for Lipiński, at least, may be the key to its location.[21]

What it does show is that the Phoenicians had access to the Red Sea and may have used the port of Ezion-geber for any number of voyages into the Indian Ocean. Of course, if Ophir is to be found in the Horn of Africa or in South Arabia, this does not negate an Indian origin of these goods, but points to it being possibly a centre of trade between the Near East and India, like *Dilmun* or *Magan* in the third and early second millennia BC.

Later on in the ninth century we also have evidence of King Jehoshaphat of Judea (871–849 BC) entering into an alliance with King Ahaziah of Israel (870–850 BC), for the purpose of undertaking maritime commerce with the Red Sea and particularly Ophir. The fleet that was equipped at Ezion-Gever was soon wrecked and a new fleet was fitted out without the cooperation of the king of Israel.[22] Although successful, the trade was not continued,[23] other than in the early sixth century, when King Azariah of Judea (*c*. 780–740 BC) conquered Elath, he may also have had the wealth of Ophir in mind.[24] Potts suggests that because of their size, all of these expeditions may have been of a genuine trading nature, taking with them eastwards wine, olive oil, honey and perhaps slaves.[25]

During the ninth to seventh centuries BC, the Near East witnesses a new regional trading system, stretching from north-west Iran and the Persian Gulf to Central Anatolia and the Eastern Mediterranean and including the west coast of India. The members of the trading system were interconnected by a complex series of overland and maritime trade routes and the ability of the Assyrians to maintain their dominant role in its functioning, except for the newly emerging trade route across the Arabian Sea and to the Near East through the Red Sea. In a westerly direction, Phoenician traders were also expanding and there is plenty of evidence for their strictly maritime contacts with the Greek world at this time,[26] where a few Indian imports into the Near East may well have reached the end of their journey. As Oliver Dickinson has demonstrated, during the ninth and eighth centuries BC in the Geometric Period, it was not a period of deterioration in exchange relations both within and without the Aegean, as there is evidence of Near Eastern goods being found both at Lefkandi in Euboea and at Knossos on Crete. The level of exchange between the Aegean and the Near East was again intensifying.[27]

Iron Age India[28]

Archaeological excavations in the last 50 years seem to indicate that the decline of the Harappan Civilisation was marked by the last part of the Late Harappan Phase, the Gandhara Grave (or Swāt) Culture[29] and the final stages of Cemetery H Culture,[30] which some believe may have continued in some form until at least 1200 BC.[31] It marked the final stage of the North Indian Bronze Age and towards the end is also likely to have seen some of the population moving eastwards. Here we now see a number of Iron Age cultures emerging such as the Ochre Coloured Pottery Culture, which lasted from approximately 1300 to 1000 BC and the Painted Grey Ware Culture, which lasted from approximately 1100 to 350 BC, which shows influences of the former. Both are associated with the first use of iron, but the former is also associated with copper hoards, a second millennium BC Bronze Age phenomenon of the Indus-Ganges (or Ganges-Yamuna) Plain.[32] Whether these later populations can be found to have been associated with proto-Hindu Indo-European population movements into Northern India, is pure conjecture,[33] but it is thought that some of the Vedic period (possibly excepting the earliest phase of the core of the Ṛgveda) is thought to lie within the twelfth to sixth centuries BC.

The Painted Grey Ware Culture was also developed in South India, such as at Hallur and Komaranhalli in modern Karnataka and Adichanallur in Tamil Nadu,[34] epitomised at each of these sites by iron working in an advanced stage. To the east, down into the valley of the River *Gangā* or Ganges, the Indo-European or Aryan heartland (known as *Brhmāvarta*), we witness the development of the Late Vedic Culture, the time of the compilation of the *Ṛgveda* and where the pace of urbanisation was significantly advanced and some of the later post-Bronze Age urban centres were being built.[35] In the north-east, there were coastal settlements at Somnath, Nagara and Nagal, which are likely to have been trading posts, but it is not possible to determine which parts of Iron Age India the Phoenicians will have come into contact. It may have been the richer Iron Age settlements of the south-western coast that were the more important trading centres for them.

The Coming of Iron: An Eastern Mediterranean Connection?

It has been speculated that knowledge of iron metallurgy in post-Harappan Civilisation India may have been diffused from the Eastern Mediterranean (which includes the Aegean) by way of the Near East, Iran and the movement of Indo-Aryan settlers.[36] This belief has been founded on the chronological development of iron smelting and the use of iron which be believed was much later in India than further west. However, there is now good evidence for iron smelting and use much earlier at the Iron Age site of Pirak near Naushahro in north-west India, where we see the introduction of iron objects as early as phase two of its occupation in *c.* 1370–1340 BC.[37] Iron tools now include arrow and spearheads, chisels, axes and knives. Copper seems now to be less common but does include pins, bangles, fishhooks and some dishes.

More recently, excavations have produced evidence of iron working in the sub-continent that goes back even earlier and throws considerable doubt on the original speculation. Excavations on the Central Ganges Plain and in the Eastern Vindhya mountains, has uncovered iron artefacts and slag in strata radiocarbon dated to between 1800–1000 BC.[38] As was suspected all along, iron working was an indigenous development in India, during the second millennium BC, alongside the copper and bronze traditions of the Harappan Civilisation and the later Ganges basin.

Trade and Contact in the Iron Age

After the end of the Bronze Age in *c.* 1000 BC, contact between Mesopotamia and north-west India was revived, using both land and sea routes, involving both the Assyrians and Neo-Babylonians, possibly by way of the Gulf,[39] with the sea route likely to have taken preference over land caravan routes. Livestock, such as hump-backed cattle, monkeys, domestic fowl, peafowl and plant commodities such as black pepper started to arrive and some were also now reared or grown in the Near East.[40] The Bactrian camel depicted on the obelisk of King Shalmaneser III of Assyria (see above) clearly points to the use of the land route. For the sea-trade from India now it comprised of precious woods and black wood, parrots, precious stones, pearls and so forth.[41] However, it is more difficult to say what would have been specifically Indian imports in the first millennium BC. Some pottery has been found, both in India and in the various steps along the trade-route, but pottery as such was hardly profitable enough to make its transportation pay; the real merchandise was probably packed in those jars, of which we are currently unable to identify.

There is, however, currently no archaeological evidence to support either of these scenarios or for Near Eastern (or further western) objects being found in India at this time. In fact, in the *Ṛgveda* there are no obvious accounts of foreign lands or people. However, it is very likely that trade through the Gulf continued well into the period of the Persian Achaemenid Empire that dominated the region down into the end of the fourth century BC, when it was ended by Hellenistic expansion and conquest.

Another indicator of contact between the Near East and India in the Iron Age is though camels. The arrival of domesticated camels into the Syro-Palestine region in the Iron Age, centres on them not being domesticated in the Near East until after the Bronze Age. Erez Ben-Yosef and Lidar Sapir-Hen of Tel Aviv University's Department of Archaeology and Near Eastern Cultures, have recently used radiocarbon dating to pinpoint the moment when domesticated camels arrived in Syro-Palestine, pushing the date forward from the twelfth to the ninth century BC. They believe that camels were probably domesticated in the Arabian Peninsula for use as pack animals sometime towards the last third of the tenth century BC or later. In the southern

Levant, the oldest known domesticated camel bones are from the Aravah Valley, an ancient centre of copper production, conformed by his 2009 (and latterly 2013) excavations. The few camel bones found in earlier archaeological layers probably belonged to wild camels, which archaeologists think were in Syro-Palestine from the Neolithic period or even earlier. Notably, all the sites active in the ninth century in the Aravah Valley had camel bones, but none of the sites that were active earlier contained them.[42]

Whilst some objects may have found the Greek world as their destination, there would still not have been any knowledge of India in the Aegean, all there might have been being what Karttunen in his lengthy discussion on the subject was a vague knowledge.[43] As regards references in the works of Homer and Hesiod to India, there is absolutely nothing in the work of either author that points to contact or even any knowledge of India, however scanty.[44]

From the Sixth Century BC

From the Geometric through to the Orientalising and Archaic Periods in Greece and the Aegean, there is currently no textual or archaeological evidence to suggest contacts with India. From the early sixth century BC, onwards, however, we have evidence of contacts between the Greek world that culminated in the conquests of King Alexander III of Macedon, better known as Alexander the Great, who with his army in the year 327–326 BC, crossed the Hindu Kush Mountains, ventured beyond Gandhara, passed through the Khyber Pass and then eventually entered the Indus Valley.

India in the Middle of the First Millennium BC

The India with which the early Greek travellers will have come into contact from the sixth century onwards was culturally and chronologically at the end of the North Indian Iron Age at the time of the establishment of the many historical kingdoms within the Maha Janapadas (*c.* 700–300 BC) and whose weakness created a vacuum that both Persians and eventually Greeks could fill. Although it was essentially Vedic in nature, this time also witnessed the early development of Buddhism on quite a considerable scale.

Around this time, the most important centre in Northern India was the Gandharan city of Taxila, or *Takṣaśilā* (Ταξίλα)[45] (Fig. 9), which was an important centre for both Hindus and Buddhists. Historically, it lay at the crossroads of three major trade routes, the *uttarāpatha*, the northern royal road that connected Gandhara in the west to the kingdom of Magadha and its capital Pāṭaliputra in the valley of the Ganges in the east; the north-western route through Bactria and the west and the *Sindu* route from Kashmir and Central Asia, across the Khunjerab pass (now known as the Karakoram Pass) to the Silk Road in the north to the Indian Ocean in the south; all traversed in later antiquity.

Figure 9. Ruins of the ancient city of Sirkap, the Indo-Greek archaeological site (Public Domain)

The city of Taxila, known to Greek travellers and subsequently Alexander, was centred on the Bhir Mound, which dates from the sixth to third centuries BC and was first excavated for the Archaeological Survey of India by Marshall between 1913 and 1925 and then Wheeler between 1944 and 1945. The site forms an irregular shape measuring around 1 km from north to south and about 600 m from east to west. The streets of the city show that they were narrow and the house plans were very irregular; there is little evidence of planning. Textual evidence points to King Darius I (521–486) taking Taxila into the Achaemenid Empire in 518 BC. Gandhara and Kamboja now constituted the seventh satrapy of Upper Indus. An inscription on Darius' tomb (DNa) at Naqš-i Rustam near Persepolis records Gandara along with other Indian possessions in the list of satrapies; but by about 380 BC, the Persian hold on the region was weakening.

He was followed nearly 200 years later in 326 BC by Alexander, when the local King Raja Ambhi entertained him and surrendered the city and offered him a body of elephant mounted cavalry. Some years later in 316 BC, King Chandragupta of Magadha, the founder of the Mauryan dynasty, conquered The Punjab and Taxila became a mere provincial city, but remained relatively important as a regional centre of administration, education and trade.

Trade and Contacts in the Sixth to Fourth Centuries BC

Between the sixth and fourth centuries BC, Greek knowledge of India was acquired by way of Persia. What Alexander the Great knew of what lay ahead for him would have been obtained from his contacts and those of his leading followers with the Achaemenid Empire, founded by King Cyrus (559–530 BC), who during his reign, incorporated Gandhara to his domains. In many ways, Persian and Indian relations were natural, sharing as they did a common and close Indo-European heritage. Some years later, King Darius I (522–486 BC) extended his domain even further southwards to incorporate Taxila, the lands of The Punjab and Sind up to the River Indus, broadening the Greek contacts with India through the medium of his empire, which now stretched from there to the Ionian coast of Asia Minor with its Greek population.[46]

India was now its 20th satrapy and the most fertile and populous part of Darius' realm. Communications between the extremities of this huge polity were now largely unimpeded by political frontiers. Moreover, Persian policies served inadvertently to promote that mixture of nationalities which so frequently provides intellectual stimulus. Large-scale deportations of peoples occurred on occasion, while slaves captured in war often came to reside in portions of the empire far removed from their original homes. The skills and labour power of all of Persia's subjects, Greeks included, were employed in imperial building projects. Many Greeks served as officials or mercenaries in the various Achaemenid provinces; on occasion, Greek physicians, such as Ctesias were employed at the Persian royal courts.

Some of the best evidence for trade between India and further westwards comes from Susa, which became part of the Achaemenid Empire between 540 and 539 BC when it was captured by King Cyrus II during his conquest of Elam, of which Susa was the capital. The epigraphical evidence mentions several imported goods such as ivory from Kush and India and wood from Carmania, Gandhara and Makran. Gold came from Bactria, carnelian and lapis lazuli from Sogdiana. There is the case of the hard-wood *Dalbergia sissoo* Roxb.[47] The Apadana relief shows Indians and Gandharans bringing various products. Cotton was certainly known to Herodotus.[48] Around 400 BC, Ctesias saw several Indian products at the Persian court, such as elephants, peacocks, swords, precious stones, drugs and poisons, dyes, even cheese and wine. At the same time, pepper again became known in Greece as an Indian or Persian medicine. Imports came overland *through Bactria; Ctesias speaks* of Bactrian merchants and by sea.

In this period, another trade route was opened. Literary sources lead us to conclude that Indian or Arabian seafarers had rather early learnt to put aside their traditional fear of the open sea and to use the regular monsoon winds to cross the Arabian Sea. This relates to the early flourish of spice trade. Cassia and cinnamon have their origin in South India and Sri Lanka (originally perhaps even in South-East Asia), but as early as before the mid-first millennium BC, they started to arrive in the West via South Arabia. This is attested as early as Sappho[49] and is referred to in the Old Testament.[50] In the Near East, the spice trade was part of the Arabian caravan and sea trade connecting the Mediterranean coast with South Arabia. We, of course, note immediately that from South Arabia there was a sea connection to India, but in the ancient West, the real origin of spices remained hidden. Ionian Greek contacts, both trade and cultural, would have produced a wealth of knowledge of Indian customs, religious and cultural beliefs and practices.

A number of mercenaries, including Greeks, served in the Achaemenid army, opposing Alexander at the Battle of Gaugamela in 331 BC and many of their predecessors served earlier in the army of King Darius I, which first invaded mainland Greece in 490 BC, but were defeated at the Battle of Marathon. These ranks of mercenaries also served in the army of King Xerxes I (485–465 BC), which invaded Greece and fought the Battles of Thermopylae and Plataea in 480–479 BC and were marshalled together with the Eastern Ethiopians from the African extremity of the Persian Empire.[51] Herodotus tells us that this included a number of native soldiers from Gandhara and The Punjab, whose cotton clothing, cane bows and arrows and modes of transport would have been quite alien to the Greeks. He writes:

> The Indians wore tree-wool (cotton) garments and carried bows of cane and iron-tipped arrows also made of cane. Such was their equipment and they marched under the command of Pharnazathres the son of Artabates.[52] (trans. Author)

and of their cavalry:

> The Medes and Cissians, who had the same equipment as their (Persian) foot-soldiers. The Indians were similarly equipped as their foot soldiers; but some rode fast horses and they had chariots, drawn either by horses or wild asses.[53] (trans. Author)

The Achaemenid presence in Afghanistan and north-west India is well established in literary sources, both Greek and Old Persian. To this can be added some numismatic evidence as Achaemenid coinage, first issued by King Darius I at the end of the sixth century BC, has been found, in addition to stray finds, in the Tchamon-i-Hazouri hoard near Kabul and at the Bhir Mound in Taxila, where urbanisation can be traced back to *c.* 1000 BC. There are also several Greek coins, which depict not only the Athenian owls (for which local forgeries have been suggested), but also coins of several Ionian, Greek and Macedonian city states. It is likely that the concept of coinage was brought by the Achaemenids to north-west India.[54]

Greeks in Ancient Sanskrit Literature

Early contacts with Greeks will have introduced them to Indian literature. Long before the arrival of Alexander the Great on India's north-western border, there are references in early Sanskrit literature calling the Greeks *Yavanas*. Pāṇini, the leading ancient Sanskrit grammarian from Pushkalavati in Gandhara,[55] was acquainted with the word *Yavana* in his composition, although nothing much is known about Pāṇini's life, not even the century in which he worked and lived, but scholarship now favours the fourth century BC. Pāṇini's grammar, known as *Ashtadhyayi*, meaning eight chapters, defines classical Sanskrit, so it is believed that Pāṇini lived at the end of the Vedic period.

An important hint for the dating of Pāṇini is the occurrence of the word *yavanānī*,[56] possibly from very early contacts with Ionian Greeks in Gandhara before the conquests of Alexander, or that the name was known from the Old Persian word *yauna*, so that the occurrence of *yavanānī* taken in isolation allows for as early as 520 BC, at the time of the Achaemenid conquests in India. Katyayana (*fl.* third century BC) was also a Sanskrit grammarian, mathematician and Vedic priest. He explains the term *yavanānī* as the script of the Yavanas. He also believed that the Old Persian term *yauna* became Sanskritised to name all Greeks and appears in the Mahabharata (*c.* 500 BC).

Early Geographers and Historians

Hecataeus of Miletos

Knowledge communicated through Persia was doubtless also the source for those few Indian names that appear in surviving remnants of the early work of the geographer Hecataeus of Miletos (*c.* 550–476 BC), *Travels Round the Earth or World Survey*, written in two books. He was born into a wealthy family and after having travelled extensively, he settled in Miletus, where he occupied a leading position at the time of the Persian invasion and devoted his time to the composition of geographical and historical works.

Although believed to have been better known in his time than Scylax, unfortunately of the number of extant fragments, numbering 374,[57] of his work only one predates the Hellenistic period, that quoted by Herodotus[58] and it makes it nearly impossible to tell precisely what he actually knew about India, although it is believed that he travelled in the Persian Empire.[59] As Karttunen reminds us, it is likely that the work was extant before the Hellenistic period and that later on, it was considered to be important enough to have been collected by one of the great Hellenistic libraries and we know it was studied by a number of scholars before being finally lost.[60] Some of the extant later fragments offer information on dress, ethnography and social conditions from overseas;[61] none of it is about Indian geography. Of the total number of fragments, only seven contain any information that relates to India, likely to have been the north-west.[62] Karttunen tells us that these few fragments are mainly etymological,[63] the most significant being the name of the people as Γανδάραι from Γανδαρική[64] or Gandhara.

Scylax of Caryanda

Scylax of Caryanda (near Halicarnassus in Caria) was a Greek geographer and alleged discoverer of shipping routes and is reputed to have travelled to India and described its geography in his work *Periplous Outside the Pillars of Heracles*.[65] Believed to have been a naval commander in the service of King Darius I,[66] he was sent by him in the years 519–512 BC to follow the course of the River Indus from Caspatyrus in Gandhara to the Indian Ocean, because Darius wished to know at what point the River Indus flows into the sea. Scylax reputedly took a fleet of ships from the headwaters of the river down to its mouth, thence westward across the ocean and into the Red Sea as far as Suez over 30 months.[67] As described by Herodotus,[68] this voyage was exploratory in nature and was later followed by Darius' conquest of the Indus territory. Scylax mentions the author Heraclides of Mylasa in his text, so he could not have died before 480 BC.[69] Unfortunately, there is good reason to question whether Scylax really made this voyage or published an account of it which was known in the Greek world. In view of the warlike population whom Alexander later encountered along this route, it is somewhat difficult to imagine a small expedition making this journey without incident.

It is alleged that in his writings he has tales of the one-eyed people and people who use their single foot as an umbrella under which they slept. This apparently stretched King Darius' credulity and perhaps also that of later readers, since only a fragment of his work survives apart from the references to the exotic races he encountered.

At the same time, extant evidence scarcely permits the alternative suggestion that Scylax's expedition formed a naval component of Darius' conquering army. More importantly, a genuine voyager cannot have believed that the Indus flows eastward, as Herodotus reports, or that the trip required two and a half years. The latter notion is explainable only upon the historian's assumption that the expedition involved the circumnavigation of India, but that is again unproven.

One solution to the problem is that while it is thought that Scylax travelled down the River Indus to a Red Sea port, he describes following the river in an easterly direction and then sailing westwards around India. Scylax does not actually mention the River Indus, it is Hecataeus of Miletos who first uses the name. Richard Stoneman has discussed this in his recent book and is generally of the conclusion that he sailed down the Ganges and at its delta, his ship turned westwards and sailed for 30 months until it reached the port which is called Libya by Herodotus.[70]

Herodotus of Halicarnassus

In the work of the historian Herodotus of Halicarnassus (484–425 BC) there is much more information on India, albeit rather chaotic, although much of what Herodotus has written on India probably originates from Hecataeus' summary of Scylax. In his extant *The Histories*,[71] which is a vivid narrative that has survived in its entirety, references to India are included in Book III, which deals mainly with the extraction and acquisition of gold, which the Indians from the Twentieth Satrapy of the Achaemenid Empire paid to the Great King in Persepolis[72] and the source of which would have been the goal of some of the earlier travellers and explorers from Greece and the Aegean.[73]

What remains is what is essentially a jumble of information on the geography, ethnography and to a limited extend the natural history of north-west India, together with what can only be described as curiosities. Further afield in South Asia, even the basin of the River Ganges was completely unknown to Herodotus and other writers. We are also reminded that any attempt at writing history has been excluded.[74]

Compared to his descriptions of Persia and Egypt, his writings on India are marginal and unimportant, but are considered to have been useful evidence of the rather strange and romantic ideas of India that may have existed in Greece and the Aegean and which Herodotus helped to spread, including Indian myths,[75] which may have been taken up by Ctesias in his *Indika*. What Herodotus could have drawn from the work of Hecataeus, who may have read and been familiar with the work of Scylax of Caryanda, is not known but it is speculated that he may have done so.

Herodotus provides an enormous variety of data about many countries, some of it derived from earlier writers. Although it is probably safe to assume that he never visited India and was an indefatigable collector of anecdotes from many sources.[76] He starts with describing the topography of India:

> It seems as if the extreme regions of the earth were blessed by nature with the most excellent productions, just in the same way that Hellas enjoys a climate more excellently tempered than any other country. In India, which, as I observed lately, is the furthest region of the inhabited world towards the east, all the four-footed beasts and the birds are very much bigger than those found elsewhere, except only the horses, which are surpassed by the Median breed called the Nisaean. Gold too is produced there in vast abundance, some dug from the earth, some washed down by the rivers, some carried off in the mode which I have but now described.[77]

He knew that India embraced diverse population groups of widely varying physical appearance, customs and languages.

> The way in which the Indians get the plentiful supply of gold which enables them to furnish year by year so vast an amount of gold-dust to the kind is the following. Eastward of India lies a tract which is entirely sand. Indeed, of all the inhabitants of Asia, concerning whom anything certain is known, the Indians dwell the nearest to the east and the rising of the sun. Beyond them the whole country is desert because the sand. The tribes of Indians are numerous and do not all speak the same language; some are wandering tribes, others not. They who dwell in the marshes along the river live on raw fish, which they take in boats made of reeds, each formed out of a single joint. These Indians wear a dress of sedge, which they cut in the river and bruise; afterwards they weave it into mats and wear it as we wear a breast-plate.[78]

Further eastwards we have a description of some funerary practices by nomadic tribesmen, such as eating raw flesh and cannibalism:

> Eastward of these Indians are another tribe, called Padaeans, who are wanderers and live on raw flesh. This tribe is said to have the following customs: If one of their number be ill, man or woman, they take the sick person and if he be a man, the men of his acquaintance proceed to put him to death, because, they say, his flesh would be spoilt for them if he pined and wasted away with sickness. The man protests he is not ill in the least; but his friends will not accept his denial; despite all he can say, they kill him and feast themselves on his

> body. So also, if a woman be sick, the women, who are her friends, take her and do with her the same as the men. If one of them reaches to old age, about which there is seldom any question, as commonly before that time they have had some disease or other and so have been put to death; but if a man, notwithstanding, comes to be old, then they offer him in sacrifice to their gods and afterwards eat his flesh.[79]

In contrast, he also describes vegetarian nomads, devoid of any funerary practices at all:

> There is another set of Indians whose customs are very different. They refuse to put any live animal to death; they sow no corn and have no dwelling houses. Vegetables are their only food. There is a plant which grows wild in their country, bearing seed, about the size of millet-seed, in a calyx: their wont is to gather this seed and having boiled it, calyx and all, to use it for food. If one of them is attacked with sickness, he goes forth into the wilderness and lies down to die; no one has the least concern either for the sick or for the dead.[80]

Here one sees in this description a possible mixture of religious practices which today might be components of Hinduism, Jainism, Zoroastrianism and Buddhism. Apparently, Herodotus also recognised the distinction between the Indo-European and Dravidian races; the latter he compares to the Ethiopians in skin colour and notes that they lived in the south and were not subjects of King Darius:

> All the tribes which I have mentioned live together like the brute beasts: they have also all the same tint of skin, which approaches that of the Ethiopians. Their country is a long way from Persia towards the south; nor had king Darius ever any authority over them.[81]

This is likely a hearsay description of tribesmen who lived to the south of the North Indian plain, in the Deccan or the coast of Kerala, with whom there were very occasional contacts with Persians or Greeks.

One of the most interesting and well-known descriptions of Herodotus, likely known to Alexander and all those that looked for wealth in India, is that gold is produced in the Indian desert by fierce ants larger than foxes:

> Besides these, there are Indians of another tribe, who border on the city of Caspatyrus and the country of Pactyica; these people dwell northward of all the rest of the Indians and follow nearly the same mode of life as the Bactrians. They are more warlike than any of the other tribes and from them the men are sent forth who go to procure the gold. For it is in this part of India that the sandy desert lies. Here, in this desert, there live amid the sand great ants, in size somewhat less than dogs, but bigger than foxes. The Persian king has several them, which have been caught by the hunters in the land whereof we are speaking. Those ants make their dwellings underground and like the Hellene ants, which they very much resemble in shape, throw up sand-heaps as they burrow. Now the sand which they throw up is full of gold. The Indians, when they go into the desert to collect this sand, take three camels and harness them together, a female in the middle and a male on either side, in a leading rein. The rider sits on the female and they are particular to choose for the purpose one that has but just dropped her young; for their female camels, can run as fast as horses, while they bear burdens very much better.[82]

> When the Indians therefore have thus equipped themselves, they set off in quest of the gold, calculating the time so that they may be engaged in seizing it during the sultriest part of the day, when the ants hide themselves to escape the heat. The sun in those parts shines fiercest in the morning, not, as elsewhere, at noonday; the greatest heat is from the time when he has reached a certain height, until the hour at which the market closes. During this space, he burns much more furiously than at midday in Hellas, so that the men there are said at that time to drench themselves with water. At noon, his heat is much the same in India as in other countries, after which, as the day declines, the warmth is only equal to that of the morning sun elsewhere. Towards evening the coolness increases, till about sunset it becomes very cold.[83]

> When the Indians reach the place where the gold is, they fill their bags with the sand and ride away at their best speed; the ants, however, scenting them, as the Persians say, rush forth in pursuit. Now these animals are, they declare, so swift, that there is nothing in the world like them; if it were not, therefore, that the Indians get a start while the ants are mustering, not a single gold-gatherer could escape. During the flight the male camels, which are not so fleet as the females, grow tired and begin to drag, first one and then the other; but the females recollect the young which they have left behind and never give way or flag. Such, according to the Persians, is the way the Indians get the greater part of their gold; some is dug out of the earth, but of this the supply is scantier.[84]

This appears at first sight to be an utter fantasy, but one explanation, amongst one of the many less imaginary, is that it may be related to the burrowing activities of one of the rodent family, the Himalayan Marmot (*Marmota himalayana*), which inhabits the Deosai (in Urdu 'land of giants') plateau on the Pakistani side of the border with India in Jammu and Kashmir. It is believed that they may have thrown up gold bearing earth as they burrowed, which was then exploited by the local population.[85]

Herodotus also recognises the cotton plant for the first time and the fabric it produces:

> and farther, there are trees which grow wild there, the fruit thereof is a wool exceeding in beauty and goodness that of sheep. The natives make their clothes of this tree-wool.[86]

The Greeks would not have seen cotton before, unless worn by an Indian or Persian with whom they came into contact. Cotton is a soft, fluffy staple fibre that grows in a boil, or protective capsule, around the seeds of cotton plants of the genus *Gossypium*. The plant is a shrub native to tropical and subtropical regions around the world, including India. It is then spun into yarn or thread and used to make a soft, breathable textile.

Overall, Herodotus emphasises the country's wealth in gold; not unsurprising as many of the early traders sought an inroad into India's great wealth. Indian birds and beasts he regards as much bigger than those existing elsewhere, except for horses.

However, Herodotus' notions of geography were understandably inaccurate: for instance, his belief that the Indus flows eastward and that India constitutes the most easterly inhabited region of Asia, with only desert wastes beyond The Punjab. Interestingly, nothing in his remarks gives the impression that India possessed much in the way of civilisation, let alone the philosophic and religious eminence for which it became noted only 100 years later, after Alexander had entered India.

Ctesias of Cnidus

The last of those Greeks before the time Alexander who are known to have written about India was Ctesias of Cnidus (405–379 BC). He is believed to have been a physician of an Aesclepiad clan, who practiced medicine for eight years (404–398/397 BC) at the court of the Achaemenid King Artaxerxes II Mnemon (404–358 BC).[87] Being close to the Achaemenid centre of power, he would have had any number of opportunities to communicate with the Persian elite and obtain detailed insight into the inner workings of their empire. Upon his eventual return to the Greek world in Ionia, Ctesias wrote a book, *Indika*, in approximately 400 BC, being a compilation of what was known or believed to have been known about India but this has not survived in its original form.

The Byzantine scholar St Photius, Patriarch of Constantinople, who probably lived between 820–893, brought together the text of *Indica* by Ctesias that we have today from known fragments and quotations from other authors (see the Appendix).[88] However, recently a more accurate and definitive translation and commentary in English has been produced by Andrew Nichols.[89]

Ctesias' credibility as a historian has been seriously questioned, as his book is full of both entertaining stories and descriptions, including what is now thought to be exaggerations, if not pure fantasy.[90] He claimed to have used the Persian royal archives in his gathering of material, but this is quite unlikely, given the legendary character of so much of what he writes.

Until the time of Alexander, he was a standard authority on the history and culture of both Persia and India. On India, whilst what Ctesias has to offer is very occasionally accurate, though mostly exaggerated, even from the vantage-point of the Persian court at Susa at this time, he showed evidence of an exotic and virtually unknown country; so, at such a distance, marvels become more credible. Why *Indika* is important is what it tells us about the Graeco-Persian views of India and the Indians, but restricted to the area of the Indus Valley, today both the Indian and Pakistani states of The Punjab.

Ctesias did take care, however, to clearly distinguish between things he had seen for himself and information he had only acquired by hearsay. He never claimed ever to have visited India, though we must naturally suppose that he had occasion to meet Indians or Achaemenid officials who had served in the empire's Indian satrapy, as well as Indian visitors and merchants. Several times he refers to meeting Bactrian merchants, from whom he learned about the silver mines of Bacteria and much else.

Presumably he had seen objects of tribute or simply gifts offered by Indian princes to the Achaemenid king and his senior courtiers. For example, he knew that India contained elephants, little monkeys with long tails, huge birds and talking parrots and silver and gold in the mountains.

Of particular interest are elephants and tigers. Ctesias, who must have seen the elephant for himself as he worked at the Achaemenid court, described the animal in his Indica. He discussed the elephant in connection with the man-eating martichora (ἀνθρωποφάγος), known to others as the manticore, a beast with the body of a lion, the head of a human head, the face of vermillion, light-blue eyes, three rows of teeth and a tail in the shape of a scorpion's sting. According to Ctesias, the sting of the martichora is fatal to all except the elephant and Indians are believed to have hunted them with spears and arrows while mounted on them. As to the identity of a martichora, it is likely that he refers to the Royal Bengal Tiger (*Panthera tigris*), which he also may have seen at court in captivity.

Ctesias in his work mainly provides an inventory of Indian tribes, together with other details. He is relatively impressed by the size of the population and is the first to tell the quite remarkable account of the so-called giant ants digging up the gold dust guarded by Griffins, which is repeated in every subsequent writing in India. Included in his description of the exotic wonders of India is a fountain that fills with liquid gold each year; dogs large enough to fight lions; a river consisting of honey: a spring in which the water curdles like cheese and if drunk becomes a truth serum; people who live as long as 200 years and others having eight fingers on each hand and ears long enough to cover their shoulders. He does not examine such tales according to any standard of accuracy, except to say that he has omitted to relate even more extraordinary matters for fear he will not be believed!

If we may judge from the wide dissemination of his works, Greek readers did not expect a sceptical or critical approach to the marvels of that sub-continent; they wanted fantastic stories and details of these marvels. The works of Ctesias, such as *Indika*, would have been well known to Alexander as it was both popular and highly influential and more importantly, would have informed the planning of his eastward conquests. In fact, Strabo believed that those who wrote about India before Alexander the Great preferred the marvellous to the true.[91]

Religion and Philosophy

There is the remote possibility that Indian religious ideas filtered into Greece and the Aegean before Alexander through the agency of wandering holy men. These itinerant ascetics had been a familiar sight in India since the beginning of that country's recorded history. Early Buddhist missionary fervour may have inspired occasional monks to proselytise beyond the Himalayas, though this is more likely from the third century BC onward, when Buddhism experienced its first great age of expansion.

One edict of the later Mauryan Emperor Ashoka (*c.* 304–232 BC) records that he sent envoys into various Hellenistic countries to propagate his Law of Piety. The fact that no Buddhist writings of this period have ever been discovered in the Greek speaking world is not conclusive evidence to the contrary; the Indian guru typically exerts his influence by means of speech and example rather than by texts as many were illiterate. Nonetheless, pre-Hellenistic sources totally fail to mention the presence of Indians of any kind among the Greeks. Not only had the Greeks no inkling that the Indians might even possess a philosophy; their contempt for 'barbarians' (*i.e.* all non-Greeks) would have hindered any mutual understanding. After the arrival of Alexander in India, it is a different story.[92]

Greeks, Macedonians and their Legacy in India

When Alexander crossed the Hindu-Kush Mountains he conquered the local principalities ruled by King Ambhi in Taxila and afterwards those of King Porus who held lands between the Rivers Jhelum and the Chenab in The Punjab at the Battle of Hydapses in 326 BC, believed to be located on the bank of the River Hydapses, also known as the River Jhelum.[93] Here there was no unifying force such as the Nanda Empire that existed in other places in north-eastern India to resist him.[94] Although it was a Macedonian victory and The Punjab was annexed and King Porus was allowed afterwards to keep his crown as a loyal satrap, Alexander went no further as he was forced in 325 BC to turn back by his exhausted and nearly mutinous army and then for home, conquering his way down the Indus to the Sea, once he reached the right bank of the River Beas.[95]

What he left behind was a legacy of the land of the five rivers being incorporated into the Bactrian and Indian extremity of the Hellenistic world. Alexander, inspired by the legends of the exploits of Dionysus and Heracles and what he had learned about the fabulous wealth of India, had a vision of where he wanted to lead his army; further to the south, beyond The Punjab, following the route of the River Ganges and then down probably across the Deccan to the south and to what is now Sri Lanka or eastwards to the Bay of Bengal. It would have been a difficult task. What the Greeks knew about India, therefore, was not very much and not at all reliable. As the result of writings like those of Hecataeus, Herodotus, Scylax and Ctesias, educated and literate Greeks of the age, undoubtedly possessed some rudimentary awareness of India's existence and presumably such information did not remain totally without effect. Knowledge of foreign peoples was a prime stimulus in causing the Greeks to examine their own traditions in a critical spirit; and this in turn had enormous importance in the development of Greek intellectual life. Stoneman discusses in detail why Alexander crossed the Hindu Kush mountains. It is likely that The Punjab and Sind had been part of the Achaemenid Empire at its greatest extent under King Darius I and that Alexander needed to conquer the whole of that Empire.[96]

Herodotus himself gives evidence of how foreign contacts might produce a challenging point of view; he notes that while each nation possesses its own customs, each also considers its own to be superior. As an example, he cites certain Indians at the court of King Darius of Persia, who considered it normal to eat their own fathers' dead bodies, but abhorrent to cremate them.[97] The Greeks, of course, held precisely the opposite view.

After Alexander, the greater portion of the Indian sub-continent was never to become directly part of the Hellenistic world. Only in the north-west did it ever become subject to direct political domination by Greeks; and it was here, naturally enough, that the Greeks exerted their greatest influence in India. For about two centuries, Bactria, just north of the Hindu Kush, was ruled by Greeks; first as part of the Seleucid Empire based in Persia and Mesopotamia, later as an independent polity. For a time during the second century BC, Greek kings also dominated The Punjab. Greek rule then disappeared forever from this region.

Alexander had certainly intended north-west India to become a permanent part of his empire. Prior to his withdrawal from the region, he established about a dozen satrapies with Macedonian governors and garrisoned troops at strategic points to support them. As in his other conquered territories, he also founded several cities. In India, itself, however, these arrangements survived his death, by no more than two years. By 321 BC, the territories lying east of the River Indus had become virtually independent. Shortly after this the Indian conqueror, King Chandragupta Maurya (321–297 BC), founder of the Mauryan Empire, incorporated this territory into an empire that ultimately covered more than two-thirds of the sub-continent.[98]

Despite the classical Greeks' ignorance of India, some significance presumably attaches to the fact that much Greek philosophy originated in the cities of Ionia on Asia Minor's western shore; that portion of the Greek world in closest touch with the East. Admittedly, this circumstance scarcely permits any inferences regarding Indian influence upon the Greeks. The inter-cultural communication and even acculturation that the policies of the Persian Empire certainly facilitated, however, would have given impetus to intellectual creativity; an impetus that cannot have remained without effect upon the life of Greece and the Greek World.

Notes

1 Possehl 2012, 769. For cotton see Oppenheim 1964, 94; Talon 1986, 75–78.

2 Brunswig *et al.* 1983, 102.

3 Drews 1988, 61.

4 Mayrhoffer 1966.

5 Karttunen 1989, 23.

6 It may be the multi-coloured bird called in Sumerian DHA.JAMUŠEN which is sometimes identified as a peacock, see Falkenstein 1964, 75. But as Kartunnen points out, there are other multi-coloured birds in India, see Karttunen 1989, 14 n.35, but this does not negate the fact that that the fowl originated in India.

7 Karttunen 1989, 24–25. For details see Brentjes 1981, 145–148; 1988, 163–167; Schmidt 1980, 45. In the annals of King Tiglathpileser III (*c.* 745–727 BC) for the year 738 BC there is recorded as being 'birds of heaven with blue wings' among the tributes, which may well be peacocks, see Karttunen 1989, 25.

8 Potts 1993a, 1452.

9 British Museum, inv. no. ME 118885.

10 Potts 1993a, 1460.

11 The Biblical references are: 'And they came to Ophir and fetched from thence gold, four hundred and twenty talents and brought [it] to king Solomon' (1 *Kings* 9.28); 'And the navy also of Hiram, that brought gold from Ophir, brought in from Ophir great plenty of almug

trees and precious stones' (1 *Kings* 10.11); 'And Huram sent him by the hands of his servants ships and servants that had knowledge of the sea; and they went with the servants of Solomon to Ophir and took thence four hundred and fifty talents of gold and brought [them] to king Solomon' (2 *Chronicles* 8.18); 'And the servants also of Huram and the servants of Solomon, which brought gold from Ophir, brought algum trees and precious stones' (2 *Chronicles* 9.10). There is further Biblical evidence for the great wealth of Ophir: '[Even] three thousand talents of gold, of the gold of Ophir and seven thousand talents of refined silver, to overlay the walls of the houses [withal]' (1 *Chronicles* 29.4); 'It cannot be valued with the gold of Ophir, with the precious onyx, or the sapphire' (*Job* 28.16); 'Kings' daughters [were] among thy honourable women: upon thy right hand did stand the queen in gold of Ophir' (*Psalm* 45.9); 'I will make a man more precious than fine gold; even a man than the golden wedge of Ophir' (*Isaiah* 13.12). All biblical references are to the Authorised Version of 1603.

12 1 *Kings* 10.22.

13 Potts 1993a, 1460.

14 Potts 1993a, 1460.

15 Lipiński 2004, for Ophir see 189–224.

16 Groom 1981, 480–54; Barnett 1982, 9 and n.4.

17 Barnett 1957, 168.

18 Karttunen believes there is no evidence of any contacts of Phoenicians with India and the ships of Hiram bringing the gold and other products of Ophir, as related in the Old Testament, probably did not go as far as that, but rather to South Arabia or North-East Africa, see Karttunen 1989, 146. He also notes that the Egyptian accounts of the Punt expeditions, wherever it was exactly located and the less-detailed evidence of the Phoenician activity at least show the existence of a trade connection in the Red Sea area, see Karttunen 2014, 331 and Salles 1996, 251–267.

19 Maisler (Mazar) 1951, 266–267 and pl. XI B; Renz and Rölling 1996, 229–231.

20 This dispenses with the need to even consider that Ophir was a fantasy. See Lipiński 2004, 196 n.41.

21 Lipiński 2004, 196–197.

22 The reference to the failure of King Jehoshaphat of Judah to sail to Ophir may also refer to the closure of the eastern trade route, or even possibly to the failure of the venture that was carried out without the benefit of experienced Phoenician sailors and navigators.

23 I *Kings*, 22.48–49; 2 *Chronicles* 20.35–37.

24 Potts 1993a, 1460–1461.

25 Potts 1993a, 1460–1461.

26 Korou 2008, 305–364. See also Lipiński 2004, 145–188.

27 Dickinson 2006, 215–216; Sherratt 2020, 199–200.

28 For a comprehensive survey of India in the Iron Age, see Uesugi 2018.

29 Tusa 1977, 675–695.

30 Kenoyer 1991a, 1–64; 1991b, 29–60; Shaffer 1992, Volume I, 441–464, Volume II, 425–446.

31 Shaffer 1993, 53–67.

32 Yule 1985a; 1989, 193–275; Sharma 2002. See also Shaffer and Lichtenstein 1999, 239–260.

33 For a review of the debate concerning the arrival of the Indo-Europeans see Bryant and Patton 2005.

34 Kenoyer 1991a, 331–385; 1995, 213–257.

35 Allchin and Allchin 1982, 311–325.

36 Wertime 1980, 7–8.

37 Allchin and Allchin 1982, 233–234.

38 Tewari 2003, 536–545.

39 Kennedy 1898, 241–288.

40 Karttunen 1989, 25–26. For peacocks see Rybatzky 2008, 187–207. For monkeys, see Barnett 1973, 1–10; Mendleson 1983, 81–83.
41 Karttunen 2014, 332; Salles 1996, 256.
42 Ben-Yosef and Sapir-He 2014.
43 Karttunen 1989, 11, 157–160.
44 Karttunen 1989, 103–108.
45 Marshall 1951; Puri 1966; Dar 1984; Dani *et al.* 1986.
46 Arrian, *Indika,* viii.1.3. For a better understanding of the relations between the Greek and Persian worlds see Drews 1973, 45–96 and Briant 1990, 69–114. The Achaemenid Empire satrapy was called Hindush (or *Hi*^{n}*dūš*), following their conquest of the Indus Valley in around 500 BC. It is believed that the name *Hindush* derives from *Sindhu*, the Sanskrit name of the Indus river as well as the region at the lower Indus basin (modern Sindh). The Greeks of Asia Minor, who were also part of the Achaemenid Empire, called the province 'India'; more precisely, they called the people of the province as 'Indians' ('Ινδοι, *Indoi*).
47 Gershevitch 1957, 317–320; Maxwell-Hyslop 1983, pl. 23.
48 Herodotus, iii.106.
49 Sappho, F.44.
50 *Exodus* 30.23, *Proverbs* 7.17, *Song of Solomon* 4.14. See also Herodotus, iii.111.
51 Herodotus, vii.70.
52 Herodotus, vii.65. An inscription on the tomb of King Darius I (DNa) at Naqš-i Rustam near Persepolis, records Gandara along with other Indian possessions in the list of satrapies. An Indian foot soldier is also included on the frieze of the tomb depicting the bearers of the coffin of King Darius, similar to those that were included in the armies that invaded the Greek mainland. See 'Naqš-i Rustam' *Encyclopaedia Iranica,* http://www.iranicaonline.org/articles/naqs-e-rostam.
53 Herodotus, vii.86. See also vii.187; viii.113. Herds of wild asses can still be found in the Rann of Kutch in Rajasthan, India.
54 Morgenstierne 1974, 273; Baghbidoi 2006, 143–166.
55 [55] Böhtlingk 1887; Katre 1987; Joshi 1991. For a survey of the evidence for the life of Pānini, see Stoneman 2019, 30–31.
56 *Pāṇini*, 4.1.49, 'Greek woman' or 'Greek script'.
57 Nenci 1954.
58 Herodotus, ii.143, telling us about a visit by Hecataeus to Egypt. See Jacoby 1923, 1–47 (no. 1); Karttunen 1989, 144–160; West 1991, 144–160.
59 Karttunen 1989, 49, n.329.
60 Karttunen 1989, 69.
61 Karttunen 1989, 72, n.52.
62 Karttunen 1989, 72.
63 Karttunen 1989, 72, n.53–58.
64 Karttunen 1989, 82, n.53.
65 (Greek Original) Σκύλαξ, Καρυανδεύς [πόλις δ' ἐστὶ τῆς Καρίας πλησίον Ἁλικαρνασσοῦ τὰ Καρύανδα], μαθηματικὸς καὶ μουσικός. Περίπλουν τῶν ἐκτὸς τῶν Ἡρακλέους στηλῶν, Τὰ κατὰ Ἡρακλείδην τὸν Μυλασσῶν βασιλέα, Γῆς περίοδον, Ἀντιγραφὴν πρὸς τὴν Πολυβίου ἱστορίαν. Although only a few fragments of Scylax survive, his travels as a geographer were well known in his time see Herodotus, iv.44 and later Aristotle, *Politics,* vii.13.2. For the seven fragments on India ascribed to him, see Jacoby 1958, no. 709. See also Gisinger 1923, volume 5A, 619–646. There is some confusion as to what can be ascribed to Scylax. The travels of Skylax of Caryanda at the behest of King Darius I are mentioned by Herodotus, iv.44, but this is not to be confused with the author of the *Circumnavigation of the Inhabited Sea* that survives under Scylax's name,

perhaps as a tribute, since from internal evidence it must be fourth century BC, at least in its present form. Accordingly, it is known as *Pseudo-Skylax*. See Shipley 2011.
66 Fritz 1967.
67 Fritz 1967, volume I, 14–16, 33 and 52–55, volume II, 634; Herodotus, iv.44.
68 Herodotus, iv.44.
69 Gisinger 1923, volume 5A, 634.
70 Stoneman 2019, 25–28.
71 Unless otherwise indicated, the translations of Herodotus are after Herodotus, *History of the Greek and Persian War*, translated by George Rawlinson, edited and abridged with an introduction by W. G. Forrest, London, New English Library, 1966.
72 Herodotus, iii.94.
73 Herodotus, iii. 98; Asheri *et al.* 2007, 496–497.
74 Asheri *et al.* 2007, 496.
75 Asheri *et al.* 2007, 497. For Greek notions of India at the time immediately before Alexander, see Reese 1914; Puskás 1983, 201–207; Karttunen 1989, 157–160; and Lenfant 1995, 307–336.
76 Dihle 1990, 41–68.
77 Herodotus, iii.106.
78 Herodotus, iii.98.
79 Herodotus, iii.99.
80 Herodotus, iii.100.
81 Herodotus, iii.101.
82 Herodotus, iii.102.
83 Herodotus, iii.104.
84 Herodotus, iii.105.
85 Peissel 1984.
86 Herodotus, iii.106.
87 For life of Ctesias of Cnidus, see Nichols 2011, 13–18.
88 McCrindle 1882. For discussion of the work of St Photius, see Bigwood 1989, 302–316. See also Wilson 1836; Gardiner-Garden 1987; Lenfant 2004; Stronk 2010; Llewellyn-Jones and Robson 2012.
89 Nichols 2011. This work is particularly useful for an understanding of the sources and influence of Ctesias.
90 The reliance of both Ctesias and Herodotus on a simple acquaintance with Indian mythology as an alternative to visiting the region is apparent, see for example, Herodotus, ii.157.
91 Strabo, 2.I.9 and 15.i.28.
92 Stoneman 2019, 289–331.
93 Diodorus Siculus, xvii.88.2–3; Arrian, *Anabasis Alexandri*, v.17.3; Curtius, viii.14.16; Devine 1987, 91–113; Holt 2003, 50–56, 71–82, 100–111, 150–156.
94 Sharma 2005, 154–155.
95 Diodorus Siculus, xvii.19.4; Arrian, *Anabasis Alexandri*, v.27.1–29; Curtius, ix.3.3–5; x.2.8–4.3. One of the reasons Alexander's army was frightened was the prospect of crossing the River Ganges and then facing yet another giant Indian army in the Ganges Plain. Further south he would have met in battle the troops and mounted elephant cavalry of the Nanda Empire that existed between 345 and 331 BC, before being eventually incorporated into the Mauryan Empire of King Chandragupta Maurya. This army is vividly described by Plutarch (*Alexander*, lxii.1–3): 'As for the Macedonians, however, their struggle with Porus blunted their courage and stayed their farther advance into India. For having had all they could do to repulse an enemy who mustered only twenty thousand infantry and two thousand horse, they violently opposed Alexander when he insisted on crossing the river Ganges also, the width of which,

as they learned, was thirty-two furlongs, its depth a hundred fathoms, while its banks on the farther side were covered with multitudes of men-at-arms and horsemen and elephants. For they were told that the kings of the Ganderites and Praesii were awaiting them with eighty thousand horsemen, two hundred thousand footmen, eight thousand chariots and six thousand fighting elephants' (Translation after Perrin 1900).

96 Stoneman 2019, 36–79.

97 Herodotus, iii.99.

98 Eggermont 1956; Thapar 1998.

Appendix: *Indica* by Ctesias of Cnidus

The text of *Indica* by Ctesias was assembled during his lifetime by the Byzantine scholar St Photius, Patriarch of Constantinople (St Photius the Great), who probably lived between 820–893. The translation below is based on that of Freese (1920). Some of the text is believed to be interpolations, which have been removed. In the text 'he' is the author Ctesias. Readers are also referred to the translation by Nichols (2011). Ctesias became a byword in antiquity for unreliability and improbability. The precision of his reports, reproduced below, have been interpreted in modern times either as ridiculous or as a form of a series of jokes (see Stoneman 2019, 32).

[§1] In regard to the River Indus, he says that, where it is narrowest, it is seven, where it is widest it is thirty-five kilometres broad.

[§2] He declares that the population of India is almost greater than that of the whole world.

[§3] He also mentions a worm found in this river, the only living creature which breeds there.

[§4] Beyond India there are no countries inhabited by men.

[§5] It never rains there, the country being watered by the river.

[§6] He says of the *pantarba*, a kind of seal-stone, that four hundred and seventy-seven seal-stones and other precious stones, belonging to a Bactrian merchant that had been thrown into the river, were drawn up from the bottom, all clinging together, by this stone.

[§7] He also speaks of elephants which knock down walls, of little apes with tails four cubits long and of cocks of very large size.

[§8] Of the parrot about as large as a hawk which has a human tongue and voice, a dark red beak, a black, beard and blue feathers up to the neck which is red like cinnabar. It speaks Indian like a native and if taught Greek, speaks Greek.

[§9] He next mentions a fountain which is filled every year with liquid gold, from which a hundred pitcherfulls are drawn. These pitchers have to be made of earth, since the gold when drawn off becomes solid and it is necessary to break the vessel in order to get it out. The fountain is square, sixteen cubits in circumference and a fathom deep. The gold in each pitcher weighs a talent. At the bottom of the fountain there is iron and the author says that he possessed two swords made from it, one given him by the king, the other by his mother, Parysatis. If this iron be fixed in the ground, it keeps off clouds and hail and hurricanes Ctesias declares that the king twice proved its efficacy and that he himself was a witness to it.

[§10] The Indian dogs are very large and even attack lions.

[§11] There are great mountains, from which are dug sardonyx, onyx and other seal-stones.

[§12] It is intensely hot and the sun appears ten times larger than in other countries; large numbers of people are suffocated by the heat.

[§13] The sea is as large as that of Greece; it is so hot on the surface and to a depth of four fingers that fish cannot live near it but keep on the bottom.

[§14] The River Indus flows across plains and between mountains, where the Indian reed [bamboo] grows. It is so thick that two men can hardly get their arms round it and as tall as the mast of a merchant-ship of largest tonnage. Some are larger, some smaller, as is natural considering the size of the mountain. Of these reeds some are male, others female. The male has no pith and is very strong, but the female has.

[§15] The *martikhora* is an animal found in this country. It has a face like a man's, a skin red as cinnabar and is as large as a lion. It has three rows of teeth, ears and light-blue eyes like those of a man; its tail is like that of a land scorpion, containing a sting more than a cubit long at the end. It has other stings on each side of its tail and one on the top of its head, like the scorpion, with which it inflicts a wound that is always fatal. If it is attacked from a distance, it sets up its tail in front and discharges its stings as if from a bow; if attacked from behind, it straightens it out and launches its stings in a direct line to the distance of a thirty meter. The wound inflicted is fatal to all animals except the elephant. The stings are about a foot long and about as thick as a small rush. The *martikhora* is called in Greek *anthropophagos* [man-eater], because, although it preys upon other animals, it kills and devours a greater number of human beings. It fights with both its claws and stings, which, according to

Ctesias, grow again after they have been discharged. There are a great number of these animals in India, which are hunted and killed with spears or arrows by natives mounted on elephants.

[§16] Observing that the Indians are extremely just, Ctesias goes on to describe their manners and customs.

[§17] He mentions a sacred spot in an uninhabited district, which they honour under the name of the sun and the moon. It is a fifteen days' journey from mount Sardo.

[§18] Here the sun is always cool for thirty-five days in the year, so that his votaries my attend his feast and after its celebration may return home without being scorched. In India there is neither thunder, lightning, nor rain but winds and hurricanes, which carry along everything that comes in their way, are frequent. The sun, after rising, is cool for half the day, but for the remainder is excessively hot in most parts of the country.

[§19] It is not the heat of the sun that makes the Indians swarthy; they are so naturally. Some of them, both men and women, are very fair, though they are fewer in number. Ctesias says that he himself saw five white men and two white women.

[§20] (Not relevant to India).

[§21] In the middle of India there are black men, called pygmies, who speak the same language as the other inhabitants of the country. They are very short, the tallest being only two cubits in height, most of them only one and a half. Their hair is very long, going down to the knees and even lower and their beards are larger than those of any other men. When their beards are full grown they leave off wearing clothes and let the hair of their head fall down behind far below the knees, while their beard trails down to the feet in front. When their body is thus entirely covered with hair they fasten it round them with a girdle, so that it serves them for clothes. They are snub-nosed and ugly.

[§22] Their sheep are no bigger than lambs, their oxen, asses, horses, mules and other beasts of burden about the size of rams.

[§23] Being very skilful archers, three thousand attend the king of India.

[§24] They are very just and have the same laws as the Indians. They hunt the hare and the fox, not with dogs, but with ravens, kites, crows and eagles.

[§25] There is lake one hundred and forty kilometres in circumference, the surface of which, when riot ruffled by the wind, is covered with floating oil. Sailing over it in little boats, they ladle out the oil with little vessels and keep it for use. They also use oil of sesame and nut oil, but the oil from the lake is best. The lake also abounds in fish.

[§26] The country produces much silver and there are numerous silver mines, not very deep, but those of Bactria are said to be deeper. There is also gold, not found in rivers and washed, as in the River Pactolus, but in many large mountains which are inhabited by griffins. These are four-footed birds as large as a wolf, their legs and claws resembling those of a lion; their breast feathers are red, those of the rest of the body black. Although there is abundance of gold in the mountains, it is difficult to get it because of these birds.

[§27] The Indian sheep and goats are larger than asses and as a rule have four young ones, sometimes six, at a time. There are neither tame nor wild pigs.

[§28] The palm trees and dates are three times as large as those of Babylon.

[§29] There is a river of honey that flows from a rock.

[§30] The author speaks at length of the Indians' love of justice, their loyalty to their kings and their contempt of death.

[§31] He also mentions a fountain, the water from which, when drawn off, thickens like cheese. If three obols weight of this thick mass be crushed, mixed with water and given to anyone to drink, he reveals everything that he has ever done, being in a state of frenzy and delirium the whole day. The king makes use of this test when he desires to discover the truth about an accused person. If he confesses, he is ordered to starve himself to death; if he reveals nothing, he is acquitted.

[§32] The Indians are not subject to headache, ophthalmia, or even toothache; to ulcers on the mouth, or sores in any other part of the body. They live one hundred and twenty, one hundred and thirty, one hundred and fifty and some even two hundred years.

[§33] There is a serpent a span in length, of a most beautiful purple colour, with a very white head and without teeth. It is caught on the burning mountains, from which the sardonyx is dug. It does not sting, but its vomit rots the place where it falls. If it is hung up by the tail it discharges two kinds of poison, one yellow like amber, when it is alive, the other black, when it is dead. If one drinks only as much of the former as a grain of sesame dissolved in water, his brain runs out through his nose and he dies immediately; if the other poison is administered, it brings on consumption, which does not prove fatal for at least a year.

[§34] There is a bird called *dicaerus* ('just'), the size of a partridge's egg. It buries its excrement in the ground in order to hide it. If anyone finds it and takes only a morsel of it about the size of a grain of sesame in the morning, he is overcome by sleep, loses consciousness and dies at sunset.

[§35] There is also a tree called *parebus*, about the size of an olive, which is only found in the royal gardens. It bears neither flowers nor fruit and has only fifteen very stout roots, the smallest of which is as thick as a man's arm. If a piece of this root, about a span in length, be put near anybody of matter, gold, silver, brass, stones, in fact, everything except amber, it attracts it; if a cubit's length of it be used, it attracts lambs and birds, the latter being generally caught in this way. If you wish to solidify a gallon of water, you need only throw in a piece of the root the weight of an obol; the same with wine, which can be handled like wax, although on the next day it becomes liquid again. The root is also used as a remedy for those suffering from bowel complaints.

[§36] There is a river that flows through India, not large, but about three hundred and fifty metres broad. It is called the River Hyparchus in Indian, meaning in Greek 'bestowing all blessings.' During thirty days in the year it brings down amber. It is said that in the mountains there are trees on the banks of the river where it passes through, which at a certain season of the year shed tears like the almond, fir, or any other tree, especially during these thirty days. These tears drop into the river and become hard. This tree is called in Indian *siptakhora*, meaning in Greek 'sweet' and from it the inhabitants gather amber. It also bears fruit in clusters like grapes, the stones of which are as large as the nuts of Pontus.

[§37] On these mountains there, live men with the head of a dog, whose clothing is the skin of wild beasts. They speak no language, but bark like dogs and in this manner make themselves understood by each other. Their teeth are larger than those of dogs, their nails like those of these animals, but longer and rounder. They inhabit the mountains as far as the river Indus. Their complexion is swarthy. They are extremely just, like the rest of the Indians with whom they associate. They understand the Indian language but are unable to converse, only barking or making signs with their hands and fingers by way of reply, like the deaf and dumb. They are called by the Indians *calystrii*, in

Greek *cynocephali* or 'dog-heads.' They live on raw meat. They number about one hundred and twenty thousand.

[§38] Near the sources of this river grows a purple flower, from which is obtained a purple dye, as good in quality as the Greek and of an even more brilliant hue.

[§39] In the same district there is an animal about the size of a beetle, red as cinnabar, with very long feet and a body as soft as that of a worm. It breeds on the trees which produce amber, eats their fruit and kills them, as the wood louse destroys the vines in Greece. The Indians crush these insects and use them for dyeing their robes and tunics and anything else they wish. The dye is superior to the Persian.

[§40] The *Cynocephali* living on the mountains do not practice any trade but live by hunting. When they have killed an animal, they roast it in the sun. They also rear numbers of sheep, goats and asses, drinking the milk of the sheep and whey made from it. They eat the fruit of the *siptakhora*, whence amber is procured, since it is sweet. They also dry it and keep it in baskets, as the Greeks keep their dried grapes. They make rafts which they load with this fruit together with well-cleaned purple flowers and two hundred and sixty talents of amber, with the same quantity of the purple dye and thousand additional talents of amber, which they send annually to the king of India.

[§41] They exchange the rest for bread, flour and cotton stuffs with the Indians, from whom they also buy swords for hunting wild beasts, bows and arrows, being very skilful in drawing the bow and hurling the spear. They cannot be defeated in war since they inhabit lofty and inaccessible mountains. Every five years the king sends them a present of three hundred thousand bows, as many spears, one hundred and twenty thousand shields and fifty thousand swords.

[§42] They do not live in houses, but in caves. They set out for the chase with bows and spears and as they are very swift of foot, they pursue and soon overtake their quarry. The women have a bath once a month and the men do not have a bath at all, but only wash their hands. They anoint themselves three times a month with oil made from milk and wipe themselves with skins. The clothes of men and women alike are not skins with the hair on, but skins that are tanned and very fine. The richest wear linen clothes, but they are few in number. They have no beds, but sleep on leaves or grass. He who possesses the greatest number of sheep is considered the richest and so in regard to their other possessions. All, both men and women, have tails above their hips, like dogs, but longer and hairier.

[§43] They are just and live longer than any other men, one hundred and seventy and sometimes two hundred years.

[§44] It is said that beyond their country, above the sources of the river, there are other men, black like the rest of the Indians. They do no work, do not eat grain nor drink water, but rear large numbers of cattle, cows, goats and sheep, whose milk is their only food. When they drink milk in the morning and then again at mid-day, they eat a sweet root which prevents the milk from curdling in the stomach and at night makes them vomit all they have taken without any difficulty.

[§45] In India there are wild asses [rhinoceroses] as large as horses, or even larger. Their body is white, their head dark red, their eyes bluish and they have a horn in their forehead about a cubit in length. The lower part of the horn, for about two palms distance from the forehead, is quite white, the middle is black, the upper part, which terminates in a point, is a very flaming red. Those who drink out of cups made from it are proof against convulsions, epilepsy and even poison, provided that before or after having taken it they drink some wine or water or other liquid out of these cups. The domestic and wild asses of other countries and all other solid-hoofed animals have neither knuckle bones nor gall bladder, whereas the Indian asses have both. Their knuckle bone is the most beautiful that I have seen, like that of the ox in size and appearance; it is as heavy as lead and of the colour of cinnabar all through. These animals are very strong and swift; neither the horse nor any other animal can overtake them. At first they run slowly, but the longer they run their pace increases wonderfully and becomes faster and faster. There is only one way of catching them. When they take their young to feed, if they are surrounded by a large number of horsemen, being unwilling to abandon their foals, they show fight, but with their horns, kick, bite and kill many men and horses. They are at last taken, after they have been pierced with arrows and spears; for it is impossible to capture them alive. Their flesh is too bitter to eat and they are only hunted for the sake of the horns and knuckle bones.

[§46] In the River Indus a worm is found resembling those which are usually found on fig trees. Its average length is seven cubits, though some are longer, others shorter. It is so thick that a child who is ten years old could hardly put his arms round it. It has two teeth, one in the upper and one in the lower jaw. Everything it seizes with these teeth it devours. By day it remains in the mud of the river, but at night it comes out, seizes whatever it comes across, whether ox or camel, drags it into the river and devours it all except the intestines. It is caught with a large hook baited with a lamb or kid attached by iron chains. After it has been caught, it is hung up for thirty days with vessels placed underneath, into which as much oil from the body drips as would fill ten Attic kotylae. At the end of the thirty days, the worm is thrown away, the vessels of oil are sealed arid taken as a present to the king of India, who alone is allowed to use it. This oil sets everything alight -wood or animals- over which it is poured and the flame can only be extinguished by throwing a quantity of thick mud on it.

[§47] There are trees in India as high as cedars or cypresses, with leaves like those of the palm tree, except that they are a little broader and have no shoots. They flower like the male laurel but have no fruit. The tree is called by the Indians *carpios*, by the Greeks *myrorodon* (unguent rose); it is not common. Drops of oil ooze out of it, which are wiped off with wool and then squeezed into stone alabaster boxes. The oil is reddish, rather thick and so fragrant that it scents the air to a distance of nine hundred metres. Only the king and his family are allowed to use it. The king of India sent some to the king of Persia and Ctesias, who saw it, says that he cannot compare the perfume with any other.

[§48] The Indians also have very excellent cheese and sweet wine, both of which Ctesias tested himself.

[§49] There is a square fountain in India, about five ells in circumference. The water is in a rock, about three cubits' depth down and the water itself three fathoms. The Indians of highest rank, men, women and children, bathe in it not only for cleanliness, but as a preventive of disease. They plunge feet foremost into the water and when they jump into it, it throws them out again on to dry land, not only human beings, but every animal, living or dead, in fact, everything that is thrown into it except iron, silver, gold and copper, which sink to the bottom. The water is very cold and agreeable to drink; it makes a loud noise like that of water boiling in a caldron. It cures leprosy and scab. In Indian it is called *ballade* and in Greek *ophelime* or 'useful.'

[§50] In the mountains where the Indian reed grows dwells a people about thirty thousand in number. Their women only have children once in their life, which are born with beautiful teeth in the upper and lower jaw. Both male and female children have white hair, on the head and eyebrows. Up to the age of thirty the men have white hair all over the body; it then begins to turn black and at the age of sixty it is quite black. Both men and women have eight fingers and eight toes. They are very warlike and five thousand of them, bowmen and spearmen, accompany the king of India on his military expeditions. Their ears are so long that their arms are covered with them as far as the elbow and also their backs and one ear touches the other.

[§51] Ctesias relates these fables as perfect truth, adding that he himself had seen with his own eyes some of the things he describes and had been informed of the rest by eye witnesses. He says that he has omitted many far more marvellous things for fear that those who had not seen them might think that his account was utterly untrustworthy.

Bibliography

Allchin, R. (1962) 'Upon the antiquity and methods of gold mining in Ancient India' *Journal of the Economic and Social History of the Orient*, 5: 195–211.

Allchin, R. and Allchin, B. (1982) *The Rise of Civilisation in India and Pakistan*, Cambridge, Cambridge University Press.

Alexiou, S. and Warren, P. (2004) *The Early Minoan Tombs of Lebena, Southern Crete*, Sāvedalen, Paul Åströms Förlag, (*Studies in Mediterranean Archaeology*, 30).

Alram-Stern, E. (2004) 'Die Frühbronzezeit in Griechenland mit Ausnahme von Kreta' in Alram-Stern, E. (ed.), *Die Ägäische Frühzeit, Forschungsbericht 1975–2002*, Vienna, Österreichische Akademie der Wissenschaften Mykenische Kommission, pp. 453–456.

Anastasiadou, M. (2011) *The Middle Minoan Three-Sided Soft Stone Prism: A Study of Style and Iconography*, *Corpus der minoischen und mykenischem Siegel*, Beiheft 9, Volume I, Mainz, von Zabern.

Antonova, I., Tolstikov, V. and Treister, M. (1996) *The Gold of Troy: Searching for Homer's Fabled Troy*, London, Thames and Hudson.

Arkel, A. (1936) 'Cambay and the Bead Trade' *Antiquity*, 10: 292–305.

Aruz, J. (1984) 'The Silver Cylinder Seal from Mochlos' *Kadmos*, 1984, 23: 186–188.

Aruz, J. (ed.) (2003) *Art of the First Cities: The Third Millennium BC from the Mediterranean to the Indus*, New York and New Haven, Metropolitan Museum of Art and Yale University Press.

Aruz, J. (2008) *Marks of Distinction: Seals and Cultural Exchange Between the Aegean and the Orient (ca. 3500–1360 BC)*, Mainz, Philipp von Zabern (*Corpus der minoischen und mykenischem Siegel*, Beiheft 7).

Asheri, D., Lloyd, A. B., Corcella, A., Murray, O. and Moreno, A. (2007) *A Commentary on Herodotus Books I–IV*, Oxford, Oxford University Press.

Aston, B. G., Harrell, J. A. and Law, I. (2000) 'Stone' in Nicholson, P. T. and Shaw, I. (eds), *Ancient Egyptian Materials and Technology*, Cambridge, Cambridge University Press.

Astour, M. C. (1973) 'Ugarit and the Aegean: a brief summary of archaeological and epigraphical evidence' in Hoffner, H. A., Jr. (ed.), *Orient and Occident. Essays Presented to Cyrus H. Gordon on the Occasion of his Sixty-fifth Birthday*, Kevelaer, Butzon and Bercker (*Alter Orient und Altes Testament* 22), pp. 17–27.

Baghbidoi, H. R. (2006) 'Iranian elements in Sanskrit' in Tikkanen, B. and Hettrich, H., 'Themes and Tasks in Old and Middle Indo-Aryan Linguistics' *Papers of the 12th World Sanskrit Conference*, Delhi, Motilal Banarsidass, pp. 143–166.

Barnett, R. D. (1957) *A Catalogue of the Nimrud Ivories: With Other Examples of Ancient Near Eastern Ivories in the British Museum*, London, Trustees of the British Museum.

Barnett, R. D. (1973) 'Monkey Business' *The Journal of the Ancient Near Eastern Society of Columbia University (JANES)*, 5: 1–10.

Barnett, R. D. (1982) *Ancient Ivories in the Near East*, Jerusalem, Institute of Archaeology, Hebrew University of Jerusalem.

Bar-Yosef, M., Porat, N., Gal, Z., Shalem, D. and Smithline, H. (2004) 'Steatite beads at Peqi'in: long distance trade and pyro-technology during the Chalcolithic of the Levant' *Journal of Archaeological Science*, 31: 493–502.

Ben-Yosef, E. and Sapir-He, L. (2014) 'Archaeologists pinpoint the date when domesticated camels arrived in Israel' *PhysOrg* (University of Tel Aviv), 3 February 2014, at https://phys.org/news/2014-02-archaeologists-date-domesticated-camels-israel.html.

Benzi, M. (1992) *Rodi e la civiltà micenea*, Rome, Gruppo editoriale internazionale.

Bernabò Brea, L. (ed.) (1964) *Poliochni, Città preistorica nell'isola di Lemnos*, Volume 1, Rome, 'L'Erma' di Bretschneider.

Bernabò Brea, L. (ed.) (1976) *Poliochni, Città preistorica nell'isola di Lemnos*, Volume 2, Rome, 'L'Erma' di Bretschneider.

Betancourt, P. B. (1985) *History of Minoan Pottery*, Princeton, Princeton University Press.

Bignasca, A. M. (2000) *I kernoi circolari in Oriente e in Occidente: strumenti di culto e immagini cosmiche*, Frieburg and Göttingen, Universitätsverlag Freiburg and Vandenhoeck and Ruprecht (*Orbis Biblicus et Orientalis* 19).

Bigwood, J. M. (1989) 'Ctesias' *Indica* and Photius' *Phoenix*, 43: 302–316.

Bilgen, A. N. (ed.) (2015) *Seyitömer Höyük*, Istanbul, Arkeoloji ve Sanat Yayınları.

Birtacha, K. (2007) 'Ornaments' in Renfrew, C., Doumas, C., Marangou, L. and Gavalas, G. (eds), *Keros, Dhaskalio Kavos: the investigations of 1987-1988*, Cambridge, McDonald Institute of Archaeological Research (*Keros I*).

Bisht, R. S. (1993) 'Excavations at Banawali: 1974–1977' in Possehl, G. L. (ed.), *Harappan Civilisation: A Recent Perspective*, second edition, New Delhi, Oxford and IBH Publishing (for the American Institute of Indian Studies), pp. 113–124.

Blegen, C. W. (1928) *Zygouries: A Prehistoric Settlement in the Valley of Cleonae*, Cambridge, Mass., Harvard University Press (for American School of Classical Studies at Athens).

Blegen, C. W., Boulter, C. G., Caskey, J. L. and Rawson, M. (1958) *Troy IV. The Settlements, VIIA, VIIB and VIII*, Princeton, Princeton University Press.

Blegen, C. W., Caskey, J. L., Rawson, M. and Sperling, J. (1950) *Troy I: General Introduction and the First and Second Settlements*, Volume I, Princeton, Princeton University Press (for the University of Cincinnati).

Boardman, J. (1970) *Greek Gems and Finger Rings*, London, Thames and Hudson.

Böhtlingk, O. von (1887) *Pāṇini's Grammatik*, Leipzig, H. Haessel.

Bosanquet, R. C. (1896–1897) 'Notes from the Cyclades: so-called kernoi' *Annual of the British School at Athens*, 3: 57–61.

Boyadziev, Y. D. (1995) 'Chronology of Prehistoric Cultures in Bulgaria' in Bailey, D. W. and Panayotov, I. (eds), *Prehistoric Bulgaria*, Madison, Prehistory Press (*Monographs in World Archaeology* No. 22).

Branigan, K. (1966) 'Byblite daggers in Cyprus and Crete' *American Journal of Archaeology*, 70: 123–126.

Branigan, K. (1967) 'Further Light on prehistoric relations between Crete and Byblos' *American Journal of Archaeology*, 71: 117–121.

Branigan, K. (1967) 'The Early Bronze Age daggers of Crete' *Annual of the British School at Athens*, 62: 211–239.

Branigan, K. (1974) *Aegean Metalwork of the Early and Middle Bronze Age*, Oxford, Oxford University Press.

Brentjes, B. (1981) 'The Mittanians and the peacock' in Asimiov, M. A. (ed.), *Etnicheskie problemy istorii Tsentral'noĭ Azii v drevnosti (II tysi͡acheletie do n.ė.)* (*Ethnic Problems of the History of Central Asia (Second Millennium BC)*, Moscow, Academy of Sciences of the USSR and the Soviet Commission for UNESCO (International Symposium on Ethnic Problems of the Ancient History of Central Asia (Second Millennium BC), Dushanbe, Tajikistan, 17–22 October 1977), pp. 145–148.

Brentjes, B. (1988) 'Die "baktrischen Bronzen" und Vorderasien-Probleme der Kunstgeschlichte des 2. Jahrtausends v. u. Z' *Iranica Antiqua*, 23: 163–167.

Briant, P. (1990) 'Hérodote et la société perse' in Nenci, G. and Reverdin, O. (eds), *Hérodote et les peoples non-grecs*, Vandoeuvres-Geneva, Fondation Hardt (*Entretiens sue l'Antiquité Classique* Volume 35), pp. 69–114.

Broodbank, C. (2000) *An Island Archaeology of the Early Cyclades*, Cambridge, Cambridge University Press.

Brunel, F. (1972) *Jewellery of India: Five Thousand Years of Tradition*, New Delhi, National Book Trust.

Brunswig, R. H., Parpola, A. and Potts, D. T. (1983) 'New Indus type and related seals from the Near East' in Potts, D. T. (ed.), *Dilmun: New Studies in the Archaeology and Early History of Bahrain*, Berlin, D. Reimer, pp. 101–115.

Bryant, E. F. and Patton, L. L. (2005) *The Indo-Aryan Controversy: Evidence and Inference in Indian History*, London, Routledge.

Buccellati, G. and Kelly-Buccellati, M. (1983) 'Terqa: the first eight seasons' *Les annales archéologiques arabes syriennes*, 33: 47–67.

Casal, J.-M. (1961) *Fouilles de Mundigak*, two volumes, Paris, Librairie C. Klincksieck (*Memoires de la Delegation Archaeologique Français en Afghanistan* 17).

Casanova, M. (1995) 'Le lapis-lazuli dans l'Orient antique' in Tallon, F. (ed.), *Les Pierres précieuses de l'Orient ancien des Sumériens aux Sassanides*, Paris, Editions de la Réunion des musées nationaux (*Musée du Louvre, Dossier du département des Antiquités orientales* 49), pp. 15–20.

Casanova, M. (1999) 'Le lapis lazuli dans l'Orient ancien' in Caubet, A. (ed.), *Cornaline et pierres précieuses: La Méditerranée, de l'Antiquité à l'Islam. Actes du Colloque organisé au musée du Louvre par le Service culturel les 24 et 25 novembre 1995*, Paris, Musée du Louvre, pp. 189–210.

Casanova, M. (2013) *Le lapis-lazuli du l'orient ancient: production et circulation du néolithique au IIe millénaire av. J.-C.*, Paris, Éditions du Comité des travaux historiques et scientifiques (CTHS Documents préhistoriques 27).

Chakrabarti, D. K. (1978) 'Lapis lazuli in Early India' *Man and Environment*, 2: 51–58.

Chakrabarti, D. K. (1993) 'Long-barrel-cylinder beads and the issue of Pre-Sargonic contact between the Harappan Civilization and Mesopotamia' in Possehl, G. L. (ed.), *Harappan Civilization: A Recent Perspective*, second edition, New Delhi, Oxford and IBH Publishing, pp. 265–270.

Chakrabarti, D. K. (1995) *India: An Archaeological History*, New Delhi, Oxford University Press.

Chakrabarti, D. K. and Lahiri, N. (1996) *Copper and its Alloys in Ancient India*, New Delhi, Munshiram Manoharlal.

Chaplin, A. P. and Pareja, M.-N. (2020) 'Peacocks or Poppycock? Investigations into exotic animal imagery in Minoan and Cycladic Art' in Davis, B. and Laffineur, R. (eds), Νεωτερος. *Studies in Bronze Age Aegean Art and Archaeology in Honor of Professor John G. Younger on the Occasion of his Retirement*, Leuven-Liège, Peeters Publishers (*Aegaeum* 44), pp. 215–226.

Childe, V. G. (1936) 'The Axes from Maikop and Caucasian metallurgy' *Liverpool Annals of Archaeology and Anthropology*, 23: 113–119.

Cierny, J. and Weisgerber, G. (2003) 'The Bronze Age tin mines in Central Asia' in Giumlia-Mair, A. and Lo Schiavo, F. (eds), *Le problème de l'étain à l'origine de la métallurgie/The Problem of Early Tin*, Oxford, Archaeopress (*British Archaeological Reports International Series* 1199), pp. 23–31.

Clayden, T. (2019) *Blue - Lapis and Glass in Kassite Babylonia.* Lecture given to the Egyptology and Ancient Near Eastern Studies Seminar of the Oriental Institute of the University of Oxford, 19 February 2019.

Cleuziou, S. and Berthold, T. (1982) 'Early tin in the Near East' *Expedition*, 25: 14–19.

Cline, E. H. (1994) *Sailing the Wine-Dark Sea: International Trade and the Late Bronze Age Aegean*, Oxford, Tempus Reparatum (*British Archaeological Reports International Series* 591).

Cline, E. H. (2007) 'Rethinking Mycenaean International Trade with Egypt and the Near East' in Galaty, M. L. and Parkinson, W. A. (eds), *Rethinking Mycenaean Palaces II*, revised and expanded second edition, Los Angeles, Cotsen Institute of Archaeology, University of California (Monograph 50), pp. 190–200.

Cohen, M. (1975) 'Ur.sag.me.sar.ur4' *Die Welt des Orients*, 8: 22–36.

Colburn, C. S. (2008) 'Exotica and the Early Minoan elite: eastern imports in Pre-Palatial Crete' *American Journal of Archaeology*, 112: 203–224.

Colburn, C. S. (2012) 'Bodily adornment in the Early Bronze Age Aegean and Near East' in Nosch, M.-L. and Laffineur, R. (eds), *Kosmos, Jewellery, Adornment and Textiles in the Aegean Bronze Age*, Leuven, Peeters (*Aegaeum* 33), pp. 369–378.

Collon, D. (2008) 'The Aegina Treasure: Near Eastern Connections' in Fitton, J. L. (ed.), *The Aegina Treasure: Aegean Bronze Age Jewellery and a Mystery Revisited*, London, British Museum Press, pp. 43–45.

Coningham, R. and Young, R. (2015) *The Archaeology of South Asia: From the Indus to Asoka, c.6500 BCE to 200 CE*, Cambridge, Cambridge University Press.

Cullen, H. M. and Demenocal, P. B. (2000) 'North Atlantic influence on Tigris–Euphrates streamflow' *International Journal of Climatology*, 20: 853–863.

Cullen, H. M., Kaplan, A. and Arkin, P. A. (2002) 'Impact of the North Atlantic Oscillation on Middle Eastern climate and streamflow' *Climate Change*, 55: 315–338.

Dales, G. F. (1968) 'The South Asia Section' *Expedition*, 11: 38–45.

Dales, G. F. and Kenoyer, J. M. (1986) *Excavations at Mohenjo Daro, Pakistan: The Pottery* (with an account of the pottery from the 1950 excavations by Sir Mortimer Wheeler, by Leslie Alcock), Philadelphia, University Museum, University of Philadelphia (*University Museum Monographs* 53).

Damick, A. and Woodworth, M. (2015) 'Steatite beads from Tell Fadous-Kfarabida: A case study in Early Bronze Age technology in Northern Coastal Lebanon' *Journal of Archaeological Science: Reports*, 3: 603–614.

Dani, A. H., Higashi, Y., Bunkja, A. and Senta, K. (1986) *The Historic City of Taxila*, Tokyo, Centre for East Asian Cultural Studies and Paris, UNESCO.

Dar, S. (1984) *Taxila and the Western World*, Lahore, l-Wagar Publishers.

Davaras, C. (1975) 'Early Minoan Jewellery from Mochlos' *Annual of the British School at Athens*, 70: 101–114.

Davaras, C. (2003) *Parallels and Affinities between Crete and India in the Bronze Age: some speculations*, Amsterdam, Adolf Hakkert (*Cretan Studies* Supplementum 1).

Davaras, C. (2005) 'Bronze Age Crete and India' *Indian Historical Review*, 32: 126–139.

David, H. S. (1956) 'Some further contacts and affinities between Egypto-Minoan and the Indo-Dravido-Sumerian Culture' *Indian Culture*, 4: 56–65.

Dayalan, D. (2019) *The Origin of Silk Production.* Unpublished manuscript, New Delhi, Archaeological Survey of India.

Dayton, J. E. (1971) 'The problem of tin in the ancient world' *World Archaeology*, 3: 49–70.

Dayton, J. E. (2003) 'The problem of tin in the ancient world (Part 2)' in Giumlia-Mair, A. and Lo Schiavo, F. (eds), *Le problème de l'étain à l'origine de la métallurgie/The Problem of Early Tin*, Oxford, Archaeopress (*British Archaeological Reports International Series*, 1199), pp. 165–170.

Delmas, A. B. and Casanova, M. (1990) 'The lapis lazuli sources in the Ancient Near East' in Taddei, M. (ed.), *South Asian Archaeology 1987*, Rome, Istituto Italiano per il Medio ed Estremo Oriente, pp. 493–505.

Delougaz, P. (1952) *Pottery from the Diyala Region*, Chicago, University of Chicago Oriental Institute.

Demakopoulou, K. (1966) *The Aidonia Treasure: Seals and Jewellery of the Aegean Late Bronze Age*, Athens, Ministry of Culture (exhibition catalogue).

Demakopoulou, K. (ed.) (1988) *The Mycenaean World: Five Centuries of Early Greek Culture, 1600–1100 BC*, Athens, Ministry of Culture/ICOM (exhibition catalogue).

Demand, N. (2011) *The Mediterranean Context of Early Greek History*, Chichester, Wiley Blackwell.

Devine, A. M. (1987) 'The Battle of Hydaspes: a tactical and source-critical study' *Ancient World*, 1, 16: 91–113.

Dickinson, O. (2006) *The Aegean from Bronze Age to Iron Age: Continuity and Change Between the Twelfth and Eighth Centuries BC*, London, Routledge.

Dihle, A. (1987) 'Dionysos in Indien' in Pollet, G. (ed.), *India and the Ancient World: History, Trade and Culture before A.D. 650* (Professor P. H. L. Eggermont Jubilee Volume, presented on the occasion of his seventieth birthday), Leuven, Department of Oriëntalistiek (*Orientalia Lovaniensia Analecta* 25), pp. 47–57.

Dihle, A. (1990) 'Arabien and Indien' in Nenci, G. and Reverdin, O. (eds), *Hérodote et les peoples non-grecs*, Vandoeuvres-Geneva, Fondation Hardt, (*Entretiens sue l'Antiquité Classique* Volume 35), pp. 41–68.

Dikaios, P. (1953) *Khirokitia*. Oxford, Oxford University Press.

Dikshit, K. N. and Mani, B. R. (2013) 'The origin of Indian civilization buried under sands of the "lost" River Saraswati' *Dialogue*, 15: 47–59.

Dixit, Y., Hodell, D. A. and Petrie, C. (2014) 'Abrupt weakening of the summer monsoon in northwest India ~4100 yr ago' *Geology*, 42: 339–342.

Dörpfeld, W. (1927) *Alt-Ithaka: ein Beitrag zur Homer-Frage, Studien und Ausgrabungen aus der insel Leukas-Ithaka*, Munich, R. Uhde.

Dossin, G. (1970) 'La route de l'étain en Mésopotamie au temps de Zimri Lim' *Revue d'Assyriologie et d'archaéologie orientale*, 64: 97–106.

Doumas, C. (1992) *The Wall-Paintings of Thera*, Athens, The Thera Foundation.

Drews, R. (1973) *Greek Accounts of Near Eastern History*, Cambridge, Yale University Press.

Drews, R. (1988) *The Coming of the Greeks: Indo-European Conquests in the Aegean and the Near East*, Princeton, Princeton University Press.

Duff, P. (2012) *Dancing with Bulls: An Exploration of Indus Iconography Showing Dynamic Interaction Between Humans and Bulls*, Unpublished dissertation, University of Cambridge.

Dunand, M. (1937) *Fouilles de Byblos I*, Paris, P. Geuthner.

Dupree, L. (1981) 'Notes on Shortugai: a Harappan site in Northern Afghanistan' in Dani, A. (ed.), *Indus Civilization: New Perspectives*, Islamabad, Centre for the Study of the Civilization of Central Asia, Quaid-i-Azam University, pp. 103–115.

Duhoux, Y. (2008) *A Companion to Linear B: Mycenaean Greek and their World*, Volume 1, Louvain-la-Neuve, Peeters (*BCILL* 120).

During Caspers, E. C. (1985) 'A possible Harappan contact with the Aegean world' in Schotsmans, J. and Taddei, M. (eds), *South Asian Archaeology 1983*, Naples, Istituto Universitario Orientale, Dipartimento di Asiatici (*Series Minor* XXIII), pp. 435–452.

Edens, C. (1992) 'Dynamics of trade in the ancient Mesopotamian world system' *American Anthropologist*, 94: 118–139.

Eggermont, P. H. L. (1956) *The Chronology of the Reign of Asoka Moriya: A Comparison of the Data of the Asoka Inscriptions and the Data of the Tradition*, Leiden, E. J. Brill.

Effinger, M. (1996) *Minoischer Schmuck*, Oxford, Tempus Reparatum (*British Archaeological Reports International Series* 645).

Evans, Sir A. (1921) *The Palace of Minos at Knossos*, Volume I, London, Macmillan.

Fábri, C. L. (1937) 'The Cretan Bull grappling sport and the bull sacrifice and the Indus valley civilisation' in Blakiston J. F. (ed.), *Annual Report of the Archaeological Survey of India 1935–1936*, Delhi, Government of India, pp. 93–101.

Fairservis, W. A. (1975) *The Roots of Ancient India: The Archaeology of Early Indian Civilisation*, Chicago, University of Chicago Press.

Falkenstein, A. (1964) 'Sumerische religiöse Texte' *Zeitschrift für Assyriologie* (NF), 56: 44–129.

Falkenstein, A. (1966) *Die Inschriften Gudeas von Lagaš*, Volume I, *Einleitung*, Rome, Pontificium Institutum Biblicum.

Felten, F. (2007) 'Aegina-Kolonna: the history of a Greek acropolis' in Felten F., Gauss, W. and Smetana, R., *Middle Helladic Pottery and Synchronisms: proceedings of the International Workshop held at Salzburg, October 31st–November 2nd, 2004*, Vienna, Österreichische Akademie der Wissenschaften (*Ägina-Kolonna. Forschungen und Ergebnisse* 1), pp. 11–34.

Felten, F. (2008) 'Aegina-Kolonna in the Early and Middle Bronze Age' in Fitton, J. L. (ed.), *The Aegina Treasure: Aegean Bronze Age Jewellery and a Mystery Revisited*, London, British Museum Press, pp. 32–35.

Fitton, J. L., Meeks, N. and Joyner, L. (2008) 'The Aegina Treasure: Catalogue and Technical Report' in Fitton, J. L. (ed.), *The Aegina Treasure: Aegean Bronze Age Jewellery and a Mystery Revisited*, London, British Museum Press.

Foster, B. R. (1997) 'A Sumerian merchant's account of the Dilmun trade' *Acta Sumerologica Japonica*, 19: 53–62.

Foster, K. P. (1979) *Aegean Faience of the Bronze Age*, New Haven, Yale University Press.

Frahm, E. and Feinberg, J. M. (2013) 'Environment and collapse: Eastern Anatolian obsidians at Urkesh (Tell Mozan, Syria) and the third millennium Mesopotamian urban crisis' *Journal of Archaeological Science*, 40: 1866–1878.

Francfort, H.-P. (1984) 'The Harappan Settlement of Shortugai' in Lal, B. B. and Gupta, S. P. (eds), *Frontiers of the Indus Civilization* (Sir Mortimer Wheeler Commemoration Volume), New Delhi, Books and Books (on behalf of the Indian Archaeological Society, jointly with the Indian History and Culture Society), pp. 301–310.

Francfort, H.-P. (1989) *Fouilles de Shortughai, Recherches sur L'Asie Centrale Protohistorique*, two volumes, Paris, Diffusion de Boccard (Mission archéologique française en Asie centrale).

Frank, A. G. (1993) 'Bronze Age world system cycles' (and comments and reply), *Current Anthropology*, 34: 383–429.

Fritz, K. von (1967) *Die griechische Geschichtsschreibung*, two volumes, Berlin, De Gruyter.

Franke-Vogt, U. (1993) 'The Harappans and the West: some reflections on Meluhha's relations to Magan, Dilmun and Mesopotamia' *Bulletin of Archaeology, University of Kanazawa*, 20: 72–97.

Fuller, D. Q. (2008) 'The spread of textile production and textile crops in India beyond the Harappan zone: an aspect of the emergence of craft specialisation and systematic trade' in Osada, T. and Uesugi, A. (eds), *Linguistics, Archaeology and the Human Past*, 2008, Kyoto, Research Institute for Humanity and Nature (Occasional Paper 3), pp. 1–26.

Furumark, A. (1972) *Mycenaean Pottery I: Analysis and Classification*, Stockholm, Swedish Institute in Athens (*Acta Instituti Atheniensis Regni Sueciae*, series in 4°, XX:1) (reprint of 1941 edition).

Gadd, C. J. and Smith, S. (1924) 'The new links between Indian and Babylonian civilisation' *Illustrated London News*, 4 October 1924, pp. 614–616.

Gardiner-Garden, J. R. (1987) *Ktesias on Early Central Asian History and Ethnography*, Bloomington, Indiana University Research Institute for Inner Asian Studies.

Gaul, J. (1948) *The Neolithic Period in Bulgaria*, Cambridge, Mass., Peabody Museum of Harvard University (American School of Prehistoric Research, *Bulletin* 16).

Gernez, G. (2007) *Des armes et des hommes. La question des modèles de diffusion des armes au Proche-orient à l'âge du Bronze. Mobilités, immobilismes. L'emprunt et son refus*, Paris, De Boccard/Maison René-Ginouvès.

Gershevitch, I. (1957) 'Sissoo at Susa: (Opers. yakā = *Dalbergia sissoo* Roxb.)' *Bulletin of the School of Oriental and African Studies*, 19: 317–320.

Giardino, C. (2019) *Magan – The Land of Copper: Prehistoric Metallurgy of Oman*, Muscat, Ministry of Heritage and Culture.

Gill, D. W. J. (2000) 'Collecting for Cambridge: John Hubert Marshall on Crete' *Annual of the British School at Athens*, 95: 517–526.

Gisinger, F. (1923) 'Scylax' in *Paulys Real-Encyclopädie der classischen Altertumswissenschaft (Neue Bearbeitung/unter Mitwirkung zahlreicher Fachgenossen herausgegeben von G. Wissowa*, Munchen, Alfred Druckenmuller, volume 5A, pp. 619–646.

Goldman, H. (1931) *Excavations at Eutresis in Boeotia*, Cambridge Mass., Harvard University Press.

Good, I. L. (2006) 'Textiles as a medium of exchange in third millennium BCE Western Asia' in Mair, V. H. (ed.), *Contact and Exchange in the Ancient World*, Honolulu, University of Hawai'i Press, pp. 191–214.

Good, I. L., Kenoyer, J. M. and Meadow, R. H. (2009) 'New evidence for early silk in the Indus Civilisation' *Archaeometry*, 51: 457–466.

Groom, N. (1981) *Frankincense and Myrrh: A Study of the Arabian Incense Trade*, London, Longmann.

Guha, S. (2005) 'Negotiating Evidence: history, archaeology and the Indus Civilisation' *Modern Asian Studies*, 39: 399–426.

Guichard, M. (1999) 'Les mentions de la Crète à Mari'. *L'Acrobat au Taureau. Les découvertes de Tell el-Dab'a et l'archaèologie de la Mèditerranean orientale*, Paris, La Documentation Française, pp. 165–177.

Gupta, S. P. (1993) 'The Late Harappan: a study in cultural dynamics' in Possehl, G. L. (ed.), *Harappan Civilisation: A Recent Perspective*, second edition, New Delhi, Oxford and IBH Publishing (for the American *Institute of Indian Studies)*, pp. 51–59.

Haas-Lebegyev, J. and Renfrew, C. (2013) 'The other finds at Dhaskalio, Section E: Other finds of stone' in Renfrew, C., Philaniotou, O., Brodie, N., Gavalas, G. and Boyd, M. J. (eds), *The Settlement of Dhaskalio: Volume I: The Sanctuary on Keros and the Origins of Aegean Ritual Practice: The Excavations of 2006-2008*, Cambridge, McDonald Institute Monographs, pp. 662–665

Hall, M. E. and Steadman, S. R. (1991) 'Tin and Anatolia: another look' *Journal of Mediterranean Archaeology*, 4: 217–234.

Hansman, J. (1973) 'A Periplus of Magan and Meluhha' *Bulletin of the School of Oriental and African Studies* 36: 553–587.

Hansman, J. (1975) 'A further note on Magan and Meluhha (Notes and Communications)' *Bulletin of the School of Oriental and African Studies*, 38: 609–610.

Hegde, K. (1983) 'The art of the Harappan microbead' *Archaeology*, 36(3): 68, 70, 72.

Hegde, K., Karanth, R. V. and Sychanthavong, S. P. (1993) 'On the composition and technology of Harappan Microbeads' in Possehl, G. L. (ed.), *Harappan Civilisation: A Recent Perspective*, second edition, New Delhi, Oxford and IBH Publishing (for *the American Institute of Indian Studies)*, pp. 239–244.

Heimpel. W. (1987) 'Das Untere Meer' *Zeitschrift für Assyriologie*, 77: 22–91.

Hermann, G. (1968) 'Lapis Lazuli: the early phases of its trade' *Iraq*, 30: 21–57.

Heskel, D. L. (1984) Iran-Indus Valley Connections: a revaluation' in Lal, B. B. and Gupta, S. P. (eds), *Frontiers of the Indus Civilization* (Sir Mortimer Wheeler Commemoration Volume), New Delhi, Books and Books (on behalf of the Indian Archaeological Society, jointly with the Indian History and Culture Society).

Hiebert, F. T. (2000) 'Black Sea Coastal Cultures: trade and interaction' *Expedition*, 43: 11–20.

Higgins, R. (1980) *Greek and Roman Jewellery*, London, Methuen, second edition.

Higgins, R. (1981) *Minoan and Mycenaean Art*, revised edition, London, Thames and Hudson.

Hiller, S. and Panagl, O. (1976) *Die frühgriechischen Texte aus mykenischer Zeit: zur Erforschung der Linear B-Tafeln*, Darmstadt, Wissenschaftliche Buchgesellschaft (*Erträge der Forschung*).

Hoffman, B. C. and Miller, H. M.-L. (2014) 'Production and consumption of copper-base metals in the Indus Civilisation' in Roberts, B. W. and Thornton, C. P. (eds), *Archaeometallurgy in Global Perspective*, New York, Springer, pp. 697–727.

Holt, F. (2003) *Alexander the Great and the Mystery of the Elephant Medallions*, Berkeley, University of California Press.

Hood, S. (1978) *The Arts in Prehistoric Greece*, Harmondsworth, Penguin Books.

Hooijer, D. A. (1978) 'The Indian Elephant at Bronze Age Ras Shamra, Ugarit' in Schaffer, C. F.-A. (ed.), *Ugaritica 7*, (*Mission de Ras Shamra* XVIII), Paris, Librairie orientaliste Paul Geuthner (Mission archéologique de Ras Shamra), pp. 187–188.

Hughes-Brock, H. (1995) 'Seals and beads: their shapes and materials compared' in Müller, W. (ed.), *Sceaux Minoens et Mycéniens*, Berlin, Mann (*Corpus der minoischen und mykenischem Siegel* Beiheft 5), pp. 105–116.

Hughes-Brock, H. (1998) 'Beads in Early Crete' *Bead Society Trust*, 32: 3.

Hughes-Brock, H. (1999) 'Mycenaean beads: gender and social contexts' *Oxford Journal of Archaeology*, 18: 277–296.

Hughes-Brock, H. (2010) 'The many facets of seal research and the contribution of the CMS' in Müller, W. (ed.), *Die Bedeutung der minoischen und mykenischen Glyptik: VI. Internationales Siegel-Symposium aus Anlass des 50 jährigen Bestehens des Corpus der minoischen und mykenischem Siegel, Marburg, 9.-12. Oktober 2008, Corpus der minoischen und mykenischem Siegel,* Beiheft 8. Mainz, von Zabern, pp. 225–237.

Hughes-Brock, H. (2011) 'Exotic materials and objects sent to – and from? – the Bronze Age Aegean' in Vianello, A. (ed.), *Exotica in the Prehistoric Mediterranean*, Oxford, Oxbow Books, pp. 99–114.

Hughes-Brock, H. with Boardman, J. (2009) *Corpus der minoischen und mykenischem Siegel*, Band VI: Oxford, The Ashmolean Museum, Mainz, von Zabern.

Inizan, M.-L. (1995) 'Cornaline et agate: production et circulation de la préhistoire à nos jours' in Tallon, F. (ed.), *Les Pierres précieuses de l'Orient ancien des Sumériens aux Sassanides*, Paris, Editions de la Réunion des musées nationaux (*Musée du Louvre, Dossier du département des Antiquités orientales* 49), pp. 21–24.

Jablonka, P. (2018) '3rd millennium BC exchange networks between the Aegean and the Indus: connecting the dots on archaeological distribution Maps' in Ünsal, Y. (ed.), *Anatolian Metal VIII* (*Der ANSCHNITT*, Beiheft 39), Bochum, Deutsches Bergbau-Museum, 2018, pp. 139–166.

Jacoby, F. (1923) *Die Fragmente der griechischen Historiker*, Volume I, Berlin, Weidmannsche.

Jacoby, F. (1958) *Die Fragmente der griechischen Historiker*, Volume III.3, Leiden, E. J. Brill.

Joshi, J. P. (1978) 'Interlocking of Late Harappan Culture and Painted Grey Ware Culture in the light of recent excavations' *Man and Environment*, 2: 100–103.

Joshi, J. P. (1980) 'Excavation at Manda in District Jammu' in Thapar. B. K. (ed.), *Indian Archaeology 1976-1977: A Review*, New Delhi, Archaeological Survey of India (Government of India), pp. 19–21.

Joshi, J. P. and Bala, M. (1993) 'Manda: a Harappan site in Jammu and Kashmir' in Possehl, G. L. (ed.), *Harappan Civilisation: A Recent Perspective*, second edition, New Delhi, Oxford and IBH Publishing (for the American *Institute of Indian Studies)*, pp. 185–195.

Joshi, S. D. (1991) *The Aṣṭādhyāyī of Pāṇini with translation and explanatory notes*, New Delhi, Sahitya Akademi.

Karo, G. (1930–1933) *Die Schachtgräber von Mykenai*, Munich, Brockmann.

Karttunen, K. (1989) *India in Early Greek Literature*, Helsinki, Finnish Oriental Society (*Studia Orientalia* 65).

Karttunen, K. (2014) 'India and world trade: from the beginnings to the Hellenistic age' in Geller, M. J. (ed.), *Melammu. The Ancient World in an Age of Globalization*, Berlin, Max Planck Research Library for History and Development Studies, *Proceedings* 7 (Proceedings of the 6th Symposium of the Melammu Project, held in Sofia, Bulgaria, September 1–3, 2008), pp. 329–339.

Katre, S. M. (1987) *Astadhyayi of Panini*, Austin, University of Texas Press.

Kenna, V. E. G. and Thomas, E. (1974) *Corpus der minoischen und mykenischem Siegel, Band XIII, Nordamerika II: Kleine Sammalungen*, Berlin, Mann.

Kennedy, J. (1898) 'The Early Commerce of India with Babylon, 700–300 BC' *Journal of the Royal Asiatic Society*, 30: 241–288.

Kenoyer, J. M. (1989) 'Socio-economic structures of the Indus Civilization as reflected in specialized crafts and the question of ritual segregation' in Kenoyer, J. M. (ed.), *Old Problems and New Perspectives in the Archaeology of South Asia*, Madison, Department of Anthropology, University of Wisconsin-Madison (*Wisconsin Archaeological Reports*, vol. 2), pp. 183–192.

Kenoyer, J. M. (1991a) 'The Indus Valley tradition of Pakistan and Western India' *Journal of World Prehistory*, 5: 331–385.

Kenoyer, J. M. (1991b) 'Urban process in the Indus Tradition: a preliminary model from Harappa' in Meadow, R. H. (ed.), *Harappa Excavations 1986-1990: A Multidisciplinary Approach to Third Millennium Urbanism,* Madison, Prehistory Press (*Monographs in World Archaeology* No. 3), pp. 29–60.

Kenoyer, J. M. (1992) 'Ornament Styles of the Indus Tradition: evidence from recent excavations at Harappa, Pakistan' *Paleorient*, 17: 79–98.

Kenoyer, J. M. (1995) 'Interaction Systems, Specialized Crafts and Culture Change: the Indus Valley Tradition and the Indo-Gangetic traditions in South Asia' in Erdosy, G. (ed.), *The Indo-Aryans of Ancient South Asia: Language, Material Culture and Ethnicity*, Berlin, De Gruyter, pp. 213–257.

Kenoyer, J. M. (1997) 'Trade and technology of the Indus Valley: new insights from Harappa, Pakistan' *World Archaeology*, 29: 262–280.

Kenoyer, J. M. (1998) *Ancient Cities of the Indus Valley Civilisation*, Karachi, Oxford University Press/ American Institute of Pakistan Studies, pp. 126–127.

Kenoyer, J. M. (2003) 'Beads of the Indus Valley' in Aruz, J. (ed.), *Art of the First Cities: The Third Millennium BC from the Mediterranean to the Indus*, New York and New Haven, Metropolitan Museum of Art and Yale University Press, p. 398.

Kenoyer, J. M. (2008a) 'Indus and Mesopotamian trade networks: new insights from shell and carnelian artifacts' in Olijdam, E. and Spoor, R. H. (eds), *Intercultural Relations between South and Southwest Asia. Studies in Commemoration of E. C. L. During-Caspers (1934– 1996)*, Oxford, Archaeopress (*Society of Arabian Studies Monograph* No. 7; *British Archaeological Reports International* Series 1826), 19–28.

Kenoyer, J. M. (2008b) 'Indus urbanism: new perspectives on its origin and character' in Marcus, J. and Sabloff, J. A. (eds), *The Ancient City: New Perspectives on Urbanism in Old and New Worlds*, Santa Fe, School of Advanced Research Press, pp. 183–208.

Kenoyer, J. M. (2014) 'The Indus Civilisation' in Renfrew, C. and Bahn, P. (eds), *The Cambridge World Prehistory, Volume I: Africa, South and Southeast Asia and the Pacific*, Cambridge, Cambridge University Press, pp. 407–432.

Kenoyer, J. M., Vidale, M. and Bhan, K. K. (1994) 'Carnelian bead production in Khambhat India: an ethno-archaeological study' in Allchin, B. (ed.), *Living Traditions: Studies in the Ethnoarchaeology of South Asia*, Oxford, Oxbow Books.

Kenoyer, J. M. and Miller, H. M.-L. (1999) 'Metal technologies of the Indus Valley Tradition in Pakistan and Western India' in Pigott, V. C. (ed.), *The Archaeometallurgy of the Asian Old World*, Philadelphia, University Museum, University of Pennsylvania (University Museum Monograph 89), pp. 107–151.

Khan, I. (2016) 'Notes on war technology and military engineering in pre-modern India' *Studies in People's History*, 3: 1–9.

Kilian-Dirlmeier, I. (1984) *Nadeln der frühelladischen bis archaischen Zeit von der Peloponnes*, Munich, C. H. Beck'sche Verlagsbuchhandlung, (*Prähistorische Bronzefunde*, Abteilung XIII, Band 8).

Klengel, H. (1984) 'Near Eastern trade and the emergence of interaction with Crete in the third millennium BC' *Studi Micenei ed Egeo-Anatolici*, 24: 7–19

Kochhar, N., Kochhar, R. and Chakrabarti, D. K. (1999) 'A new source of primary tin ore on the Indus Civilization' *South Asian Studies*, 15: 115–118.

Korou, N. (2008) 'The evidence for the Aegean' in Sagona, C. (ed.), *Beyond the Homeland: Markers in Phoenician Chronology*, Leuven, Peeters (*Ancient Near Eastern Studies* Supplement 28), pp. 305–364.

Krzyszkowska, O. (1988) 'Ivory in the Aegean Bronze Age: Elephant Tusk or Hippopotamus Ivory?' *Annual of the British School at Athens*, 83: 209–234.

Krzyszkowska, O. (1990) *Ivory and Related Materials: An Illustrated Guide*, London, Institute of Classical Studies (*Classical Handbook* 3).

Krzyszkowska, O. (2003) 'The Seals' in Mountjoy, P. A., *Knossos: The South House*, London, British School at Athens (*Annual of the British School at Athens* Supplement 34), pp. 199–206.

Krzyszkowska, O. (2005) *Aegean Seals: An Introduction*, London, Institute of Classical Studies (*Bulletin of the Institute of Classical Studies*, Supplement 85).

Lahiri, N. (1992) *The Archaeology of Indian Trade Routes up to c.200 BC: Resource Use, Resource Access and Lines of Communication*, New Delhi, Oxford University Press.

Lahiri, N. (2005) *Finding Forgotten Cities - How the Indus Civilisation was Discovered*, London, Seagull Books.

Lamberg-Karlovsky, C. C. (1972) 'Trade mechanisms in Indus-Mesopotamian interrelations' *Journal of the American Oriental Society*, 92: 222–229.

Lambrou-Phillipson, C. (1990) *Hellenorientalia: The Near Eastern Presence in the Bronze Age Aegean. ca. 3000–1100 BC*, Göteborg, Åstrom (*Studies in Mediterranean Archaeology* Pocketbook 95).

Lauresen, S. and Steinkeller, P. (2017) *Babylonia, the Gulf Region and the Indus: Archaeological and Textual Evidence for Contact in the Third and Second Millennia BC*, Winona Lake, Eisenbrauns.

Law, R. (2006) 'Moving Mountains: the trade and transport of rocks and minerals within the Greater Indus Valley region' in Robertson, E. C., Seibert, J. D.; Fernandez, D. C. and Zender, M. U. (eds), *Space and Spatial Analysis in Archaeology*, Calgary, University of Calgary Press, pp. 301–313.

Law, R. (2014) 'Evaluating potential lapis lazi sources for ancient South Asia using sulful isotope analysis' in Lamberg-Karlovsky, C. C., Genito, B. and Cerasetti, B. (eds), *'My life is like a summer rose' Maurizio Tosi e l'archaeologia come modfo di vivere'* Oxford, Archaeopress (*British Archaeological Reports International Series 2690*), pp. 419–429.

Law, R., Carter, A., Bhan, K., Malik, A. and Glascock, M. D. (2013) 'INAA of agate sources and artifacts from the Indus, Helmand and Thailand regions' in Frenez, D. and Tosi, M. (eds), *South Asian Archaeology, 2007, Volume I: Prehistory*, Oxford, Archaeopress (*British Archaeological Reports International Series* 2454), pp. 177–184.

Lawler, A. (2012) 'The ingredients for a 4000-year-old proto-curry' *Science*, 337: 288.

Lawler, A. (2018) 'Migrants and trade spiced up Canaanite metropolis' *Science*, 62: 980–981.

Leemans, W. F. (1960) *Foreign Trade in the Old Babylonian Period as Revealed by Texts from Southern Mesopotamia*, Leiden, Brill.

Legrain, L. (1926) *Royal Inscriptions and Fragments from Nippur and Babylon*, Philadelphia, University of Pennsylvania Museum (Publications of the Babylonian Section, Volume 15).

Lenfant, D. (1995) 'L'Inde de Ctésias. Des sources aux représentations' *Topoi (Τόποι) orient-occident* (Societe des amis de la bibliotheque Salomon Reinach), 5: 307–336.

Lenfant, D. (2004) *Ctésias de Cnide. La Perse. L'Inde. Autres fragments*, Paris, Les Belles Lettres (Collection des Universités de France publiée sous le patronage de l'Association Guillaume Budé).

Leshnick, L. (1968) 'The Harappan Port Town at Lothal: another view' *American Anthropologist*, 70: 911–922.

Lipiński, E. (2004) *Itineraria Phoenicia*, Leuven, Peeters (*Orientalia Lovaniensia Analecta* 127/*Studia Phoenicia* 18).

Llewellyn-Jones, L. and Robson, J. E. (2012) *Ctesias' History of Persia: tales of the Orient*, London, Routledge.

Luci, K. (2007) 'Dating the Donja Brnjke Culture based on metal finds' in Todorova, H., Strefanovick, M. and Ivanov, G. (eds), *The Struma/Strymon River Valley in Prehistory (In the Steps of James Henry Gaul)* (Proceedings of the International Symposium *Strymon Praehistoricus*, Blagoevgrad/Serres, 22 September–1 October 2004), Volume 2, Sofia, Gerda Henkal Stieftung, pp. 347–358.

Ludvik, G. (2018) *Hard Stone Beads and Socio-Political Interaction in the Intermediate Bronze Age Southern Levant, ca. 2500–2000 BCE*, Unpublished PhD thesis, University of Wisconsin-Madison.

Ludvik, G., Kenoyer, J. M., Pieniażek, M. and Aylward, W. (2015) 'New perspectives on stone bead technology at Bronze Age Troy' *Anatolian Studies*, 65: 1–18.

Ludvik, G. E., Kenoyer, J. M. and Pieniążek, M. (2020) 'New evidence for interregional interaction in the 3rd millennium BCE Aegean: Indus-style carnelian beads at Aegina-Kolonna, Greece' *Paléorient*, 46: 161–178.

Lyonnet, B. (2005) 'Another possible interpretation of Bactro-Margiana culture (BMAC) of Central Asia: the tin trade' in Jarridge, C. and Lefèvre, V., *South Asian Archaeology 2001*, Paris, Éditions Recherche sur les Civilisations, pp. 191–200.
Mackay, E. J. H. (1925) 'Sumerian connections with Ancient India' *Journal of the Royal Asiatic Society of Great Britain and Ireland*, 4: 697–701.
Mackay, E. J. H. (1929) *A Sumerian Palace and the 'A' Cemetery at Kish, Mesopotamia*, Part II, Chicago, Field Museum of Natural History (*Anthropology Memoirs* I (2)).
Mackay, E. J. H. (1937) 'Bead-making in Ancient Sind' *Journal of the American Oriental Society*, 57: 1–15.
Mackay, E. J. H. (1938) *Further Excavations at Mohenjo-daro: being an official account of archaeological excavations at Mohenjo-daro carried out by the Government of India between the years 1927 and 1931*, Delhi, Government of India and Archaeological Survey of India.
Mackay, E. J. H. (1943) *Chanhu-daro Excavations, 1935-1936*, New Haven, Harvard University Press for American Oriental Society, American Society of Indic and Iranian Studies and the Museum of Fine Arts, Boston (American Oriental Series 20).
Mackay, E. J. H. (1948) *Early Indus Civilisations*, Luzac, Second Edition (revised by Dorothy Mackay).
Maisler, B. (Mazar) (1951) 'Two Hebrew Ostraca from Tell Qasile' *Journal of Near Eastern Studies*, 10: 265–277.
Malamat, A. (1971) 'Syro-Palestinian destinations in a Mari tin inventory' *Israel Exploration Journal*, 21: 31–38.
Mallowan, M. E. L. (1947) 'Excavations at Brak and Chagar Bazar' *Iraq*, 9: 1–259.
Marangou, L. (ed.) (1990) *Cycladic Culture: Naxos in the 3rd Millennium BC*, Athens, Nicholas P. Goulandris Foundation - Museum of Cycladic Art.
Marshall, F. H. (1911) *Catalogue of Jewellery, Greek, Etruscan and Roman in the Departments of Antiquities, British Museum*, London, Trustees of the British Museum.
Marshall, Sir J. (1924a) 'First light on a long forgotten civilisation: new discoveries of an unknown prehistoric past in India' *Illustrated London News*, 20 September 1924, pp. 528–534, 548.
Marshall, Sir J. (1924b) 'Exploration and Research, Harappa and Mohenjo-daro', in Marshall, Sir J. (ed.), *Annual Report of the Archaeological Survey of India, 1923-24*, Delhi, Government of India, pp. 47–51.
Marshall, Sir J. (1931) *Mohenjo-daro and the Indus Civilisation, being an official account of the archaeological excavations at Mohenjo-daro carried out by the Government of India between the years 1922 and 1927*, three volumes, London, Arthur Probsthain.
Marshall, Sir J. (1951) *Taxila: an illustrated account of archaeological excavations carried out at Taxila under the orders of the Government of India between the years 1913 and 1934*, three volumes, Cambridge, Cambridge University Press.
Massa, M. and Palmisano, A. (2018a) 'Change and continuity in the long-distance exchange networks between western/central Anatolia, northern Levant and northern Mesopotamia, c.3200–1.600 BC' *Journal of Anthropological Archaeology*, 49: 65–87.
Massa, M. and Palmisano, A. (2018b) 'Commercial landscapes of long-distance contacts in Western Asia, c.3200–1600 BC: perspectives from material culture' *Journal of Open Archaeology Data*, 3 (DOI: https://doi.org/10.5334/joad.45).
Masson, V. M. (1988) *Altyn-Depe*, Philadelphia, University Museum (*University Museum Monograph* no. 55).
Mathur, U. B. (2002) 'Chronology of Harappan port towns of Gujarat in the light of sea level changes during the Holocene' *Man and Environment*, 27(2): 61–67.
Maxwell-Hyslop, K. R. (1971) *Western Asiatic Jewellery, c.3000-612 BC*, London, Methuen.
Maxwell-Hyslop, K. R. (1983) '*Dalbergia sisso* Roxburgh' *Anatolian Studies*, 33: 67–72.
Mayrhoffer, M. (1966) *Indo-Arier im Altern Vorderasien* (mit einer analytischen Bibliographie), Wiesbaden, Harraassowitz.

McCown, D. E. (1942) *The Comparative Stratigraphy of Early Iran*, Chicago, Oriental Institute (*Studies in Ancient Oriental Civilization* number 23).

McCrindle, J. W. (after St Photius I, Patriarch of Constantinople (c.820–891)) (1882) *Ancient India as described by Ktêsias the Knidian, a translation of the abridgement of his 'Indika' by Phôtios and of the fragments of that work preserved in other writers* (Reproduced with additions, from the *Indian Antiquary*), London, Trübner; Calcutta, Thacker, Spink and Co.; Bombay, B. E. S. Press.

Meadow, R. H. (1991) 'The domestication and exploitation of plants and animals in the Greater Indus Valley, 7th–2nd millennium BC' in Jansen, M., Mulloy, M. and Urban, G. (eds), *Forgotten Cities on the Indus: Early Civilisation in Pakistan from the 8th to the 2nd millennium BC*, Mainz, Verlag Philipp von Zabern, pp. 51–65.

Meadow, R. H. (1996) 'The origins and spread of agriculture and pastoralism in Northwestern South Asia' in Harris, D. R. (ed.), *The Origins and Spread of Agriculture and Pastoralism in Eurasia*, London, UCL Press, pp. 390–412.

Mendleson, C. (1983) 'More Monkey Business' *Anatolian Studies*, 33: 81–83.

Menon, J. (2014) 'The transmission of craft technologies in the Bronze Age' *Studies in People's History*, 1: 127–141.

Mery, S. (1996) 'Ceramics and patterns of exchange across the Arabian Sea and the Persian Gulf in the Early Bronze Age' *Colloquia*, 32: 167–179.

Meyer, C., Todd, J. M., and Beck, C. W. (1991) 'From Zanzibar to Zagros: A Copal Pendant from Eshnunna' *Journal of Near Eastern Studies*, 50: 296–297.

Miller, H. J. (2013) 'Spiraling Interconnections: a fresh look at spiral-double-headed pins in the Indian Subcontinent' in Abraham, S. A., Gullapalli, P., Raczek, T. P. and Rizvi, U. (eds), *Connection and Complexity: New Approaches to the Archaeology of South Asia*, Walnut Creek, Left Coast Press, pp. 223–238.

Mode, H. (1944) *Indische Frühkulturen und ihre Beziehungen zum Westen*, Basel, Benno Schwabe.

Mode, H. (1959) 'The Harappa Culture and the West' *Our Heritage*, 7: 59–70.

Mode, H. (1961) *The Harappa Culture and the West*, Calcutta, Sanskrit College (*Calcutta Sanskrit College Research Series*, No. XVI).

Montero Fenollós, J.-L. (2019) 'Mari and the use of tin within the context of the Near East during the 3rd and 2nd millennia BC' *Oriens Antiquus* (n.s.), 1: 121–126.

Moorey, P. R. S. (1994) *Ancient Mesopotamian Materials and Industries: The Archaeological Evidence*, Oxford, Oxford University Press.

Moran, W. L. (1992) *The Amarna Letters*, Baltimore, Johns Hopkins University Press.

Morgenstierne, G. (1974) 'Early Iranic Influence upon Indo-Aryan' in *Acta, I. série, Commemoration Cyrus.* Vol. I. *Hommage universel, Pahlavi*, Tehran, Bibliothèque Pahlavi, pp. 271–279.

Moutsiou, T. (2021) 'Maritime connections in Eastern Mediterranean prehistory' Paper presented to the Public Lecture Series of the Archaeological Research Unit of the University of Cyprus on 27 September 2021.

Mughal, D. M. R. (1990) 'The decline of the Indus Civilization and the Late Harappan period in the Indus Valley' *Lahore Museum Bulletin*, 3: 1–17.

Muhly, J. D. (1973) 'Copper and Tin' *Transactions of the Connecticut Academy of Arts and Sciences*, 43: 155–535. (Reprinted as Copper and Tin, New Haven, Archon Books, 1963, with 'Supplement to Copper and Tin' *Transactions of the Connecticut Academy of Arts and Sciences*, 1976, 46: 77–136).

Muhly, J. D. (1983) 'Gold analysis and the sources of gold in the Aegean' *Temple University Aegean Symposium*, 8: 1–14.

Muhly, J. D. (1985) 'Sources of tin and the beginnings of bronze metallurgy, *American Journal of Aeology*, 89: 275–291.

Müller, W., Pini, I. and Sakellariou, A. (2007) *Corpus der minoischen und mykenischem, Band III.2, Siegel Iraklion, Archäologisches Museum. Sammlung Giamalakis.* Mainz, Philipp von Zabern.

Murray, A. S., Smith, A. H. and Walters, H. B. (1900) *Excavations in Cyprus*, London, Trustees of the British Museum.

Musche, B. (1992) *Vorderasiatischer Schmuck von den Anfängen bis zur Zeit der Achaemeniden (ca. 10,000–330 v. Chr.)*, Leiden, Brill (*Handbuch der Orientalistik. Abt. Kunst und Archäologie*, Volume 1 *Der alter Vordere Orient*, Part 2B/5).

Nath, J. and Kumaran, R. N. (2017) 'Khirsara – a Harappan metropolis in Western Kachchh, Gujarat, India' *Heritage: Journal of Multidisciplinary Studies in Archaeology*, 5: 541–555.

Nenci, G. (1954) *Hecataei Milesii Fragmanta*, Florence, Nuova Italia.

Nichols, A. (2011) *Ctesias on India: Introduction, Translation and Commentary*, London, Bristol Classical Press.

Oates, D. (1977) 'The Excavations at Tell Brak 1976' *Iraq*, 39: 233–244.

Özgüç, N. (1968) *Kanis Karumu Ib kati mühürleri ve mühür baskilari / Seals and Seal Impressions of Level IB from Karum Kanish*, Ankara, Türk Tarih Kurumu Basımevi, (*Türk Tarih Kurumu yayınlarından* 5), pp. 53–58.

Olijdam, E. (1997) 'Babylonian quest for lapis lazuli and Dilmun during the City III period' in Allchin, R. and Allchin, B. (eds), *South Asian Archaeology 1995*, New Delhi, Oxford and IBH Publishing (for the Ancient India and Iran Trust), pp. 119–125.

Oppenheim, A. L. (1954) 'The seafaring merchants of Ur' *Journal of the American Oriental Society*, 74: 6–17.

Oppenheim, A. L. (1964) *Mesopotamia: Portrait of a Dead Civilisation*, Chicago, Chicago University Press.

Pande, B. M. (1971a) 'A Note on the Harappan Ring-Kernoi' in Ganesan, S., Rajam, S., Ramaswami, N. S. and Sampath, M. D. (eds), *Professor K. A. Nilakanta Sastri Felicitation Volume*, Madras, K. A. Nilakanta Sastri Felicitation Committee, pp. 231–233.

Pande, B. M. (1971b) 'Harappan Ring-Kernoi: a study' *East and West*, new series 21: 311–323.

Panagiotakopulu, E., Buckland, P. C., Day, P. M., Doumas, C., Sarpakli, A. and Skidmore, P. (1997) 'A lepidopterous cocoon from Thera and evidence for silk in the Aegean Bronze Age' *Antiquity*, 71: 420–429.

Pandya, S. (1977) 'Lothal dockyard hypothesis and sea level changes' in Agrwal, D. P. and Pande, B. M. (eds), *Ecology and Archaeology of Western India*, Delhi, Concept, pp. 99–103.

Pareja, M. N., McKinney, T., Mayhew, J. A., Nash, S. D. and Heaton, R. (2020) 'A new identification of the monkeys depicted in a Bronze Age wall painting from Akrotiri, Thera' *Primates*, 61: 159–168

Parpola, A. (2015) *The Roots of Hinduism: The Early Aryans and the Indus Civilization*, Oxford, Oxford University Press.

Parpola, S. (1975) 'On the relationship of the Sumerian toponym Meluhha and Sanskrit mleccha' *Studia Orientalia*, 46: 205–238.

Parpola, S., Parpola, A. and Brunswig, R. H. Jr. (1977) 'The Meluḫḫa Village: evidence of acculturation of Harappan traders in late third millennium Mesopotamia?' *Journal of the Economic and Social History of the Orient*, 20: 129–165.

Peissel, M. (1984) *The Ant's Gold: The Discovery of the Greek El Dorado in the Himalayas*, London, Harvill Press.

Pendlebury, J. D. S. (1939) *The Archaeology of Crete: An Introduction*, London, Methuen.

Penhallurick, R. D. (1986) *Tin in Antiquity: Its Mining and Trade Throughout the Ancient World with Particular Reference to Cornwall*, London, Institute of Metals.

Pernicka, E. (1995) 'Gewinnung und Verbreitung der Metalle in prähistorische Zeit' *Jahrbuch des RGZM, Mainz*, 37: 21–134.

Pernicka, E., Begemann, F., Schmitt-Strecker, S. and Grimianis, A. P. (1990) 'On the composition and provenance of metal objects from Poliochni on Lemnos' *Oxford Journal of Archaeology*, 9: 263–298.

Perrin, B. (1900) 'Alexander' in *Plutarch: Parallel Lives*, Volume VII, (Loeb Classical Press) Cambridge Mass., Harvard University Press.

Petrie, C. A. (2017) 'Crisis, what Crisis? Adaption, resilience and transformation in the Indus Civilisation' in Cunningham, T. and Driesen, J. (eds), *Crisis to Collapse: The Archaeology of Social Breakdown*, Louvain, Presses universitaires de Louvain, pp. 43–64.

Petrie, C. A. and Singh Ravindra, N., Bates, J., Dixit, Y., French, C. A. I., Hodell, D. A., Jones, P. J., Lancelotti, C., Lynam, F., Neogi, S., Pandey, A., Parikh, D., Pawar, V., Redhouse, D. I. and Singh, D. P. (2017) 'Adaption to Variable Environments, Resilience to Climate Change: Investigating Land, Water and Settlement in Indus Northwest India' *Current Anthropology*, 58: 1–30.

Peyronel, S. L. (2015) 'A Long-Barrel Carnelian Bead from Ebla. A new evidence for long distance contacts between the Indus Valley and the Near East' in Matthiae, P. (ed.), *Studia Eblaitca* (Studies on the Archaeology, History and Philology of Ancient Syria), Volume 1, Wiesbaden, Harrassowitz Verlag, pp. 217–220.

Pfälzner, P. (2013) 'The elephant hunts of Bronze Age Syria' in Aruz, J., Graff, S. and Rakic, Y. (eds), *Cultures in Contact: From Mesopotamia to the Mediterranean in the Second Millennium B.C.*, New York, Metropolitan Museum of Art/Yale University Press, pp. 112–131.

Pickard, C. and Schoop, U.-D. (2011) 'Characterization of late Chalcolithic microbeads from Çamblibel Tarlasi, North-Central Anatolia' *Archaeometry*, 55: 14–32.

Piggott, S. (1948) 'Notes on certain pins and a mace-head in the Harappā culture' *Ancient India*, 4: 26–40.

Piggott, S. (1950) *Prehistoric India to 1000 BC*, Harmondsworth, Penguin Books.

Pini, I., Caskey, J. L., Caskey, M., Pelon O., Heath-Wiencke, M. and Younger, J. G. (1975) *Corpus der minoischen und mykenischem Siegel*, Band V:2, *Kleinere griechische Sammlungen*, Berlin, Mann.

Pinnock, F. (1988) 'Observations on the trade of lapis lazuli in the third millennium BC' in Waetzoldt, Ha. and Haupmann, H. (eds), *Wirtschaft und Gesellschaft von Ebla: Akten der Internationalen Tagung, Heidelberg, 4–7 November 1986*, Heidelberg, Heidelberger Orientverlag (*Heidelberger Studien zum alten Orient* 2), pp. 107–110.

Piperno, M. and Tosi, M. (1975) 'The Graveyard of Shahr-I Sokhta' *Archaeology*, 28: 186–197.

Platon, N. (1969) *Corpus der minoischen und mykenischem Siegel* Band II:1, *Iraklion Archäologisches Museum, Die Siegel der Vorpalastzeit*, Berlin, Mann.

Platon, N. and Pini, I. (1984) *Corpus der minoischen und mykenischem Siegel*, Band II:3, *Iraklion, Archäologisches Museum: Die Siegel der Neupalastzeit*, Berlin, Mann.

Platon, N., Pini, I. and Salies, G. (1969) *Corpus der minoischen und mykenischem Siegel*, Band II:2 *Iraklion, Archäologisches Museum: Die Siegel der Altpalastzeit*, Berlin, Mann.

Pokharia, A. K., Agnihotri, R., Sharma, S., Bajpai, S., Nath, J., Kumaran, R. N. and Negi, B.C. (2017) 'Altered cropping pattern and cultural continuation with declined prosperity following abrupt and extreme arid event at ~4,200 yrs BP: Evidence from an Indus archaeological site Khirsara, Gujarat, western India' *Plos One*, 12(10): e0185684.

Porada, E. (1981–1982) 'Cylinder Seals Found at Thebes in Boeotia' *Archiv für Orientforschung*, 28: 1–70.

Possehl, G. L. (1988) 'Sociocultural complexity without the state: the Indus Civilization' in Feinman, G. M. and Joyce, M. (eds), *Archaic States*, Santa Fe, School of American Research Press, 1988, pp. 261–291.

Possehl, G. L. (1990) 'Revolution in the urban revolution: the emergence of Indus urbanization' *Annual Review of Anthropology*, 19: 261–282.

Possehl, G. L. (1996) 'Meluhha' in Reade, J. (ed.), *The Indian Ocean in Antiquity*, London, Kegan Paul International in association with the British Museum, pp. 133–208.

Possehl, G. L. (1997a) 'Seafaring Merchants of Meluhha' in Allchin, R. and Allchin, B. (eds), *South Asian Archaeology 1995*, New Delhi, Oxford and IBH Publishing (for the Ancient India and Iran Trust), pp. 87–100.

Possehl, G. L. (1997b) 'The transformation of the Indus Civilisation' *Journal of World Prehistory*, 11: 425–471 (reproduced in *Man and Environment*, 1999, 24(2): 1–33).

Possehl, G. L. (1999) 'An Harappan outpost on the Amu Darya: Shortughai. Why was it there?' *Indologica Tauriensia*, 23–24: 57–70.

Possehl, G. L. (2002a) 'Fifty years of Harappan Archaeology: the study of Indus Civilisation since Indian independence' in Settar, S. and Korisettar, R. (eds), *Indian Archaeology in Retrospect, Volume II, Protohistory: Archaeology of the Harappan Civilization*, New Delhi, Manohar (for Indian Council of Historical Research), pp. 1–46.

Possehl, G. L. (2002b) *The Indus Civilization: A Contemporary Perspective*, Lanham, Altamira Press.

Possehl, G. L. (2002c) 'Indus-Mesopotamian Trade: the record of the Indus' in Potts, D. T. (ed.), *Ingenious Man, Inquisitive Soul: Essays in Iranian and Central Asian archaeology for C.C. Lamberg-Karlovsky on the occasion of his 65th birthday by a selection of his students, colleagues and friends, Iranica Antiqua*, 37: 325–342.

Possehl, G. L. (2012) 'India's relations with western empires, 2300–600 BC' in Potts, D. T. (ed.), *A Companion to the Archaeology of the Ancient Near East*, Volume II, Oxford, Wiley-Blackwell, pp. 758–769.

Potts, D. T. (1990) *The Arabian Gulf in Antiquity*, Oxford, Oxford University Press.

Potts, D. T. (1993a) 'Distant shores: ancient Near Eastern trade with South Asia and northeast Africa' in Sasson, J. M. (ed.), *Civilisations of the Ancient Near East*, Volume III, New York, Scribner, pp. 1451–1463.

Potts, D. T. (1993b) 'A new Bactrian Find from Southeastern Arabia' *Antiquity*, 1993: 591–596.

Potts, D. T. (1993c) 'Rethinking some aspects of trade in the Arabian Gulf' *World Archaeology*, 24: 423–440.

Potts, D. T. (1994) 'South and Central Asian elements at Tell Abraq (Emirate of Umm al-Qaiwain, United Arab Emirates), c. 2200 BCE–CE 400' in Parpola, A. and Koskikallio, P. (eds), *South Asian Archaeology 1993* (Proceedings of the Twelfth International Conference of the European Association of South Asian Archaeologists held in Helsinki University, 5–9 July 1993), Helsinki, Suomalainen Tiedeakatemia, pp. 615–628.

Potts, D. T. (2000) *Ancient Magan. The Secrets of Tell Abraq*, London, Trident Press.

Potts, D. T. (2007) 'Differing modes of contact between India and the West: some Achaemenid and Seleucid examples' in Ray, H. P. and Potts, D. T. (eds), *Memory as History: The Legacy of Alexander in Asia*, New Delhi, Aryan Books International, pp. 122–130.

Potts, D. T. (2016) 'Cultural, economic and political relations between Mesopotamia, the Gulf and India before Alexander' in Wiesehöfer, J., Brinkhaus, H., and Bichler, R. (eds), *Megasthenes und seine Zeit*, 2016, Wiesbaden, Harrassowitz Verlag (*Classica et Orientalia* Band 13), pp. 109–118.

Potts, D. T. (2017) 'Resource origins and resource movement in and around the Persian Gulf' in Schotz, A., Bartelheim, M., Hardenberg, R. and Staeckler, J. (eds), *Resource Cultures: Sociocultural Dynamics and the Use of Resources - Theories, Methods, Perspectives*, Tübingen, Ressourcen Kulturen Band 5, pp. 133–142.

Potts, T. F. (1994) *Mesopotamia and the East. An Archaeological and Historical Study of Foreign Relations ca. 3400–2000 BCE*, Oxford, Oxford University Press/Oxford Committee for Archaeology (*Oxford Committee for Archaeology Monograph* 37).

Pulak, C. (2001) 'The cargo of the Uluburun ship and evidence for trade with the Aegean and beyond' in Bonfante, L. and Karageogrhis, V. (eds), *Italy and Cyprus in Antiquity: 1500–450 BC*, Nicosia, the Costakis and Leto Severis Foundation, pp. 12–61.

Puri, B. N. (1966) *Cities of Ancient India*, Meerut, Meenakshi Prakashan, 1966.

Puskás, I. (1983) 'Herodotus and India' *Oikoumene*, 4: 201–207.

Rahmstorf, L. (2006a) 'In Search of the Earliest Balance Weights, Scales and Weighing Systems from the East Mediterranean, the Near and Middle East' in Alberti, M. E., Ascalone, E. and Peyronel, L. (eds), *Weights in Context. Bronze Age Weighing Systems of the Eastern Mediterranean: Chronology, Typology, Material and Archaeological Contexts, Proceedings of the International*

Colloquium, Rome, 22-24 November 2004, Rome, Istituto Italiano di Numismatica (*Studi e Materiali* 13), pp. 9–45.
Rahmstorf, L. (2006b) 'Zur Ausbreitung vorderasiatischer Innovation in die frühbronzezeitliche Ägäis' *Prähistorische Zeitschrift*, 81: 49–96.
Rahmstorf, L. (2010) 'The concept of weighing during the Bronze Age in the Aegean, the Near East and Europe' in Morley, I. and Renfrew, C. (eds), *The Archaeology of Measurement: Comprehending Heaven, Earth and Time in Ancient Societies*, Cambridge, Cambridge University Press, pp. 88–105.
Rahmstorf, L. (2017) 'The use of bronze objects in the 3rd Millennium BC: a survey between Atlantic and Indus' in Maran, J. and Stockhammer, P. (eds), *Appropriating Innovations: Entangled Knowledge in Eurasia, 5000-1500 BCE*, Oxford, Oxbow Books, pp. 184–210.
Rao, S. R. (1973) *Lothal and the Indus Civilisation*, Bombay, Asia Publishing House.
Rao, S. R. (1979) *Lothal: A Harappan Port Town, 1955-1962*, Volume 1, New Delhi, Archaeological Survey of India (*Memoirs of the Archaeological Survey of India* 78(1)), pp. 123–136.
Rao, S. R. (1985) *Lothal: A Harappan port town, 1955-1962*, Volume 2, New Delhi, Archaeological Survey of India (*Memoirs of the Archaeological Survey of India* 78(2)).
Ratnagar, S. (2001) 'The Bronze Age: unique instance of a pre-industrial world system?' *Current Anthropology*, 42: 351–379.
Ratnagar, S. (2002) *The End of the Great Harappan Tradition*, Delhi, Manohar (Heras Memorial Lectures 1998, Heras Institute of Indian History and Culture, Mumbai).
Ratnagar, S. (2004) *Trading Encounters: From the Euphrates to the Indus in the Bronze Age*, New Delhi, Oxford University Press (revised edition of *Encounters: The Westerly Trade of the Harappan Civilisation*, New Delhi, Oxford University Press, 1981).
Ratnagar, S. (2016) *Harappan Archaeology: Early State Perspectives*, Delhi, Primus Books.
Reade, J. (1979) *Early Etched Beads and the Indus-Mesopotamia Trade*, London, British Museum (British Museum Occasional Paper No. 2).
Reese, W. (1914) *Die griechischen Nachrichten über Indien bis zum Feldzuge Alexanders des Grossen: eine Sammlung der Berichte und ihre Untersuchung*, Leipzig, B. G. Teubner.
Reinholdt, C. (2003) 'The Early Bronze Age Jewelry Hoard from Kolonna, Aegina' in Aruz, J. (ed.), *Art of the First Cities: the third millennium BC from the Mediterranean to the Indus*, New York and New Haven, Metropolitan Museum of Art and Yale University Press, p. 260.
Reinholdt, C. (2008) *Der frühbronzezeitliche Schmuckhortfund van Kap Kolonna: Ägina und die Ägäis im Goldzeitalter des 3. Jahrtausends v. Chr.* (*Ägina - Kolonna: Forschungen und Ergebnisse* Band II), Vienna, Österreichische Akademie der Wissenschaften (*Denkschriften der Gesamtakademie* LVI and *Contributions to the Chronology of the Easterm Mediterranean* XV).
Renfrew, C. (1972) *The Emergence of Civilisation: The Cyclades and the Aegean in the Third Millennium BC*, London, Methuen.
Renfrew, C. (1977) 'Alternative Models for Exchange and Spatial Distribution' in Earle, T. K. and Ericson, J. E. (eds), *Exchange Systems in Prehistory*, New York, Academic Press, pp. 71–89.
Renz, J. and Rölling, W. (1996) *Handbuch der althebräischen Epigraphik*, Darmstadt, Wissenschaftliche Buchgesellschaft, Volume I.
Ritchie, P. D. (1935) *Spectrographic Studies on Ancient Glass*, Unpublished paper, Courtauld Institute of Art (University of London), now believed lost owing to enemy action during the London Blitz.
Roth, M. T. (1968) *The Assyrian Dictionary of the Oriental Institute of the University of Chicago (CAD)*, Volume 1, A, part 2, Chicago, Oriental Institute of the University of Chicago.
Rybatzky, V. (2008) 'Farbigkeit und Vielfalt. Einiges zum Pfau und seinen Beziehungen in den zentralasiatischen Sprachen' *Studies on the Inner Asian Languages*, 13: 187–207.
Şahoğlu, V. (2005) 'The Anatolian Trade Network and the Izmir Region during the Early Bronze Age' *Oxford Journal of* Archaeology, 24: 339–361.

Şahoğlu, V. and Sotirakopoulou, P. (eds) (2011) *Across: The Cyclades and Western Anatolia during the 3rd millennium BC*, Istanbul, Sabanci University Sakip Sabanci Museum (exhibition catalogue).

Sakellariou, A. (1964) *Corpus der minoischen und mykenischem Siegel*, Band I.1, *Die minoiischen und mykenischen Siegel des Nationalmuseums in Athen*, Berlin, Mann.

Salles. J. F. (1996) 'Achaemenid and Hellenistic Trade in the Indian Ocean' in Reade, J. (ed.), *The Indian Ocean in Antiquity*, London, Kegan Paul International in association with the British Museum, London, pp. 251–267.

Sarianidi, V. I. and Kowalski, L. H. (1971) 'The Lapis lazuli route in the ancient east' *Archaeology*, 24: 12–15.

Sarpaki, A. (2001) 'Condiments, Perfume and Dye Plants in Linear B: a look at the textual and archaeobotanical evidence' in Michailidou, A. (ed.), *Manufacture and Measurement: Counting, Measuring and Recording Craft Items in Early Aegean Societies*, Athens, Research Centre for Greek and Roman Antiquity, National Hellenic Research Foundation (*Μελετηματα* 33), pp. 195–265.

Sayce, A. H. (1924) 'Remarkable discoveries in India' *Illustrated London News*, 27 September 1924, p. 566.

Schliemann, H. (1880) *Ilios, the City and Country of the Trojans*, London, John Murray.

Schmidt, H. (1902) *Heinrich Schliemann's Sammlung trojanischer Altertümer*, Berlin, G. Reimer (for K. Museen. Museum für Völkerkunde).

Schmidt, H. (1937) *Excavations at Tepe* Hissar, Philadelphia, University Museum.

Schmidt, H.-P. (1980) 'The Sēnmurw. Of birds and dogs and bats' *Persica*, 1980, 9: 1–85.

Schug, G. R., Gray, K., Mushrif-Tripathy, V. and Sankhyan, A. R. (2012) 'A peaceful realm? Trauma and social differentiation at Harappa' *International Journal of Paleopathology*, 2: 136–147.

Schug, G. R., Blevins, K. E., Cox, B., Gray, R. and Mushrif-Tripathy, V. (2013) 'Infection, disease and biosocial processes at the end of the Indus Civilization' *PLoS ONE*, 8(12): e84814.

Scott, A., Power, R. C., Altmann-Wendling, V., Artzy, M., Martin, M. A. S., Eisenmann, S., Hagan, R., Salazar-Garcia, D. C., Salmon, Y., Yegorov, D., Milevski, I., Finkelstein, I., Stockhammer, P. W. and Warinner, C. (2021) 'Exotic foods reveal contact between South Asia and the Near East during the second millennium BC' *Proceedings of the National Academy of Sciences of the United States of America*, 12 January, 118 (2): e2014956117 (https://doi.org/10.1073/pnas.2014956117).

Seager, R. B. (1912) *Excavations in the Island of Mochlos*, Boston and New York, American School of Classical Studies at Athens.

Serpico, M. and White, R. (2000) 'Oil, fat and wax' in Nicholson, P. T. and Shaw, I. (eds), *Ancient Egyptian Materials and Technology*, Cambridge, Cambridge University Press, pp. 390–429.

Shaffer, J. G. (1978) *Prehistoric Baluchistan*, Delhi, B & R Publishing.

Shaffer, J. G. (1987) 'One hump or two: the impact of the camel on Harappan Society' in Curaverunt, E., Gnoli, G. and Lanciotti, L. (eds), *Orientalia Josephi Tucci Memoriae Dicata*, Volume 3, Rome, Istituto Italiano per il Medo e Estremo Oriente (*Orientale Roma*, 56(2)), pp. 1315–1328.

Shaffer, J. G. (1992) 'The Indus Valley, Baluchistan and Helmand traditions: Neolithic through Bronze Age' in Ehrich, R. W., *Chronologies in Old World Archaeology*, second edition, Chicago, University of Chicago Press, Volume I, pp. 441–464, Volume II, pp. 425–446.

Shaffer, J. G. (1993) 'Reurbanization: The Eastern Punjab and beyond' in Spodek, H. and Rinivasan, D. M. S. (eds), *Urban Form and Meaning in South Asia: The Shaping of Cities from Prehistoric to Precolonial Times*, Hanover, University Press of New England, pp. 53–67.

Shaffer, J. G. and Lichtenstein, D. A. (1999) 'Migration, Philology and South Asian Archaeology' in Bonkhurst, J. and Depande, M. M. (eds), *Aryan and Non-Aryan in South Asia: Evidence, Interpretation and Ideology*, Cambridge, Harvard University (*Harvard Oriental Series* 3, Opera Minora, Department of Sanskrit and Indian Studies), pp. 239–260.

Shanks, E. (2005) 'Evidence for Anatolian Relations in Crete in Early Minoan I-IIA' in Laffineur, R. and Greco, E. (eds), *Emporia: Aegeans in the Central and Eastern Mediterranean. Proceedings of the 10th*

International Aegean Conference/10e Rencontre égéenne internationale, Italian School of Archaeology in Athens, 14–18 April 2004), Liège, Histoire de l'art et archéologie de la Grèce antique, University of Liège (*Aegaeum* 22), pp. 103–108.

Sharma, D. P. (2002) *Newly Discovered Copper Hoard, Weapons of South Asia (c.2800–1500 BC)*, Delhi, Bharatiya Kala Prakashan.

Sharma, R. S. (2005) *India's Ancient Past,* New Delhi, Oxford University Press.

Sherratt, S. (2010) 'The Aegean and the wider world: some thoughts on a world-systems perspective' in Galatay, M. and Parkinson, W. (eds), *Archaic State Interaction: The Eastern Mediterranean in the Bronze Age*, Santa Fe, School for Advanced Research Press, pp. 81–106.

Sherratt, S. (2020) 'From the Near East to the Far West' in Lemos, I. S. and Kotsonas, A. (eds), *A Companion to the Archaeology of Early Greece and the Mediterranean*, in two volumes, Hoboken, John Wiley & Sons, Volume 1, pp. 188–215.

Shipley, G. (2011) *Pseudo-Skylax's Periplous; The Circumnavigation of the Inhabited World: Text, Translation and Commentary*, Exeter, Exeter University.

Singh, R. N. and Singh, D. P. (2016) 'A note on metallurgy at Khanak: an Indus site in Tosham Mining Area, Haryana' *International Journal of Environmental, Chemical, Ecological, Geological and Geophysical Engineering*, 10: 847–856.

Soles, J. S. (1992) *The Prepalatial Cemeteries at Mochlos and Gournia and the House Tombs of Bronze Age Crete,* Princeton, American School of Classical Studies at Athens, (*Hesperia* Supplement 24). pp. 42–51.

Sollberger, E. and Kupper, J. R. (1971) *Inscriptions Royales Sumériennes et Akkadiennes*, Paris, Éditions du Cerf (*Littératures anciennes du Proche-Orient* 3).

Sowada, K. N. and Grave, P. (2009) *Egypt in the Eastern Mediterranean during the Old Kingdom. An Archaeological Perspective,* Fribourg, Academic Press (*Orbis biblicus et orientalis* 237).

Srinivasan, L. (2005) 'Mycenaean names and land and people in the Rigveda and in Indian myth' *Man and India*, 85: 1–24.

Stech, T. and Pigott, V. C. (1986) 'The metals trade in Southwest Asia in the third millennium BC' *Iraq*, 48: 39–64.

Stone, J. F. S. (1949) 'A second fixed point in the chronology of the Harappa Culture' *Antiquity*, 23: 201–205.

Stoneman, R. (2019) *The Greek Experience of India: from Alexander to the Indo-Greeks*, Princeton, Princeton University Press.

Strange, J. (1980) *Caphtor/Keftiu: A New Investigation*, Leiden, Brill (*Acta Theologica Danica* 14), pp. 90–91 (33).

Stronk, J. P. (2010) *Ctesias' Persian History,* Dusseldorf, Wellen (*Reihe Geschichte* Band 2).

Symeneoglou, K. (1973) *Kadmeia I*, Göteborg, Paul Åströms Förlag, (*Studies in Mediterranean Archaeology*, 35).

Taddei, M. (ed.) (1979) *South Asian Archaeology 1977,* Volume I, Naples, *Instituto Universitario Orientale, Seminario di Studi Asiatici* (Series Minor VI).

Talon, P. (1986) 'Le cotton et la soie en Mesopotamie?' *Akkadica*, 47: 75–78.

Taylour, Lord W. (1981) *Well Built Mycenae, The Helleno-British Excavations within the Citadel at Mycenae, 1959–1969,* Fascicule I: *The Excavations*, Warminster, Aris and Phillips.

Tenberg, M. and Potts, D. T. (1999) '^{giš}mes.má-gan-na (*Dalbergia sissoo* Roxb.) at Tell Abraq' *Arabian Archaeology and Epigraphy,* 10: 129–133.

Tewari, R. (2003) 'The origins of iron-working in India: new evidence from the Central Ganga Plain and the Eastern Vindhyas' *Antiquity*, 77: 536–545.

Thapar, B. K. (1993) 'The Harappan Civilization: some reflections on its environments and resources and their exploitation' in Possehl, G. L. (ed.), *Harappan Civilization: A Recent Perspective*, Second Edition, New Delhi, Oxford and IBH Publishing (and the American Institute of Indian Studies), pp. 3–13.

Thapar, R. (1975) 'A possible identification of Meluḫḫa, Dilmun and Makan' *Journal of the Economic and Social History of the Orient*, 18: 1–42.
Thapar, R. (1998) *Aśoka and the Decline of the Mauryas*, second edition, New Delhi, Oxford University Press.
Tobler, A. J. (1950) *Excavations at Tepe Gawra II: Levels IX–XX*, Philadelphia, Pennsylvania University Press.
Tosi, M. (1969) 'Excavations at Shahr-I Sokhta' *East and West*, 19: 371–374.
Tosi, M. (1974) 'The lapis lazuli trade across the Iranian Plateau in the third millennium BC' in *Gururājamañjarikā: studi in onore di Giuseppe Tucci*, Volume I, Naples, Istituto Universitario Orientale, pp. 3–22.
Tosi, M. (1991) 'The Indus Civilisation beyond the Indian Subcontinent' in Jansen, Michael; Mulloy, Màire and Urban, Günter (eds), *Forgotten Cities on the Indus: early civilisation in Pakistan from the 8th to the 2nd millennium BC*, Mainz, Verlag Philipp von Zabern, pp. 111–128.
Tosi, M. and Vidale, M. (1990) '4th millennium BC lapis lazuli working at Mehrgarh, Pakistan' *Paléorient*, 16: 89–99.
Touloupa, E. (1965) *Ἀρχαιολογικόν Δελτίον*, 20: B'1 Χρονικά, p. 230.
Tsountas, C. (1898) 'Κυκλαδικα' *Ἐφημερίς Ἀρχαιολογική*, 1898, cols. 137–212.
Tsountas, C. (1899) 'Κυκλαδικα II' *Ἐφημερίς Ἀρχαιολογική*, 1899, cols. 73–134.
Tusa, S. (1977) 'The Swat Valley in the 2nd and 1st millennia BC: a question of marginality' *South Asian Archaeology*, 6: 675–695.
Uesugi, A. (ed.) (2018) *Iron Age in South Asia*, Osaka, Research Group for South Asian Archaeology, Archaeological Research Unit, Kansai University.
Umesao, T. (2000) *Indus Civilization Exhibition*, Tokyo, Nippon Hoso Kyokai.
van de Mieroop, M. (2007) *The Eastern Mediterranean in the Age of Ramesses II*, Oxford, Blackwell.
Vats, M. S. (1940) *Excavations at Harappa: Being an Account of Archaeological Excavations at Harappa Carried Out Between the Years 1920-21 and 1933-34*, Delhi, Government of India and Archaeological Survey of India.
Ventris, M. and Chadwick, J. (1973) *Documents in Mycenaean Greek*, second edition, Cambridge, Cambridge University Press.
Vidale, M. (1989) 'A steatite-cutting atelier on the surface of Moenjodaro' *Annali*, 49: 29–51.
Vermaak, P. S. (2008) 'Guabba, the Meluhhan Village in Mesopotamia' *Journal for Semitics*, 17: 553–570.
Wenke, R. J. and Olszewski, D. J. (2007) *Patterns in Prehistory: Humankind's First Three Million Years*, fifth edition, Oxford, Oxford University Press.
Weeks, L. R. (1999) 'Lead isotope analysis from Tell Abraq, United Arab Emirates: new data regarding the "tin problem" in Western Asia' *Antiquity*, 3: 49–64.
Weeks, L. R. (2004) *Early Metallurgy of the Persian Gulf: Technology, Trade and the Bronze Age World*, Leiden, Brill
Wertime, T. A. (1980) 'The pyrotechnological background' in Wertime, T. A. and Muhly, J. D. (eds), *The Coming of the Age of Iron*, New Haven, Yale University Press.
West, S. (1991) 'Herodotus' portrait of Hecataeus' *Journal of Hellenic Studies*, 111: 144–160.
Wheeler, M. (1947) 'Harappa 1946: the defences and Cemetery R-37' *Ancient India*, 3: 58–130.
Wheeler, M. (1968) *The Indus Civilisation*, third edition, Cambridge, Cambridge University Press (Supplementary Volume 10 to *The Cambridge History of India*).
Wiener, M. H. (2013) 'Contracts: Crete, Egypt and the Near East circa 2000 B.C.' in Aruz, J., Graff, S. and Rakic, Y. (eds), *Cultures in Contact: From Mesopotamia to the Mediterranean in the Second Millennium B.C.*, New York, Metropolitan Museum of Art/Yale University Press, pp. 34–43.
Wilkinson, T. C. (2014) *Tying the Threads of Eurasia: Trans-regional Routes and Material Flows from Transcaucasia, Eastern Anatolia and Western Central Asia, c.3000-1500 BC*, Leiden, Sidestone Press.

Wilson, E. J. (1996) *The Cylinders of Gudea: Transliteration, Translation and Index*, Kevelaer, Verlag Butzon and Bercker (*Alter Orient und Altes Testament* 244).
Wilson, H. H. (1836) *Notes on the Indica of Ctesias,* Oxford, Ashmolean Society (Printed by Samual Collingwood, Printer to the University).
Witzel, M. (2000) 'A first link between the Ṛgvedic Panjab and Mesopotamia: *śimbala/śalmali* and *GIŠgišimmar?*' in Karttunen, K. and Koskikallio, P. (eds), *Vidyarnavandanam: Essays in Honour of Asko Parpola*, Helsinki, Finnish Oriental Society (*Studia Orientalia,* 94), pp. 497–508.
Woolley, C. L. (1934) *Ur Excavations, Volume II, The Royal Cemetery: A Report on the Predynastic and Sargonid Graves Excavated between 1926 and 1931*, London, British Museum (Joint Expedition of the British Museum and of the Museum of the University of Pennsylvania to Mesopotamia).
Wright, M. (1988) 'Contacts between Egypt and Syro-Palestine during the Old Kingdom' *Biblical Archaeologist*, 51: 143–161.
Wright, R. P. (2010) *The Ancient Indus: Urbanism, Economy and Society*, Cambridge, Cambridge University Press.
Wright, R. P., Lentz, D. L., Beaubien, H. P. and Kimbrough, C. K. (2012) 'New evidence for jute (*Corchorus capsularis* L.) in the Indus civilization' *Archaeological and Anthropological Science*, 4: 137–143.
Wylock, M. (1972) 'Les aromates dans les tablettes Ge de Mycenès' *Studi micenei ed egeo-anatolici*, 15: 105–146.
Xanthoudides, S. (1905–1906) 'Cretan Kernoi' *Annual of the British School at Athens*, 12: 9–23.
Xanthoudides, S. (1924) *The Vaulted Tombs of Mesara*, London, University Press of Liverpool.
Younger, J. G. (1979) 'Semi-precious stones to the Aegean' *Archaeological News* (Tallahassee, Florida), 8: 40–44 (*Archaeology of Trade in the Near East*, a symposium held at Duke University, University of North Carolina at Chapel Hill on 23–24 February 1979).
Younger, J. G. (2010) 'Review of J. Lesley Fitton (ed.), *The Aegina Treasure: Aegean Bronze Age Jewellery and a Mystery Revisited*, London, British Museum Press, 2008' in *Bryn Mawr Classical Review* (http://bmcr.brynmawr.edu/2010/2010-2-64.html).
Yule, P. (1985a) *Metalwork of the Bronze Age in India,* Munich, C. H. Beck'sche Verlagsbuchhandlung (*Prähistorische Bronzefunde,* Abteilung XX, Band 8).
Yule, P. (1985b) *Figuren, Schmuckformen und Täfelchen der Harappa-Kulture*, Munich, C. H. Beck'sche Verlagsbuchhandlung (*Prähistorische Bronzefunde,* Abteilung I, Band 6).
Yule, P. (1989) *The Copper Hoards of the Indian Subcontinent: Preliminaries for an Interpretation*, Mainz, Römisch-Germanischen Zentralmuseum (*Jahrbuch des RGZM* 36).
Yule, P. and Schürmann Yule, K. (1981) 'Technical observations on glyptic' in Pini, I. (ed.), *Studien zur Minoischen und Helladischen Glyptik,* Berlin, Mann (*Corpus der minoischen und mykenischem Siegel* Beiheft 1), pp. 39.
Zarins, J. (1992) 'Pastoral Nomadism in Arabia: Ethnoarchaeology and the Archaeological Record – a case study' in Bar-Yosef, O. and Khazanov, A. (eds.), *Pastoralism in the Levant. Archaeological Materials in Anthropological Perspectives*, Madison, Prehistory Press (*Monographs in World Archaeology*, 10), pp. 219–240.